THE OFFICIAL BBCSPORT GUIDE

FORMULA ONE 2016

www.bbc.co.uk/sport/formula1
The home of Formula 1 on the BBC Sport website.
All the latest news, expert analysis and live radio coverage of every race.

This edition published in 2016
by Carlton Books Limited
20 Mortimer Street
London W1T 3JW

ISBN 978-1-78097-748-5

Editorial Director: Martin Corteel
Design Manager: Luke Griffin
Designer: Darren Jordan
Production: Maria Petalidou
Picture Research: Paul Langan

Printed in Spain

Opposite: Lewis Hamilton celebrates victory. It was a familiar sight in 2015 as the Englishman picked up ten wins.

THE OFFICIAL BBC SPORT GUIDE
FORMULA ONE 2016

BRUCE JONES

CARLTON
BOOKS

CONTENTS

4

Right: Mercedes took almost all of the glory through 2015, with Ferrari and Williams leading the chase and other teams simply scrabbling for points.

Mexican fans have always loved Formula 1 and the Mexico City circuit welcomed it back last November after a 23-year break.

ANALYSIS OF THE 2016 SEASON

Formula 1 fans won't have been sad to see the end of last year's World Championship, as not only was it a runaway for one team, Mercedes, but the sport was riven with political and economic unrest. For 2016, Mercedes will again start as favourite, but expect a far sterner challenge from Ferrari and Williams, plus hopefully a return to form for McLaren, in a series in which the championship welcomes a new team: Haas F1.

Mercedes had things its own way last year for the second season running. With the best engines, a stellar technical crew and a driving line-up made up of triple world champion Lewis Hamilton and Nico Rosberg, it's hard to see any of their rivals toppling them, but Ferrari's increasing form through 2015 at least gives hope.

Hamilton is truly in his pomp, making winning seem easy. Rosberg will have to go up a level or remain second best. Should Ferrari continue to advance, Sebastian Vettel will clearly be the one to push him, while Kimi Raikkonen remains for one more year.

This will be the third year of the 1.6-litre turbocharged V6s, and it was clear last year that the Mercedes V6 was the pick of the pack. This wasn't the sole reason for Williams ranking as the third best team, as it continues to raise its game in other areas. Valtteri Bottas seemed to go off the boil mid-season, while he was being touted as a possible Ferrari signing, but came on strong again at the end. He will be partnered for the third year by Felipe Massa, a driver who continues to be rejuvenated by the British team.

Force India continues with Mercedes engines and keeps the

same driver line-up too, in Nico Hulkenberg and Sergio Perez, both of whom are underrated. The fourth team powered by Mercedes will be Manor and expect this British team that was revived just in time to start last season to make steps forward.

With Renault's V6 being slammed by Red Bull Racing's management through much of 2015, for not matching the performance of the Mercedes power units, it came as no surprise that the French manufacturer felt aggrieved and no deal was done to continue together in 2016. Then, when it seemed that they were all set to replace them with engines supplied by Audi, Audi's parent company VW was exposed in an emission test cheating scandal in the USA and any likelihood of that deal was squashed. This meant that the team that ruled the roost from 2010 to 2013 had to look elsewhere. F1 supremo Bernie Ecclestone wanted Mercedes to step in, but the German manufacturer claimed that RBR had never even approached it. So, Ferrari V6s were the only realistic option, but even this didn't appease team owner Dietrich Mateschitz who threatened to pull out both RBR and Scuderia Toro Rosso if they weren't assured of receiving engines to the same specification and level of development as those used by Scuderia Ferrari. Luckily, RBR saw sense, ate humble pie and a deal was done to remain with Renault power after all. Daniel Ricciardo showed plenty of spark last year and he will continue to lead the RBR attack, again with Daniil Kvyat in support, while Max Verstappen is sure to continue as

F1's most exciting young gun for Scuderia Toro Rosso.

Ferrari engines are also being used this year by Sauber again as well as by the new Haas F1 team, the latest American attempt to take on the F1 establishment, with Romain Grosjean having joined to give Haas F1 a rapid and known performance benchmark. Sauber is sticking to its 2015 drivers, Marcus Ericsson and Felipe Nasr.

The Lotus F1 team showed flashes of speed with Mercedes power last year, but the money ran out and so, with Red Bull Racing spurning its engines, Renault the manufacturer has returned, taking over the team and renaming it as Renault for the first time since 2011. Pastor Maldonado stays on, but will have to step up his game to help rookie team-mate Jolyon Palmer.

And this leaves one team ploughing its own furrow: McLaren. Welcoming Honda back as its engine partner last year made older fans think back to their great years together as the 1980s fed into the 1990s, when Alain Prost and Ayrton Senna dominated. Unfortunately, hitting F1 again a year after its rivals started on their V6 turbo engines, put this pairing at a disadvantage. That was to be expected, but what shocked was the degree to which they were short on horsepower and then by the lack of progress, leaving former world champions Fernando Alonso and Jenson Button both ridiculously far off the pace. It was hard to watch.

Finally, the cars should sound better as they will have a separate wastegate for their exhaust gases, known as the "screamer pipe".

MERCEDES AMG PETRONAS

Mercedes heads into 2016 on the crest of a wave after two constructors' titles in two years, but the signs were there in the closing stages of last season that their rivals are closing the gap. It would still take a bold gamble to bet against three in a row.

Hamilton and Rosberg were close on track, but not necessarily off it, and the team will hope their disagreements are behind them in 2016.

When a team changes identity several times and then makes great strides forward, it's very easy to forget its early days, and this is very much the case with Mercedes and its silver arrows after it has just dominated two years running, taking both the drivers' and constructors' titles in 2014 and then again in 2015.

Back in 1998, Jacques Villeneuve's manager Craig Pollock was hatching plans to start a team. He bought Tyrrell's championship entry, coined the tag of "a tradition of excellence" – always intriguing for an outfit that hasn't even started a race – set up a base at Brackley and brought colour and energy to BAR's launch for 1999.

Then the team, despite having trawled the pitlane for talent, fell flat on its face, with an end-of-year tally of 32 starts but only 11 finishes and no points at all for Villeneuve and Ricardo Zonta.

The team's follow-up year was greatly improved as it changed to Honda engines and ranked fifth in 2000, equal on points

with Benetton, with Villeneuve finishing fourth four times. Sixth overall in 2001 and eighth in 2002, BAR then had a change at the top as Pollock moved on and David

Richards – head of the Prodrive concern that had achieved considerable success in rallying and touring cars – took over. With Jenson Button coming in and outshining

THE POWER AND THE GLORY

TOTO WOLFF
Toto raced in Formula Ford, then set up a private equity company. This enabled him to race again, in GTs then rallying, and he finished second in the 2006 Austrian series. In 2009, he bought a share of Williams. At this point, Toto was already on the board of Mercedes' competition arm and, after becoming an executive director of Williams in 2012, he moved on to the Mercedes F1 team in 2013 with a remit to run all Mercedes' competition programmes.

CARRYING ON FROM ITS 2014 DOMINANCE
For the second year in a row, Mercedes was the class of the field, the combination of its F1 W06 chassis, its pace-setting V6 turbo engine plus the driver line-up of Hamilton and Rosberg was simply too good for its rivals. There were races, usually in very high temperatures, when the team's cars struggled to manage their tyres, but overall they had little to worry about. As in 2014, there were disagreements between its drivers, but Wolff kept a lid on that and Hamilton got on top of qualifying in 2015 then imposed himself from there.

2015 DRIVERS & RESULTS

Driver	Nationality	Races	Wins	Pts	Pos
Lewis Hamilton	British	19	10	381	1st
Nico Rosberg	German	19	6	322	2nd

FOR THE RECORD

Country of origin:	England
Team base:	Brackley, England
Telephone:	(44) 01280 844000
Website:	www.mercedes-amg-f1.com
Active in Formula One:	As BAR 1999-2005; Honda Racing 2006-08; Brawn GP 2009; Mercedes 2010 on
Grands Prix contested:	303
Wins:	45
Pole positions:	53
Fastest laps:	32

THE TEAM

Non-executive chairman:	Niki Lauda
Head of Mercedes-Benz Motorsport:	Toto Wolff
Executive director, technical:	Paddy Lowe
MD, Mercedes-Benz AMG High Performance powertrains:	Andy Cowell
Technology director:	Geoff Willis
Engineering director:	Aldo Costa
Performance director:	Mark Ellis
Chief designer:	John Owen
Chief race engineer:	Andrew Shovlin
Chief track engineer:	Simon Cole
Sporting director:	Ron Meadows
Test driver:	tba
Chassis:	Mercedes F1 W07
Engine:	Mercedes V6
Tyres:	Pirelli

Villeneuve, the team advanced to fifth in 2003, then really motored forward in 2004. Button achieved the team's first podium by finishing third at the second round, at Sepang, improved to second in the fourth and added three more second places, but Michael Schumacher was dominant for Ferrari. Still, second overall for BAR was a huge step forward.

Although the 2005 season was less successful, Honda wanted more of a share and the team became Honda Racing for 2006, with the reward of its first victory, courtesy of an inspired drive by Button at the Hungaroring. Rubens Barrichello also trawled for points and the pair stayed on for 2007 when they were shocked to tumble down the order. With 2008 being equally poor and a global economic recession hitting, Honda then pulled the plug near the end of the season, leaving little time for anyone to take the team over. Yet, at the 11th hour, technical director Ross Brawn led a buy-out, with a little money put up by Honda, but engines from Mercedes.

So the team became Brawn GP, but what followed was magical as the team had come up with the idea of a double-deck diffuser and it worked so well that Button won the opening round in Australia and followed it up with five more wins in the next six races. Barrichello was to win three times later in the year and so the team went from zeroes to heroes, to land both drivers' and constructors' titles.

Mercedes had seen enough and gave the team its third name change. Despite the cars being painted silver, like the Silver Arrows that starred in the 1930s and mid-1950s, and the finance coming from Germany, the team remained firmly based in England. Button had sensed that this might be a one-season wonder as other teams developed their own double-deck diffusers and eclipsed Brawn, so he moved to McLaren and Barrichello to Williams.

Having strong financial backing enabled the team to sign Nico Rosberg and, to much fanfare, coax Michael Schumacher out of retirement. Showing how things keep moving, Rosberg was the better placed at season's end, seventh to Schumacher's ninth, but there were no wins. It took until 2012 for the first of these to occur, when Rosberg triumphed in the Chinese GP.

Paddy Lowe took over the technical side from Brawn in 2013, the year when Lewis Hamilton joined and immediately imposed himself on Rosberg as the team leader. They have scrapped over the position ever since, but Hamilton's 11 wins in 2014 to Rosberg's five, meant that he became the team from Brackley's second World Champion, then adding another last year.

"A World Championship isn't just about points scored. It's about many hours of hard work from every single member of the team."
Toto Wolff

Michael Schumacher raced for Mercedes from 2010 to 2012, but never won.

11

🇬🇧 LEWIS HAMILTON

His rivals ought to be afraid, as Lewis not only got his mojo back in 2015 as he raced to his third World Championship title, but appears to have discovered a steelier persona who is able to deliver time and again with Mercedes' excellent machinery.

Lewis's rise through the ranks was a combination of his natural speed and his father Anthony's sheer drive to finance his karting programme. It was a struggle, which is why it was such a pivotal moment when Lewis met McLaren boss Ron Dennis at an awards evening and cheekily asked McLaren to back him. Nothing came of this immediately, but two years later the deal was done: if Lewis kept on winning, McLaren would finance his rise towards F1.

Lewis won kart titles galore. At the end of 2001, when he'd turned 16, Lewis tried single-seaters, returning for a full campaign in 2002 when he ranked third in British Formula Renault. At his second attempt, he dominated, for his first car title.

Formula 3 was also a two-year project, with Lewis landing the 2005 European title in dominant fashion. Lewis needed just one shot at GP2 to land the 2006 crown.

Dennis was good to his word and so gave Lewis his F1 break. What a year it proved to be, as Lewis came to the final round with the points lead, but stumbled and Kimi Raikkonen won race and title for Ferrari.

Lewis got it right in 2008, winning five rounds to become Britain's first World

Lewis went from strength to strength in 2015. Can he add a fourth title this year?

Champion since Damon Hill in 1996. Always in the reckoning across the next four years, it took a move to Mercedes in 2013 to yield his second title, which he landed in 2014, and then his third in 2015 when he again got the better of team-mate Nico Rosberg.

TRACK NOTES

Nationality:	BRITISH
Born:	7 JANUARY 1985, STEVENAGE, ENGLAND
Website:	www.lewishamilton.com
Teams:	McLAREN 2007-12, MERCEDES 2013-16

CAREER RECORD

First Grand Prix:	2007 AUSTRALIAN GP
Grand Prix starts:	167
Grand Prix wins:	43

2007 Canadian GP, United States GP, Hungarian GP, Japanese GP, 2008 Australian GP, Monaco GP, British GP, German GP, Chinese GP, 2009 Hungarian GP, Singapore GP, 2010 Turkish GP, Canadian GP, Belgian GP, 2011 Chinese GP, German GP, Abu Dhabi GP, 2012 Canadian GP, Hungarian GP, Italian GP, United States GP, 2013 Hungarian GP, 2014 Malaysian GP, Bahrain GP, Chinese GP, Spanish GP, British GP, Italian GP, Singapore GP, Japanese GP, Russian GP, United States GP, Abu Dhabi GP, 2015 Australian GP, Chinese GP, Bahrain GP, Canadian GP, British GP, Belgian GP, Italian GP, Japanese GP, Russian GP, United States GP

Poles:	49
Fastest laps:	28
Points:	1867
Honours:	2008, 2014 & 2015 FORMULA ONE WORLD CHAMPION, 2007 FORMULA ONE RUNNER-UP, 2006 GP2 CHAMPION, 2005 EUROPEAN FORMULA 3 CHAMPION, 2003 BRITISH FORMULA RENAULT CHAMPION, 2000 WORLD KART CUP & EUROPEAN FORMULA A KART CHAMPION, 1999 ITALIAN INTERCONTINENTAL A KART CHAMPION, 1996 McLAREN MERCEDES CHAMPION OF THE FUTURE, 1995 BRITISH CADET KARTING CHAMPION

LEADING FROM THE FRONT

Lewis made a major step in 2015 in the pursuit of his third F1 title: he improved his form in qualifying. It had never been a glaring weak point in his armour, but Mercedes team-mate Nico Rosberg had bettered him in 2014, getting the most out of the tyres to earn the advantage of starting from pole for 11 of the 19 races. Last year, Lewis struck back and duly used that advantage to good effect. Three wins in the first four rounds, beaten only by Sebastian Vettel at Sepang when his Ferrari's tyres stood up better to the searing heat, Lewis was restored to full confidence, seemingly much more content with his life away from the circuits, and the wins that kept on coming were reward for that. Naturally, with Mercedes so dominant, there was some friction between he and Rosberg, but Lewis had that battle won by mid-season and simply strode on from there. For sheer dominance, his Italian GP gave him the most pleasure as he was fastest in every single session.

NICO ROSBERG

After two years of fighting team-mate Lewis Hamilton for supremacy and two years of losing out, this will certainly be a pivotal season for Nico as Mercedes will surely look to replace him with one of its young guns if he fails to seize the opportunity.

Nico was born into racing, as his father Keke was World Champion in 1982. So, with a childhood spent karting, it was always likely that Nico would follow suit. Unusually for a budding racer, Nico also stuck at education, landing a place to study engineering at Imperial College in London. History relates, though, that he chose to focus on racing instead and so parked his studies.

By this stage, Nico had been runner-up to Lewis Hamilton in the 2000 European Formula A kart series. Indeed, they were team-mates and did a lot of growing up together. Bucking the form books from their karting days, Nico was the first of the pair to land a car racing title, when he was the 2002 Formula BMW ADAC champion.

Formula Three followed and Nico hoped to build on a fair rookie season in the European championship with title success in 2004, but ended the year fourth, with Hamilton ranked fifth. This made Nico's 2005 season all the more extraordinary, as he turned down university and stepped up to GP2, then walked away with the title to prove that he was ready for F1.

His father's old team, Williams, offered Nico his F1 break, and Nico responded by

Nico spent much of 2015 scrapping with Lewis, but has to go for gold in 2016 or change team.

not only finishing seventh on his debut, but also setting the race's fastest lap. Sadly, the team wasn't competitive and it was without a win to his name that Nico joined Mercedes in 2010. Then it was revealed that his team-mate would be Michael Schumacher, as the

seven-time World Champion returned to F1. Yet Nico showed that he is made of stern stuff, as he outscored Schuey and gave the modern incarnation of Mercedes its first win in China in 2012. Two wins followed in 2013 and five in 2014, when he fought with new team-mate Hamilton for the title and ended the year as runner-up.

So, all this has been aiming towards Nico matching Damon Hill in becoming a second-generation World Champion, but he still has that one final step to take.

TRACK NOTES

Nationality:	GERMAN
Born: 27 JUNE 1985, WIESBADEN, GERMANY	
Website:	www.nicorosberg.com
Teams:	WILLIAMS 2006-09, MERCEDES 2010-16

CAREER RECORD

First Grand Prix:	2006 BAHRAIN GP
Grand Prix starts:	185
Grand Prix wins:	14
2012 Chinese GP, 2013 Monaco GP, British GP, 2014 Australian GP, Monaco GP, Austrian GP, German GP, Brazilian GP, 2015 Spanish GP, Monaco GP, Austrian GP, Mexican GP, Brazilian GP, Abu Dhabi GP	
Poles:	22
Fastest laps:	14
Points:	1209.5
Honours: 2014, 2015 FORMULA ONE WORLD RUNNER-UP, 2005 GP2 CHAMPION, 2003 EUROPEAN FORMULA THREE ROOKIE RUNNER-UP, 2002 FORMULA BMW ADAC CHAMPION, 2000 EUROPEAN FORMULA A KART RUNNER-UP	

THREE WINS, BUT NO TITLE

Nico had given Mercedes team-mate Lewis Hamilton a good run for his money in 2014, but had lost out in the races, five to 11. Last year, Hamilton found a way to get the most out of the Pirelli tyres in qualifying and so stole that advantage away, which was ominous for Nico. This added to tension in the Mercedes camp and there were squabbles between them, a brooding tension pervading the team in the early stages of the season. After taking until the fifth round to score a win, by which time Hamilton had three to his name, Nico immediately added two more in the next three rounds to close to within ten points in the title chase. But then it started to slip away from him and he couldn't respond to his team-mate's sustained excellence. It was disappointing. More worryingly for Nico, there were few signs that he knew how to reverse the trend, with the engine failure that ended his Italian GP adding to the gloom. The speed was there, but not the winner's edge.

The Mercedes garage is a hive of activity as one of the 2015 Contructors' Cup-winning cars is about to make its way to the pits and the track.

SCUDERIA FERRARI

Ferrari rose to Mercedes' considerable challenge through last year and heads into 2016 with Sebastian Vettel excited by the challenge of lining up a championship campaign that might help Ferrari to its first constructors' title glory since 2008.

Having worked with Sebastian Vettel through 2015, Ferrari knows he will be the driver to lead its chase after a 17th constructors' title.

There have been rich years and lean years for this most gilded of teams, but Ferrari has an image like no other. Part of the furniture since the first World Championship in 1950, Ferrari is seen as far more than just as F1's constant. It's seen as romantic and independent in an age of changes of ownership and sponsorship, its road cars adding prestige too.

The man who got it going, Enzo Ferrari, curtailed his own racing team in the 1930s to run Alfa Romeo's works team before falling out with the manufacturer and setting up his own outfit in 1946 and the team's Italian red livery with a badge denoting a black prancing horse on a yellow background has prevailed ever since. There has been sponsorship on the cars since the late 1960s, but there's never any mistaking which are the Ferraris on the grid.

Success came quickly in the World Championship, with a first grand prix win in 1951, achieved at Silverstone by Jose Froilan Gonzalez. Then came two invincible

seasons, 1952 and 1953, when F2 rules were adopted and Alberto Ascari dominated. Juan Manuel Fangio was Ferrari's second champion in 1956 when he joined from

Mercedes to land his third title in succession. Then Mike Hawthorn squeaked home for Ferrari in 1958.

It took another change of rules for 1961,

THE POWER AND THE GLORY

MAURIZIO ARRIVABENE
When Maurizio took over the helm of Ferrari's F1 team from Stefano Domenicali in 2014, few in the sport knew much about him, but he appears to have done a good job as team principal since then as Ferrari has turned around its fortunes. The 58-year-old Italian's background is not in motorsport, but in marketing and promotion, and he rose up through the ranks at Philip Morris, Marlboro's parent company, to become head of its global communications and has sat on the F1 Commission since 2010, representing all F1's sponsors.

FERRARI FINDS ITS FEET AGAIN UNDER ALLISON
At last year's opening round it looked as though it was going to be Mercedes' year. Then Ferrari coped best with the heat of Sepang to win round 2. That was a false dawn and, although Vettel was usually the best of the rest, there was little to cheer until he won again in Hungary eight rounds later. Yet, Ferrari's technical crew did a great job and left Mercedes in the shade in Singapore, proving that the greatest success had been the rejig of the team.

2015 DRIVERS & RESULTS

Driver	Nationality	Races	Wins	Pts	Pos
Fernando Alonso	Spanish	19	3	278	3rd
Kimi Raikkonen	Finnish	19	0	150	4th

FOR THE RECORD

Country of origin:	Italy
Team base:	Maranello, Italy
Telephone:	(39) 536 949111
Website:	www.ferrari.com
Active in Formula One:	From 1950
Grands Prix contested:	889
Wins:	224
Pole positions:	208
Fastest laps:	232

THE TEAM

President:	Sergio Marchionne
Team principal:	Maurizio Arrivabene
Technical director:	James Allison
Chief designer:	Simone Resta
Power unit director:	Mattia Binotto
Chief designer, power unit:	Lorenzo Sassi
Head of aerodynamics:	Dirk de Beer
Director of aerodynamics:	Loic Bigois
Sporting director:	Massimo Rivola
Operations director:	Diego Ioverno
Reserve driver:	tba
Chassis:	Ferrari F16 T
Engine:	Ferrari V6
Tyres:	Pirelli

with the adoption of a 1500cc maximum engine capacity, for Ferrari to come out on top again, with Phil Hill crowned champion after team-mate Wolfgang von Trips was killed. Three years later, John Surtees edged out Lotus ace Jim Clark to become champion.

Then there was nothing of note for years as Ferrari went into decline, chosing to put more priority on its sportscar programme and falling prey to union unrest that even caused it to miss races. However, Niki Lauda galvanized the team and Luca di Montezemolo got hold of the management side of things and turned the tide. Lauda was crowned in 1975 and 1977, and would have been champion in 1976 too, but for suffering dreadful burns in the German GP.

In 1979, Jody Scheckter benefitted from Ferrari learning ground effect technology and beat team-mate Gilles Villeneuve to the title. But then Ferrari couldn't keep up with the teams that Enzo had once derided as "garagistes", as the likes of Williams, Brabham and McLaren ruled the roost, each benefitting from being smaller outfits that existed purely to go racing, rather than simply being an arm of a larger body. Because of this, they had no interference from above, as internal politics continued to make Ferrari less than efficient.

It took until 1996, when Michael Schumacher joined Ferrari from Benetton for things to turn around. In tandem with Jean Todt and technical chief Ross Brawn, they got Ferrari firing on all cylinders again and the wins started to flow. Williams' Jacques Villeneuve and McLaren's Mika Hakkinen resisted Schumacher's aspirations, but he and Ferrari hit the highest note in 2000, then followed this up with titles in the next four seasons, peaking with 15 wins from 17 rounds in a truly dominant 2002 campaign.

At this point, with Schumacher in his pomp, it seemed that Ferrari would never be toppled, but F1 doesn't work like that, not even for the team around which so many of the rules have been shaped by the sport's governing body.

Kimi Raikkonen grabbed the 2007 title at the final round, but then McLaren and Brawn GP moved ahead again before Red Bull Racing topped them all, through until Mercedes' ascent to the top in 2014.

Politics became prevalent at Ferrari in the wake of Red Bull's domination, and Stefano Domenicali decided that he'd had enough early in 2014, followed by Ferrari president di Montezemolo. Their departure left the way clear for a rejig of the technical side of the team, with James Allison setting in place a more effective line-up.

"Mercedes are the ones to beat, but as long as there is a chance, we have to go for it, just focus on looking after ourselves and do everything that we can."

Sebastian Vettel

17

Jody Scheckter leads Gilles Villeneuve at Monza in Ferrari's doubly triumphant 1979 season.

Sebastian returned Ferrari to winning ways after it had drawn a blank in 2014. In doing so, he bounced back from being outscored by Daniel Ricciardo at Red Bull Racing and showed the pace and passion that suggest this will be a good year.

It felt extraordinary in 2014 to watch Sebastian, fresh from winning four F1 titles, being outscored by team-mate Daniel Ricciardo. Also, when things weren't going his way, people saw a petulant side that hadn't been seen before. So, it was great to see the old Sebastian back last year with Ferrari, racing hard, smiling and winning.

European junior karting champion at 14, Sebastian landed his first car title three years later, dominating Germany's Formula BMW ADAC series and Red Bull was quick to get him onto its books.

Sebastian was the top rookie in the 2005 European F3 series. He returned in 2006 and finished runner-up to Paul di Resta. Yet he was encouraged by two stunning races in Formula Renault 3.5 in which he turned up at Misano and took two wins.

Returning to Formula Renault 3.5 in 2007, Sebastian won the third race, but pulled out to graduate to F1 when Robert Kubica was injured. His debut came at Indianapolis, and he came eighth. Kubica returned, but Sebastian did the final four races for Toro Rosso after it dropped Scott Speed.

A full season followed in 2008 and Sebastian gave the team its first win at the

Sebastian's first year with Ferrari was impressive and he is sure to progress more.

Italian GP, proving that he was ready to step up to Red Bull Racing. He duly gave RBR its first win too, at the Chinese GP, and added three more wins to end the year as runner-up to Brawn's Jenson Button.

The next four years were all about Sebastian and Red Bull, as he became F1's youngest champion at 23 in 2010, then continued to sweep the board.

TRACK NOTES

Nationality:	GERMAN
Born:	3 JULY 1987, HEPPENHEIM, GERMANY
Website:	www.sebastianvettel.de
Teams:	BMW SAUBER 2007, TORO ROSSO 2007-08, RED BULL RACING 2009-14, FERRARI 2015-16

CAREER RECORD

First Grand Prix:	2007 UNITED STATES GP
Grand Prix starts:	158
Grand Prix wins:	42

2008 Italian GP, 2009 Chinese GP, British GP, Japanese GP, Abu Dhabi GP, 2010 Malaysian GP, European GP, Japanese GP, Brazilian GP, Abu Dhabi GP, 2011 Australian GP, Malaysian GP, Turkish GP, Spanish GP, Monaco GP, European GP, Belgian GP, Italian GP, Singapore GP, Korean GP, Indian GP, 2012 Bahrain GP, Singapore GP, Japanese GP, Korean GP, Indian GP, 2013 Malaysian GP, Bahrain GP, Canadian GP, German GP, Belgian GP, Italian GP, Singapore GP, Korean GP, Japanese GP, Indian GP, Abu Dhabi GP, United States GP, Brazilian GP, 2015 Malaysian GP, Hungarian GP, Singapore GP

Poles:	46
Fastest laps:	25
Points:	1896
Honours:	2010, 2011, 2012 & 2013 FORMULA ONE WORLD CHAMPION, 2009 FORMULA ONE RUNNER-UP, 2006 EUROPEAN FORMULA THREE RUNNER-UP, 2004 GERMAN FORMULA BMW ADAC CHAMPION, 2003 GERMAN FORMULA BMW ADAC RUNNER-UP, 2001 EUROPEAN & GERMAN JUNIOR KART CHAMPION

CHASING THE TWO MERCEDES

It was clear from last year's opening round that it was going to be, like in 2014, Mercedes against the rest. Ferrari team leader Fernando Alonso had ended that season sixth, but third place for Sebastian at the opening round suggested that he might manage to beat that. And so it proved, especially at the following race, at Sepang, where Sebastian took his first win with Ferrari. It was clear that Ferrari's engine was no match for the Mercedes unit, but it improved through the season and Sebastian was frequently the best of the rest, collecting podium finished by the handful and then grabbing another win in Hungary and a second in Singapore. There is no doubt that Sebastian felt refreshed in a new environment, and he'll have felt more that a little relieved that he'd changed team when he saw how Red Bull Racing struggled, short on power, through 2015. Life at Ferrari clearly suits him, especially with Kimi Raikkonen happy to play a secondary role. The adulation of the Tifosi also put a smile on his face.

KIMI RAIKKONEN

Kimi's 2015 campaign had all the hallmarks of being his F1 swansong before entering permanent retirement, as he was dominated by incoming team-mate Sebastian Vettel. Yet he is being kept on for one final season with Ferrari.

Kimi's path from karting to F1 was unprecedented, as it took him just 23 races in Formula Renault before he earned a surprise race seat with Sauber in 2001.

His karting career produced Finnish and Scandinavian titles, so it came as no surprise that he was more than ready to graduate to Formula Renault in 1999 when he was 19. Critically, he had been noticed by driver manager David Robertson, whose son Steve was appointed to bring him on.

After doing four races in the British series, Kimi dropped out then returned for four races in the British winter series, and thus become champion.

In 2000, Kimi dominated the British championship. Then, while most would have considered F3, Kimi's management convinced Sauber to give him an F1 test. Amazingly, he impressed the team so much he was signed for F1 for 2001. He then belied his lack of experience and came sixth on his F1 debut. McLaren soon signed Kimi for 2002, and he delivered in 2003 by scoring his first win and running Michael Schumacher close for the title.

Runner-up again in 2005, Kimi moved on to Ferrari for 2007. Against expectations,

Kimi has been retained for a final year and must wish to end his F1 career on a high.

his late-season charge took him past McLaren's Fernando Alonso and Lewis Hamilton. This drivers' title has never been equalled and, by the end of his run with Ferrari in 2009, Kimi appeared to have lost almost all his enthusiasm for F1.

Having recharged his batteries in the World Rally Championship, Kimi returned to F1 in 2012 and grabbed victory for Lotus in Abu Dhabi. After another strong campaign in 2013, Kimi started his second spell with Ferrari, but this has yielded little glory.

TRACK NOTES

Nationality:	FINNISH
Born:	17 OCTOBER 1979, ESPOO, FINLAND
Website:	www.kimiraikkonen.com
Teams:	SAUBER 2001, McLAREN 2002-06, FERRARI 2007-09, LOTUS 2012-13, FERRARI 2014-16

CAREER RECORD

First Grand Prix:	2001 AUSTRALIAN GP
Grand Prix starts:	232
Grand Prix wins:	20
	2003 Malaysian GP, 2004 Belgian GP, 2005 Spanish GP, Monaco GP, Canadian GP, Hungarian GP, Turkish GP, Belgian GP, Japanese GP, 2007 Australian GP, French GP, British GP, Belgian GP, Chinese GP, Brazilian GP, 2008 Malaysian GP, Spanish GP, 2009 Belgian GP, 2012 Abu Dhabi GP, 2013 Australian GP
Poles:	16
Fastest laps:	42
Points:	1174
Honours:	2007 FORMULA ONE WORLD CHAMPION, 2003 & 2005 FORMULA ONE RUNNER-UP, 2000 BRITISH FORMULA RENAULT CHAMPION, 1999 BRITISH FORMULA RENAULT WINTER SERIES CHAMPION, 1998 EUROPEAN SUPER A KART RUNNER-UP, FINNISH KART CHAMPION & NORDIC KART CHAMPION

A YEAR SPENT IN THE SHADE

Having been outscored 161 to 55 by team-mate Fernando Alonso in 2014, Kimi would have hoped that last year might have offered him a chance to be less of a number two at Ferrari. Yet his hopes were kept in check, as his new partner would be none other than Sebastian Vettel. When the German raced to victory in his second race with the team, he achieved something that Kimi was never to come close to achieving. Certainly Mercedes dominated almost all the races, but it was the German and not the Finn who beat them when their guard was down. He won again in Hungary and Singapore, although Kimi claimed second in Bahrain and recorded a few fastest laps, he was never consistently rapid. This led many to conclude that his input wasn't all that it should be, and with some suggesting that his approach to his second spell in F1 after spending two years away in the World Rally Championship wasn't as focused as it would have been had he felt he had a shot at the title.

WILLIAMS

Proving that its 2014 return to form was no flash in the pan, Williams did it again last year and has kept on drivers Valtteri Bottas and Felipe Massa for a further push to challenge Mercedes, Red Bull and Ferrari in 2016, with greater consistency a must.

Felipe Massa looks forward to 2016 with great positivity after rising last year to the challenge of younger team-mate Valtteri Bottas.

Of all the teams competing in the World Championship, Williams goes back further than all but Ferrari and McLaren. With 114 wins and nine constructors' titles to its name, the team also has a record to contend with. Yet, of course, this was one of the teams that Enzo Ferrari dismissed from the ranks of largely British teams that were able to take on Ferrari after the introduction of the Ford DFV V8, an off-the-shelf engine that was a match for the best.

Frank Williams hoped to make a career as a racing driver, but F3 was as high as he got, as he realized that others had more talent and, certainly, more budget. Instead, he turned to running cars for others, both in F3 then F2. In 1969, he bought a Brabham chassis with which to enter Piers Courage in F1. Two second places showed promise and they brought in sportscar manufacturer de Tomaso for 1970. Sadly, Courage crashed to his death in the Dutch GP. That knocked Williams back and he ran Henri Pescarolo in a March in 1971. In 1972, though, Williams

built its first car, called the Politoys after a sponsor. It was destroyed on its debut. In 1973, Williams tried again, this time naming its car after sportscar manufacturer Iso.

The rest of the mid-1970s was more of the same, always short of money. In 1977, though, he formed Williams Grand Prix Engineering with Patrick Head, and they

THE POWER AND THE GLORY

ROB SMEDLEY
This 42-year-old English engineer joined Pilbeam after completing a master's degree at Loughborough University. From there, he worked for Peugeot in touring cars, then moved to the Williams-run Renault touring car team. His F1 break came in 1999 with Stewart GP and, from there, Rob became a track engineer for Jordan in 2002. After a spell with Ferrari's test team, Rob stepped up to its race outfit, as race engineer for Massa. In 2014, he followed the Brazilian driver to Williams, as head of performance engineering.

FIRMLY BACK WHERE IT BELONGS
Williams was generally there or thereabouts about last year, snapping at the heels of Ferrari in the pursuit of Mercedes. Yet, it took until the seventh round to earn even a podium position, for Bottas, followed next time out by one for Massa. There was a time when rumours of Ferrari's interest in Bottas unsettled the Finn, but when they died down he refocused. The team reported that the FW37 had a problem on low-speed circuits and reckoned at the Singapore GP that it had sorted it.

2015 DRIVERS & RESULTS

Driver	Nationality	Races	Wins	Pts	Pos
Valtteri Bottas	Finnish	19	0	136	5th
Felipe Massa	Brazilian	19	0	121	6th

FOR THE RECORD

Country of origin:	England
Team base:	Grove, England
Telephone:	(44) 01235 777700
Website:	www.williamsf1.com
Active in Formula One:	From 1972
Grands Prix contested:	700
Wins:	114
Pole positions:	128
Fastest laps:	133

THE TEAM

Team principal:	Sir Frank Williams
Co-founder:	Patrick Head
Deputy team principal:	Claire Williams
Chief executive officer:	Mike O'Driscoll
Chief technical officer:	Pat Symonds
Head of performance engineering:	Rob Smedley
Chief designer:	Ed Wood
Head of aerodynamics:	Jason Somerville
Chief engineer:	Andrew Murdoch
Race engineers:	Jonathan Eddolls & Dave Robson
Sporting manager:	Steve Nielsen
Test drivers:	Alex Lynn & Lance Stroll
Chassis:	Williams FW38
Engine:	Mercedes V6
Tyres:	Pirelli

never looked back. With proper backing for the first time, from Saudia, they got to grips with ground effects and Clay Regazzoni scored the first Williams win in the 1979 British GP. It was Alan Jones who was the more successful driver, though, and he landed the 1980 drivers' title, with the team taking the constructors' honours as well.

Keke Rosberg was Williams' second World Champion two years later, but after Nigel Mansell was pipped in 1986 and Nelson Piquet crowned in 1987, it played second fiddle to McLaren until it did a deal to run with Renault engines and Mansell dominated the 1992 campaign, with Alain Prost replacing him for 1993 and making it two titles in a row for the team from Grove.

Damon Hill was denied the opportunity to make it three in a row in 1994, when Michael Schumacher drove into him at the final round, but the team still landed its seventh constructors' title. Hill did get his crown two years later, followed by Jacques Villeneuve keeping Williams on top in 1997.

What was amazing through the decade was the fact that Frank had had a serious car accident early in 1986 and was paralysed from the chest down, yet continued to run the team in tandem with the engineering genius of Head. In 1994, too, the team had to stay strong after disaster, with new signing Ayrton Senna being killed at Imola.

Williams was knighted in 1999, but he would rather that the team had remained competitive, as it lost ground to McLaren and Ferrari after losing its works Renault deal. BMW then came on board and Ralf Schumacher won three races in 2001 but, after Juan Pablo Montoya claimed the 2004 season-closer in Brazil, eight years passed before the team triumphed again. This came at the 2012 Spanish GP, at which Pastor Maldonado shocked by qualifying on pole and then going on to win. There have been no further Williams wins. But since fitting Mercedes engines after the change to turbo V6s in 2014, it's getting closer all the time. Another reason for this has been the arrival of Pat Symonds to restructure the team and its approach to racing.

"We had a really good 2015 season and finished a solid third again, which is important for the growth of the team."
Rob Smedley

Nigel Mansell took his first F1 win with Williams at Brands Hatch at the end of 1985.

VALTTERI BOTTAS

It seemed likely through much of 2015 that Valtteri would be replacing fellow Finn Kimi Raikkonen at Ferrari in 2016, but instead he's staying on at Williams and will need to shine more than he did in 2015 to keep his career momentum going.

A star of the Scandinavian karting scene, Valtteri ventured further from home in 2007 when he ranked third in the Northern European Formula Renault Championship for a team run by fellow Finns, the Koiranens. He followed this up with the title in 2008 and the major European one too after overhauling Daniel Ricciardo, marking himself out as one to watch.

Moving up to the European Formula Three Championship in 2009, Valtteri failed to win a round, but still ranked third overall, albeit some way behind his ART Grand Prix team-mate Jules Bianchi.

Deciding to stay on and finish the job in European F3, Valtteri returned with ART in 2010 and won twice, but again had to settle for third overall behind Edoardo Mortara and Marco Wittmann. He did, though, win the F3 Masters invitation race at Zandvoort for the second time.

Without the money to move up to Formula Renault 3.5 or GP2 in 2011, Valtteri took a shot at GP3, a single-seater category roughly equivalent to F3 that had been introduced in 2010. The move paid off, as he took four wins and the title, then rounded out the year with a prize that went to the

Valtteri has enjoyed the patronage of Williams is desperate to start winning in 2016.

champion, an F1 test with Williams.

This proved key to Valtteri's future, as the team had seen enough of his abilities to give him regular runs in the Friday morning practice sessions at grands prix through the season.

This led to a race seat in 2013 and the team's faith was rewarded when he qualified third in the wet for the Canadian GP, before tumbling to 14th in the race as his car had no pace in the dry. However, he showed an affinity for North America later in the year by collecting his only points when he finished eighth at the United States GP at the Circuit of the Americas.

If his form in 2013 impressed, Valtteri really shone in 2014 and his run of third place in Austria followed by a pair of seconds at Silverstone and Hockenheim really made people pay attention. Three more podium visits helped him to edge past reigning World Champion Sebastian Vettel to rank fourth overall in the final standings.

PICKING UP THE POINTS

A few years ago, as the team endured a slump, a Williams driver scoring championship points was a revelation. However, as impressive as Valtteri's run of good point-scoring positions in the early rounds last year was, with a good third place in the Canadian GP, there were some in the F1 paddock who noted that he wasn't leaving his veteran team-mate Felipe Massa in his wake. Indeed, there was little to separate them as the Williams FW37 often proved to be best of the rest behind the Mercedes pair of Hamilton and Rosberg. Popular though Massa is, he's considered never to have been as good since his head injury in Hungary in 2009, and so some started questioning whether Valtteri really is the best of the new generation of drivers. As a result, Valtteri lost the chance to replace compatriot Raikkonen at Ferrari in 2016, putting extra pressure on him to shine this year or risk his best shot at landing a ride with a title-winning team being snatched by another young gun.

TRACK NOTES

Nationality:	FINNISH
Born:	28 AUGUST 1989, NASTOLA, FINLAND
Website:	www.valtteribottas.com
Teams:	WILLIAMS 2013-2016

CAREER RECORD

First Grand Prix:	2013 AUSTRALIAN GP
Grand Prix starts:	57
Grand Prix wins:	0
(best result: 2nd, 2014 British & German GPs)	
Poles:	0
Fastest laps:	1
Points:	326
Honours:	2011 GP3 CHAMPION,
	2010 & 2009 MASTERS FORMULA 3 WINNER,
	2008 EUROPEAN & NORTHERN EUROPEAN
	FORMULA RENAULT CHAMPION

FELIPE MASSA

Felipe appeared rejuvenated at Williams last year and one of the pitlane's most popular drivers is back for more in 2016, eager to gun for more podium visits after a year in which he displayed that he is certainly not ready to step back into retirement.

It's strange to report, but F1 team bosses aren't always much good at spotting rising talent. Felipe is one such driver who almost slipped their net, for he took an unusual route to F1 and many were surprised when he was given his F1 break by Sauber in 2002.

Felipe took the standard approach by moving up from racing karts in his native Brazil to claim the country's junior single-seater Formula Chevrolet title in 1999. With ambitions beyond stepping up to the South American F3 series, he headed for Europe when still 18. It was worth the separation from home life, as this overseas foray yielded both the European and Italian Formula Renault crowns.

Then came the unusual step of bypassing F3 to race instead in the more powerful F3000 category. However, there's a major distinction, as he didn't race in the FIA F3000 Championship, F1's feeder formula. Instead, Felipe competed in the inferior Formula 3000 Euro Championship. When he landed the title, few paid much attention. Yet, Felipe convinced Sauber to give him an F1 test and he landed a ride for 2002.

Felipe was immediately quick but wild, and lost his ride to become a test driver

Felipe was super consistent in 2015 and will want to claim more podiums, even a win.

in 2003. Impressively, though, this was for Ferrari, thanks to Felipe being managed by Ferrari F1 chief Jean Todt's son Nicolas.

Back racing in F1 with Ferrari-powered Sauber in 2004, Felipe showed marked improvement and so became a fully-fledged

Ferrari driver in 2006. Winning in Turkey and Brazil, he showed that he wasn't always prepared to be Michael Schumacher's number two. Although he added nine more wins over the next two seasons, Felipe's hopes of becoming Ferrari's number one were never realized. Then he suffered a head injury in Hungary in 2009.

Although Felipe returned in 2010 and stayed for four years, it was only when he joined Williams in 2014 that he felt able to be anything than a number two.

TRACK NOTES

Nationality:	BRAZILIAN
Born:	25 APRIL 1981, SAO PAULO, BRAZIL
Website:	www.felipemassa.com
Teams:	SAUBER 2002 & 2004-05, FERRARI 2006-13, WILLIAMS 2014-16

CAREER RECORD

First Grand Prix:	2002 AUSTRALIAN GP
Grand Prix starts:	230
Grand Prix wins:	11
	2006 Turkish GP, Brazilian GP, 2007 Bahrain GP, Spanish GP, Turkish GP, 2008 Bahrain GP, Turkish GP, French GP, European GP, Belgian GP, Brazilian GP
Poles:	16
Fastest laps:	6
Points:	1071
Honours:	2008 FORMULA ONE RUNNER-UP, 2001 EUROPEAN FORMULA 3000 CHAMPION, 2000 EUROPEAN & ITALIAN FORMULA RENAULT CHAMPION, 1999 BRAZILIAN FORMULA CHEVROLET CHAMPION

AIMING TO BE BEST OF THE REST

It's safe to say that Felipe enjoyed the 2015 World Championship. For, far from buckling under the burgeoning form of younger team-mate Valtteri Bottas, he rose to the challenge. After starting his second year with Williams strongly, the 34-year-old Brazilian claimed a podium finish at the Austrian GP, then, four rounds later, another third-place finish at Monza when his confidence had already been boosted by the signing of a contract extension for 2016. At this point in the season, Felipe had shown that he could really take the battle to Bottas – something that hadn't been the case in 2014 or even the early-season races of 2015. It was a real feather in his cap. To some it came as a surprise, but it emphasized how Felipe was thriving in the atmosphere at Williams, a team rejuvenated by its return to the sharp end of the grid. As a famously emotional driver, it showed that he performs better when feeling valued, which wasn't always the case when he drove for Ferrari.

RED BULL RACING

There was a lot of noise coming from Red Bull Racing last year that its Renault engines were no match for the Mercedes V6. However, after a lenthy search for a new engine supplier, the team will have Renault V6s again in 2016, badged as TAG Heuers.

Daniel Ricciardo raced as hard as he had in 2014, yet wasn't rewarded with any wins. Engine choice will dictate whether he does or not in 2016.

Like the Mercedes team, this is an outfit that has been entered under different names in the past. Like Mercedes, it appears cosmopolitan, but remains rooted in F1's crescent of excellence, in Milton Keynes.

Dietrich Mateschitz made his fortune from the Red Bull energy drink and his love of racing brought him into F1 as a sponsor of Sauber. However, fellow Austrian Helmut Marko helped him boost his involvement and their joint idea was Red Bull Racing. The perfect vehicle to make this happen fast was to take over an established team, and so it did in 2005, rebranding Jaguar Racing.

Jaguar Racing wasn't the team's first identity, as it had been created by three-time World Champion Jackie Stewart and his elder son Paul, taking a step up in 1997 after years of running teams in F3 then F3000.

The team ran Rubens Barrichello and Jan Magnussen in 1997 but, apart from Barrichello's second place at Monaco, its Ford-powered cars had no answer to the Williams or the Ferraris. It was the same in 1998, but Johnny Herbert joined in 1999 and won the European GP at the Nurburgring. This helped Stewart to rank fourth and the Stewart family then sold the team to Ford.

For 2000, the team re-emerged as Jaguar Racing after the Ford bosses decided to boost its Jaguar brand. Herbert was joined by Eddie Irvine, but they didn't fare well.

THE POWER AND THE GLORY

ROB MARSHALL
Red Bull's chief engineering officer went from rebuilding a 1930s motorbike as a teenager to design work at Rolls Royce. Then, in 1998, he moved from aerospace to F1, gaining kudos as his work helped Benetton to win again once it changed its name to Renault, culminating in Alonso's 2005 title. Joining Red Bull as chief designer for 2005, Rob has remained ever since, and now is in control in conjunction with aerodynamicist Dan Fallows as Newey steps back.

CLOSING THE YAWNING GAP TO MERCEDES
When Red Bull could claim only a sixth place at the opening round of 2015 as Mercedes dominated, things looked bleak. Horner started complaining about the lack of power from the Renault V6. Mateschitz and Marko soon followed suit, even making noises about moving on from F1, annoying some of the sport's bosses. Behind the scenes, though, the team was making progress and, while it looked for a new engine partner for 2016, Ricciardo and Kvyat excelled, with each claiming a second-place finish as the team worked hard to cut the deficit.

2015 DRIVERS & RESULTS

Driver	Nationality	Races	Wins	Pts	Pos
Daniel Ricciardo	Australian	19	0	92	8th
Daniil Kvyat	Russian	19	0	95	7th

FOR THE RECORD

Country of origin:	England
Team base:	Milton Keynes, England
Telephone:	(44) 01908 279700
Website:	www.redbullracing.com
Active in Formula One:	As Stewart GP 1997-99; Jaguar Racing 2000-04; Red Bull Racing 2005 on
Grands Prix contested:	319
Wins:	48
Pole positions:	58
Fastest laps:	41

THE TEAM

Chairman:	Dietrich Mateschitz
Team principal:	Christian Horner
Chief technical officer:	Adrian Newey
Chief engineering officer:	Rob Marshall
Head of aerodynamics:	Dan Fallows
Chief engineer, car engineering:	Paul Monaghan
Chief engineer, performance engineering:	Pierre Wache
Head of electronics:	Paul Everington
Team manager:	Jonathan Wheatley
Chief engineer:	Guillaume Rocquelin
Test driver:	tba
Chassis:	Red Bull RB12
Engine:	Renault V6
Tyres:	Pirelli

For 2001, former Indycar champion Bobby Rahal was given the reins and Irvine was its main point-scorer, but this and 2002 were hard years. Mark Webber joined for 2003 and showed fighting form in qualifying, but the team continued to rank seventh.

So it was that Red Bull found a team going nowhere fast and struck its deal, putting former F3000 racer turned team chief Christian Horner in charge. David Coulthard was signed as its lead driver, but the team finished seventh again, then again in 2006. However, Coulthard had convinced Adrian Newey to join from McLaren and the design ace soon gave the team upward momentum as Coulthard and Webber guided it to fifth. In 2008, the team suffered the embarrassment of Dietrich's back-up team, Scuderia Toro Rosso, being the first from his stable to win, thanks to Sebastian Vettel starring at Monza.

For 2009, Vettel was on board and he duly gave Red Bull Racing its first win, in the wet at Shanghai. With Webber claiming his first win at the Nurburgring, the team ended the year second only to Brawn GP.

Then came its golden years, with Vettel edging out Webber and Ferrari's Fernando Alonso to land the 2010 title. The team also landed its first constructors' title. In 2011, Vettel was in a class of his own and so two more titles were added as Red Bull ended up 153 points clear of McLaren. Renault-powered Red Bull then collected two more titles and Vettel another brace. However, F1 had new rules for 2014, making teams run 1.6-litre turbocharged V6 engines, and Renault's best wasn't good enough, allowing Mercedes to shine and Red Bull to slip. Interestingly, Daniel Ricciardo joined from Toro Rosso and took three wins to Vettel's none.

Another element of this changing of the guard was that Newey was pulling back, keen to try his hand at other things, but Rob Marshall has been doing well since. Then, with Red Bull criticizing Renault through 2015, it looked for a new engine, but the VW emissions scandal hit hopes of a deal with Audi, leaving Red Bull to race with TAG-Heuer badged Renault V6s.

25

"Our shared values of innovation and a desire to stand out from the crowd make our partnership with TAG Heuer one of the most exciting in F1."
Christian Horner

Conditions were foul in the 2009 Chinese GP, but Sebastian Vettel took RBR's first victory.

DANIEL RICCIARDO

In 2014, Daniel proved himself by beating his then Red Bull Racing team-mate Sebastian Vettel. In 2015, with Renault engines holding him back, he failed to win even once, and he will be determined to redress that balance in the season ahead.

Daniel won all he could in karting in Western Australia and advanced to Formula Ford once he turned 16. Then, with his home city of Perth so far from other Australian cities, he opted not to compete in the Australian championship, but to contest the Formula BMW Pacific Championship in 2006 instead at circuits including Sepang and Shanghai, ranking third in that.

The next step in 2007 required even more travelling as Daniel headed to Europe and based himself in Italy to race in its Formula Renault Championship. Racing against the likes of Jaime Alguersuari, he did well enough to attract Red Bull's talent spotters, and he landed the backing for a crack at the European series in 2008, finishing second to Valtteri Bottas.

Having been pipped to the title by Valtteri Bottas, he was anxious to keep the momentum going, so in 2009 Daniel trod the well-worn path to the British F3 Championship. He duly followed in the wheeltracks of numerous future World Champions in landing the title and this acted as his springboard into more powerful single-seaters. It also earned him his first F1 test courtesy of Red Bull.

Daniel has proved himself a winner, and will strike when he is next given the equipment.

Impressing in Formula Renault 3.5 in 2010, he was edged out by Mikhail Aleshin.

Daniel stayed for a second crack at Formula Renault 3.5 in 2011, but his programme was interrupted midseason when the HRT F1 team asked him to replace Narain Karthikeyan, allowing backers Red Bull to finance valuable F1 track time.

Joining Scuderia Toro Rosso for 2012, Daniel finished ninth in the opening round and was kept on for 2013, doubling his points tally, to rank 14th. A pair of seventh-place finishes gave him the nod ahead of team-mate Jean-Eric Vergne to be promoted to Red Bull Racing for 2014.

He was expected to stay in his team-mate Sebastian Vettel's shadow, but he amazed everyone in the F1 paddock when he outscored him three wins to none to end the year behind only Mercedes drivers Lewis Hamilton and Nico Rosberg.

TRACK NOTES

Nationality:	AUSTRALIAN
Born:	1 JULY 1989, PERTH, AUSTRALIA
Website:	www.danielricciardo.com
Teams:	HRT 2011, TORO ROSSO 2012-13, RED BULL RACING 2014-16

CAREER RECORD	
First Grand Prix:	2011 BRITISH GP
Grand Prix starts:	88
Grand Prix wins:	3
2014 Canadian GP, Hungarian GP, Belgian GP	
Poles:	0
Fastest laps:	4
Points:	360
Honours:	2010 FORMULA RENAULT 3.5 RUNNER-UP, 2009 BRITISH FORMULA THREE CHAMPION, 2008 EUROPEAN FORMULA RENAULT RUNNER-UP & WESTERN EUROPEAN FORMULA RENAULT CHAMPION

GIVING IT A GO, REGARDLESS

It was clear from the outset of last season that Daniel's second season with Red Bull Racing was going to be a challenge. After his wonderful first campaign with the team, in which he ranked third overall, behind only the Mercedes drivers, but importantly two positions ahead of Sebastian Vettel, his target had to be to improve on the three wins he collected in 2014. However, sixth place in Melbourne was a sign of things to come, with simply not enough horsepower being provided by the Renault V6 behind his shoulders to match the Mercedes- and Ferrari-powered cars ahead of him. With a problem this fundamental, things didn't improve, although third place and fastest lap at the Hungaroring was a sign that his skill was still of the highest order. Three rounds later, Daniel went one place better by finishing second on the streets of Singapore. In the end, though, people simply had to admire Daniel's determination to go for it even in a less than competitive car, and the smile that seldom left his face.

DANIIL KYVAT

After a solid if not always spectacular first season with Red Bull Racing, this 21-year-old Russian is back to see if he can improve on his 2015 peak result of second place in Hungary and take the battle more consistently to Daniel Ricciardo.

In the past few years, summarizing an F1 driver's career takes fewer words than it used to, as they all spend their childhood racing karts before they vault in as few leaps as possible through the junior single-seater formulae to F1.

Daniil's four-year passage from Formula BMW to F1 is impressive but not unique, even though he was still only 19 when he made his F1 debut in 2014. Yet, the fact that Max Verstappen who followed him to Toro Rosso, did it in just one year from karts to F1 shows how things have changed.

Competing in karting meant undertaking a considerable amount of travel from his home in Ufa, but Daniil did enough to make his mark and advanced to car racing as he turned 16. His first single-seater campaign was in European Formula BMW and Daniil ranked tenth, but vitally picked up Red Bull backing. That winter, he contested the Toyota Racing Series in New Zealand, winning a round and ranking fifth.

A season of European Formula Renault was his main exercise for 2011, and it yielded three wins and third place behind Robin Frijns and Carlos Sainz Jr. With the aim of taking the European title in 2012,

Daniil is adding experience to his speed and should shine in his third year of F1.

Daniil remained with Koiranen Motorsport and he and Stoffel Vandoorne dominated, before the Belgian pipped him. Daniil did claim one title, though, as he landed the middle European ALPS Formula Renault crown to take his 2012 wins tally to 14.

Daniil raced to the GP3 title with MW Arden in 2013, coming on strong to win three of the last six races in the 16-round series. Looking to gain maximum experience, he also contested most of the European F3 Championship with Carlin. He did well in that as well, taking five poles and winning a race at Zandvoort.

Then, with a vacancy at Scuderia Toro Rosso for 2014, Daniil was selected to skip GP2 and go directly to F1. He made no mistakes, finishing ninth on his debut in the Australian GP. Daniil wasn't fazed by F1 at all, adding two more points finishes before the year was out.

TRACK NOTES

Nationality:	RUSSIAN
Born:	26 APRIL 1994, UFA, RUSSIA
Website:	www.daniilkvyat.me
Teams:	TORO ROSSO 2014, RED BULL RACING 2015-16

CAREER RECORD	
First Grand Prix:	2014 AUSTRALIAN GP
Grand Prix starts:	38
Grand Prix wins:	0
	(best result: 2nd, 2015 Hungarian GP)
Poles:	0
Fastest laps:	0
Points:	103
Honours:	2013 GP3 CHAMPION, 2012 EUROPEAN FORMULA RENAULT RUNNER-UP & ALPS CHAMPION, 2011 FORMULA RENAULT NORTHERN EUROPE RUNNER-UP, 2009 WSK KART RUNNER-UP

SETTLING IN VERY NICELY

In 2014, Daniel Ricciardo stepped up from Toro Rosso to Red Bull Racing and outperformed his team-mate, winning three races to his rival's none. This was impressive, and especially so as that team-mate was four-time World Champion and long-time team number one Sebastian Vettel. Daniil wasn't able to achieve that same feat against Ricciardo last year after being similarly promoted from Toro Rosso to Red Bull Racing, but he stayed close enough on points through the year to impress. Wins were out of the question for both as their Renault V6s weren't competitive enough for that, failing to allow them to keep up with their Mercedes- and Ferrari-engined rivals. Yet, when a lack of power was less of an issue, on twistier tracks, Daniil showed well. Fourth place at Monaco was topped by second at the Hungaroring, in a race where he kept his head while others around him were losing theirs. Fourth place next time out on the high-speed Spa-Francorchamps was clear evidence of his improving form.

FORCE INDIA

Financial problems for Lotus and Toro Rosso struggling with Renault V6s, plus the dramatic decline at McLaren, left Force India able to cement fifth place in the constructors' rankings.

Nico Hulkenberg and Sergio Perez ran strongly through the second half of 2015 and will again provide a very strong driver pairing.

The Jordan team made such an impact in its first decade that it's easy to forget the two team iterations that followed, Midland and Spyker. Yet, as it's now entering its ninth season with the team's fourth identity, Vijay Mallya's Force India team now very much has an identity of its own.

Few teams have made as much of a splash as Jordan did in its debut year, 1991. Not only did its cars have a strong visual identity, but they were fast too, with Bertrand Gachot setting the fastest lap of the race at the Hungarian GP and then Andrea de Cesaris retiring from second place next time out in the Belgian GP at Spa-Francorchamps.

Entered by former F3 racer Eddie Jordan, whose F3000 team had helped the likes of Jean Alesi, Johnny Herbert and Martin Donnelly on their way to F1, the team took a backward step in 1992 when it ran Yamaha engines. Only when it paid for Hart engines did it progress, with Rubens Barrichello ranking fifth in 1994. He and Eddie Irvine finished second and third in

Canada in 1995, but their Peugeot engines were never a match for those from Renault, Ferrari or newcomers Mercedes. However, it all came together in 1998, when the

team changed to using Mugen engines and Damon Hill led home Ralf Schumacher at Spa-Francorchamps for the team's first win. Heinz-Harald Frentzen added two more wins

THE POWER AND THE GLORY

ROBERT FERNLEY

Bob and Vijay Mallya go back a long way. Bob went into business with Bob Howlings and formed Amco Motor Racing, a company that bought and sold old F1 cars. One of his customers was Mallya, for whom they ran an Ensign in Indian racing for five years. Bob then ran Jim Crawford in the British F1 series in 1982 and later in CanAm. Mallya called him in when he took over Spyker in 2007 and Bob now fills in as team boss at any grand prix not attended by Mallya.

MOVING AHEAD OF McLAREN TO FIFTH

Not so many years ago, Force India was delighted to receive some engineering advice from McLaren when it changed over to using Mercedes engines. Yet last year, as McLaren struggled with Honda power, the advice could have gone in the opposite direction. While McLaren floundered, Nico Hulkenberg and Sergio Perez were able to harvest points at most races to stay ahead of Lotus in their battle to rank fifth overall. Stability in team personnel helped the Silverstone-based to keep a clear focus, with Andrew Green producing a competitive car.

2015 DRIVERS & RESULTS

Driver	Nationality	Races	Wins	Pts	Pos
Nico Hulkenberg	German	19	0	58	10th
Sergio Perez	Mexican	19	0	78	9th

FOR THE RECORD

Country of origin:	England
Team base:	Silverstone, England
Telephone:	(44) 01327 850800
Website:	www.astonmartinracing.com
Active in Formula One:	As Jordan 1991-2004, Midland 2005-06, Spyker 2007; Force India 2008-16
Grands Prix contested:	435
Wins:	4
Pole positions:	3
Fastest laps:	5

THE TEAM

Team principal & managing director:	Vijay Mallya
Deputy team principal:	Robert Fernley
Chief operating officer:	Otmar Szafnauer
Technical director:	Andrew Green
Production director:	Bob Halliwell
Aerodynamics director:	Simon Phillips
Chief designers:	Akio Haga & Ian Hall
Aerodynamics director:	Simon Phillips
Sporting director:	Andy Stevenson
Chief engineer:	Tom McCullough
Test driver:	Alfonso Celis Jr
Chassis:	Force India VJM09
Engine:	Mercedes V6
Tyres:	Pirelli

in 1999 and Jordan finished the year in its best-ever final ranking: third.

After that, Jordan couldn't compete financially and slipped to mid-table finishes, with only Giancarlo Fisichella's victory in the 2003 Brazilian GP bringing cheer, and so ebullient showman Jordan decided to sell up and move on. For 2005, Russian steel magnate Alex Shnaider bought the team and renamed it Midland, but he soon lost interest and sold a share to the Mol family, who renamed it Spyker after a long-standing Dutch car manufacturer that wanted to promote its road-going sportscars.

This didn't bring much of a change of fortune as the team continued to bump along at the back of the pack. Its one good result in these years - third and fourth places in the 2005 US GP - came only as all but six cars withdrew before the start because of tyre safety concerns.

In late 2007, industrialist Mallya joined forces with the Mols and the team was renamed Force India for 2008, being used to promote the many product brands that Mallya's family sell in South-East Asia.

With James Key working well with design chief Mark Smith, the team made progress in 2009, with the arrival of Mercedes engines and technical assistance from McLaren helping in no small part.

With its cars run in India's colours of white, orange and green, marked progress was shown when Giancarlo Fisichella qualified on pole position for the Belgian GP and finished just a second behind winner Kimi Raikkonen's Ferrari.

Finishing just one place behind Williams in 2010, in seventh, showed more strong form, with the team going one place better in 2011. Nico Hulkenberg and Paul di Resta picked up a fourth place each in 2012. However, as shown from 2013 to 2015, the team seems to be stuck at this level, unable to challenge Ferrari, McLaren and Williams for wins as it did when Eddie Jordan was at the helm. A lack of money has long troubled the team as it tries to stay ahead of the likes of Sauber and Toro Rosso, but it has no hope of toppling the top teams. This is why talks were entered into to rename it Aston Martin Racing, not only to offer the supercar manufacturer F1 technology for its road cars but to attract much needed sponsorship. This has no connection with Aston Martin's other foray into F1 from 1959-60.

"Aston Martin is one of the most famous British brands. It has a good amount of stature, attracts more sponsors and makes what is Force India today more marketable."
Vijay Mallya

Barrichello and Irvine celebrate on the podium in Canada in 1995 when the team raced as Jordan.

NICO HULKENBERG

Nico broke F1's mould last year when he won the Le Mans 24 Hours for Porsche, reminding fans of the 1970s when drivers would race anything, any time, anywhere. For 2016, his day job will again be trying to propel Force India up the points table.

Nico has won more titles on his climb from karting to F1 than most F1 drivers, delivering whenever his equipment has been competitive. Yet, somehow, he still has found no opening with a top team and many feel that it's because he's too tall and too heavy for a sport that likes its drivers to be small and light.

The signs of his abundant talent were clear from when Nico landed the German Junior Kart title aged 15. Following up by taking the senior title in 2003, Nico duly won the Formula BMW ADAC title in his first year in single-seaters, just ahead of Sebastien Buemi.

For almost two decades, Dallara has been the chassis of choice in F3 and yet Nico did well enough in a Ligier in 2006 to land a test with the German A1GP team. Having been fastest of all in an open test at Silverstone, he landed the ride and was the series' star driver, clinching the title.

This helped Nico to land a ride in the 2007 European F3 Championship and he ended the year third overall behind Romain Grosjean and Buemi as the top rookie. In 2008, though, Nico scored almost twice the points of any rival and was a dominant

Nico had some frustrating equipment failures in 2015, but the speed was clear for all to see.

champion, earning an F1 test with Williams.

The next step was to GP2 and Nico became a rare thing: a champion at the first attempt, winning five races to leave his vastly more experienced team-mate Pastor Maldonado in the shade.

Pole position in the wet at Interlagos was the highlight of his first F1 season with Williams, but Maldonado's money bought his ride for 2011, forcing Nico onto the sidelines. After a year as Force India test driver, Nico was back racing again in 2012 when he demonstrated again that he would deliver if given competitive machinery. Frustratingly for him, this was in short supply again in 2013 when he joined Sauber and has been ever since with Force India.

TRACK NOTES

Nationality:	GERMAN
Born: 19 AUGUST 1987, EMMERICH, GERMANY	
Website:	www.nicohulkenberg.net
Teams:	WILLIAMS 2010, FORCE INDIA 2012,
	SAUBER 2013, FORCE INDIA 2014-16

CAREER RECORD

First Grand Prix:	2010 BAHRAIN GP
Grand Prix starts:	96
Grand Prix wins:	0 (best result: 4th,
	2012 Belgian GP, 2013 Korean GP)
Poles:	1
Fastest laps:	1
Points:	290
Honours:	2009 GP2 CHAMPION, 2008
	EUROPEAN FORMULA THREE CHAMPION,
	2007 FORMULA THREEE MASTERS WINNER,
	2006/07 A1GP CHAMPION, 2005 GERMAN
	FORMULA BMW ADAC CHAMPION & GERMAN
	FORMULA BMW RUNNER-UP, 2003 GERMAN
	KART CHAMPION, 2002 GERMAN JUNIOR
	KART CHAMPION

HELD BACK BY HIS EQUIPMENT

With Mercedes dominating the past two seasons of F1, it means that few other drivers have had a realistic shot at winning, and Force India, despite having Mercedes engines, was held back by a traditional lack of competitive budget. The result was that it was probably only the fifth most competitive outfit. Thus it comes as little surprise that Nico and team-mate Sergio Perez could usually fight only for the minor point-scoring positions. Nico's best finish was sixth in the Austrian GP and later at both Suzuka and Interlagos, backed up by seventh-place finishes at Silverstone and Monza. Mid-season, Nico did something that no F1 driver has done for a couple of decades: he took time out to race for Porsche in the famous 24-hour race at Le Mans. At a stroke, he gave sportscar fans a chance to see how F1 drivers stack up against their stars and Nico did himself proud by being part of Porsche's winning trio, finishing one place ahead of F1 retiree Mark Webber, who drove one of Porsche's two regular entries.

SERGIO PEREZ

Back for a third campaign with Force India, Sergio will be looking at the very least to win the internal battle with Nico Hulkenberg again and hope that the VJM09 will be competitive enough throughout the season to help him record more podium finishes.

In his early years of single-seater racing, Sergio didn't look as though he had the outstanding ability required to reach F1, as he was seldom the pick of the pack in the junior formulae. However, here he is, lined up for his sixth season in the sport's top category, and he is far from out of place. It goes to show that not every driver develops at the same pace.

Mexico has long had a liberal approach to drivers graduating to car racing, so Sergio was able to step up to cars at the age of just 14. Making the move seem all the more daunting for a young teenager, he did it abroad, racing in the Barber Dodge series in the United States. That was in 2004 and it clearly didn't stretch him enough as, the next year, Sergio moved to Germany to race in its Formula BMW championship.

After a learning year, Sergio came back and ranked sixth as Christian Vietoris dominated the season. What impressed Sergio at year's end was having a run in Mexico's more powerful A1GP car and he returned to Europe to race in British F3 in 2007. Running in the "national" class, Sergio won this junior sub-class. Returning to race

Sergio came on strong through 2015, boosting his confidence as he hit his very best F1 form.

in the main class in 2008, Sergio finished fourth for T-Sport as Jaime Alguersuari took the crown for dominant Carlin.

GP2 was next, but ranking only 12th as future Force India team-mate Hulkenberg

took the 2009 title wasn't part of his masterplan. Fortunately for Sergio, it was a case of second time lucky as he was runner-up to category veteran Pastor Maldonado in 2010, boosted by five wins.

Sergio's step into F1 in 2011 came with Sauber and he improved from an overall ranking of 16th in 2011 to 10th in 2012 in a campaign that peaked with three podium visits, the best of which was for hunting down Fernando Alonso's Ferrari at Sepang.

Joining Jenson Button at McLaren in 2013, Sergio finished a disappointing 11th. So he moved to Force India and was classified one place higher, which wasn't bad.

TRACK NOTES

Nationality:	MEXICAN
Born:	26 JANUARY 1990, GUADALAJARA, MEXICO
Website:	www.sergioperezf1.com
Teams:	SAUBER 2011-12, McLAREN 2013, FORCE INDIA 2014-16

CAREER RECORD	
First Grand Prix:	2011 BAHRAIN GP
Grand Prix starts:	93
Grand Prix wins:	0 (best result: 2nd, 2012 MALAYSIAN GP)
Poles:	0
Fastest laps:	3
Points:	266
Honours:	2010 GP2 RUNNER-UP, 2007 BRITISH FORMULA THREE NATIONAL CLASS CHAMPION

CONSISTENT FORM AT LAST

What marked out Sergio's 2015 season from his previous four seasons of F1 was that he dropped the silly moments that used to cost him points and added consistency to his attack. Famously light on his tyres, Sergio came good in the second half of the season after the team introduced development parts and then the B-spec VJM08. There was a scare when rear suspension failure in practice in Hungary put the Mexican's car on its head, but the car came good, enabling him to collect a useful run of points for fifth-, sixth- and seventh-place finishes in the consecutive races in Belgium, Italy and Singapore, then peak with third place in Sochi. With team-mate Nico Hulkenberg suffering a counterbalancing run of non-finishes, this tilted the intra-team balance in his favour. There was talk circulating of Sergio perhaps moving to Renault for 2016, but uncertainty around the future of the team encouraged him to wrap up a deal before last September's Japanese GP to stay on for a third season of his Force India partnership with Hulkenberg.

RENAULT

The financial cloud that hung over the Lotus team last year has been lifted by Renault taking it over for 2016 to give the team from Enstone its second spell as the French manufacturer's outfit. Sadly, it has lost its number one, Romain Grosjean.

Pastor Maldonado is staying on for a third year with the team and needs to step up to take on the team leader's role if he is to impress.

In the upheaval of last year, the rich history of this British team was easy to forget. Was it Lotus, was it to become Renault, was it anything? Well, last autumn it became Renault for a second time, but its past can be celebrated. It has a history with a great pedigree and no fewer than four drivers' and three constructors' titles to its name.

Toleman was its starting point, with the team founded by car transporter magnate Ted Toleman after it had dominated F2 in 1980. Progress was made as Rory Byrne shaped ever-sleeker chassis. Ayrton Senna spent his rookie F1 year with Ioleman in 1984 and came second in Monaco. However, he moved on and the team stalled, but investment from knitwear firm Benetton propelled it to a higher stage in 1986 and Gerhard Berger used BMW turbo power to good effect to give it its first win. There were to be no more wins until 1989 when Alessandro Nannini took the Japanese GP after McLaren's Senna was disqualified.

Two wins in the last two races of 1990

by Nelson Piquet helped the team rank third, as it had in 1988, but what pushed Benetton to glory was the arrival of Michael Schumacher. He gelled with Byrne and tech chief Ross Brawn and pushed Williams' Damon Hill out of the way to land the 1994 crown. In 1995, with Renault engines, they did it again, taking the constructors'

THE POWER AND THE GLORY

BOB BELL
Once it became clear last year that Renault was taking over the Lotus team, personnel changes were mooted. One of the first heavy hitters to arrive was Bob, a technical chief who had worked for the team from 2001 to 2010. He started off at McLaren back in 1982, working on its aborted land speed project. In 1997, he joined Benetton as senior aerodynamicist, had a spell at Jordan, then returned to become technical director. Since 2010, he has worked itinerantly, most recently helping the Manor team find its feet.

PRESSING ON REGARDLESS
Two non-finishes at the opening round last year might have been a forewarning, as the team would struggle to finish the year. However, it soon got going, with Grosjean in particular collecting points drives as he went. In the second half of the year, as money troubles bit, he finally bought real cheer with third place in the Belgian GP. Maldonado was not as effective, and there was the embarrassment of being locked out in Japan as bills hadn't been settled, but the team kept going.

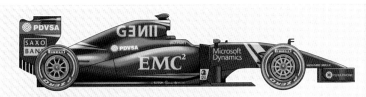

2015 DRIVERS & RESULTS

Driver	Nationality	Races	Wins	Pts	Pos
Romain Grosjean	French	19	0	51	11th
Pastor Maldonado	Venezuelan	19	0	27	14th

FOR THE RECORD

Country of origin:	England
Team base:	Enstone, England
Telephone:	(44) 01608 678000
Website:	www.renaultf1team.com
Active in Formula One:	As Toleman 1981-85, Benetton 1986-2001, Renault 2002-11 & 2016, Lotus 2012-15
Grands Prix contested:	572
Wins:	48
Pole positions:	34
Fastest laps:	54

title too, helped by two wins from Johnny Herbert to take their year's tally to 11.

Schumacher moved on and Benetton was offered hope by Giancarlo Fisichella and Alex Wurz, but Williams moved ahead then McLaren, then Ferrari, led by Schumacher.

Flavio Briatore returned to lead the team and, in 2002, it was renamed Renault. This wasn't to be confused with the Renault team that ran from 1977 to 1985, from Viry-Chatillon. It was only a name change for the team from Enstone. The extra finance that came with this change helped a lot. Fernando Alonso chose the right time to join, taking his first win in 2003. Two years later, he was champion and this "mock" Renault team gave the French manufacturer its first constructors' title in its own right, rather than as an engine partner. Alonso and Renault did it again in 2006.

It has never been as sweet again and there was a fourth name change when the team was rebranded as Lotus for 2012, two years after being taken over by venture capitalists Genii Capital. However, not even the return to F1 from rallying of Kimi Raikkonen could propel it back to the top, although he ranked third after winning in Abu Dhabi. The Lotus name had been brought back to F1 by Tony Fernandes' team in 2010, but as a branding exercise only,

as there was no bloodline back to Colin Chapman's team that shaped F1 between 1958 and 1994. The now Malaysian-owned Lotus car company didn't like this, and so Fernandes' team had to be renamed Caterham, with the Lotus name being transferred to this team from Enstone.

It remained fourth in 2013, but money was short by 2014 and its competitiveness dropped away as Renault's engine couldn't match the Mercedes V6 when the engine rules changed, and it fell to eighth.

Last autumn, though, Renault bought a 65 percent stake in the team, thus its latest name change and conversion to a full manufacturer entry rather than just racing under a badge of convenience as it did with Lotus. Renault has pledged to be involved for a minimum of five years.

THE TEAM

Team principal:	Frederic Vasseur
Chief executive officer:	Matthew Carter
Chief operating officer:	Thomas Mayer
Deputy team principal:	Federico Gastaldi
Technical director:	Bob Bell
Operations director:	Alan Permane
Chief designer:	Martin Tolliday
Head of aerodynamics:	Nicolas Hennel de Beaupreau
Chief engineer:	Ayao Komatsu
Team manager:	Paul Seaby
Chief mechanic:	Greg Baker
Test driver:	tba
Chassis:	Renault
Engine:	Renault V6
Tyres:	Pirelli

"As well as having a great future ahead of him behind the wheel, Jolyon is also an intelligent and highly marketable asset to the team."

Gerard Lopez

Gerhard Berger celebrates the team's first victory, when it raced as Benetton, in Mexico in 1986.

PASTOR MALDONADO

Lotus was in constant financial difficulty in 2015, but Pastor has brought his considerable backing to ensure a third year with the team that will now race as Renault in the hope that he will finish both more often and higher up the order.

Top international racing drivers from Venezuela are few and far between. Johnny Cecotto was the first of note, a motorbike world champion in the 1970s who moved across to car racing and raced in F1 until breaking his legs at Brands Hatch in 1984. Then there were decades before Pastor started climbing the ladder, helped in no small part by considerable financial backing from the government.

Basing himself in Italy from the age of 18, Pastor won the Italian Formula Renault title at his second attempt, also showing race-winning speed in the European championship. That was in 2004 and Pastor stepped up to the World Series by Renault, thus bypassing the more usual step of trying Formula 3 next. Clearly loving the extra power, he also raced in Italian F3000 and won a race in that. For 2006, though, Pastor's focus was the World Series and he ranked third overall behind Alx Danielsson and Borja Garcia.

Advancing to GP2 – the final step before F1 – Pastor showed great speed to qualify on pole position at Monaco and then go on to win. However, he was inconsistent and

Pastor faces the challenge of having a new team-mate in his third year with the team.

didn't finish the season. Hoping for better in 2008, Pastor won at Spa-Francorchamps, but showed a propensity to crash and ranked fifth overall at year's end.

Back for a third year in 2009, Pastor fell to sixth, being shown the way by team-mate Nico Hulkenberg who claimed the title in his rookie year. Finally, in 2010, Pastor landed the GP2 title, taking six wins to runner-up Sergio Perez's five.

Seizing this boost, Pastor was given his F1 break by Williams in 2011. One point for tenth at Spa was followed by 45 in 2012, but importantly 25 of those came from a surprise victory from pole at the Spanish GP. That Pastor's next best result that year was a fifth place showed how inconsistency continued to dog his career.

The next two years produced just three points, with even a change to Lotus for 2014 offering no more career momentum.

TRACK NOTES

Nationality:	VENEZUELAN
Born:	9 MARCH 1985, MARACAY, VENEZUELA
Website:	www.pastormaldonado.com
Teams:	WILLIAMS 2011-13, LOTUS 2014-15, RENAULT 2016

CAREER RECORD

First Grand Prix:	2011 AUSTRALIAN GP
Grand Prix starts:	96
Grand Prix wins:	1
	2012 Spanish GP
Poles:	1
Fastest laps:	0
Points:	76
Honours:	2010 GP2 CHAMPION, 2004 ITALIAN FORMULA RENAULT CHAMPION, 2003 ITALIAN FORMULA RENAULT WINTER SERIES CHAMPION

TOO FEW RACE FINISHES

If Pastor had thought that his second season with Lotus would run better than his first, he was to be disappointed, as 2015 was perhaps even more of a struggle until the second half of the season. There were way too many retirements. As ever, some were due to mechanical failure, others to Pastor's over exuberance and lack of judgement. Certainly, with the team in increasing financial difficulties, the atmosphere wasn't one that made things easy, as there were times when the team didn't know if it would still be racing at the next round or perhaps be under new ownership. A pair of seventh-place finishes in Canada then Hungary indicated progress, but he could only be judged against team-mate Romain Grosjean, and this comparison went against Pastor when Grosjean finished third in the Belgian GP. That this was followed by Pastor retiring his car with damage from a first-corner clash at the next race in Monza didn't reflect well. Still, with a welcome tranche of sponsorship available for 2016, Pastor was re-signed by the team before the season was out.

JOLYON PALMER

Former grand prix racer Jonathan Palmer's elder son Jolyon has worked extremely hard to make it to Formula One and, now he's here, he could surprise people as he brings an intelligent approach to his racing and already knows the team well.

It's not a given that racing drivers propel their offspring away from standard business careers and into racing, but it appears the rule rather than the exception. Thus Jonathan Palmer – 84 grands prix between 1983 and 1989 for Williams, RAM, Zakspeed and Tyrrell – has been followed out onto the circuits by sons Jolyon and Will. Although busy running his cluster of British circuits, including Brands Hatch, Jonathan's famously studious and analytical approach is being passed down to the next generation.

Jolyon, the older son by six years, followed a spell in karting by going car racing in 2005 in T-Cars, a special series for young teenagers in silhouette racers.

From here, he graduated to the Formula Palmer Audi single-seater series instigated by his father in 2007. Jolyon ranked third in his second season, then advanced to another Palmer-initiated series, Formula Two, in 2009. Runner-up in this in 2010, Jolyon prepared for the next step by testing for several GP2 teams.

What followed, was planned as a two-year bid for GP2 glory – one for learning and then one for landing the title – but it took

Jolyon can expect to receive plenty of parental advice for his first year as an F1 racer.

two years longer than that. After scoring no points in 2011, Jolyon took his first GP2 win in 2012 with iSport International at Monaco, to rank 11th. In 2013, he doubled up to win twice at the Hungaroring and Singapore, for Carlin, moving forward to seventh overall.

Then, in 2014, Jolyon transferred to DAMS in a final bid for glory and doubled his tally again, to four wins – at Sakhir, Monaco again, Monza and Sochi. With this impressive haul, he deservedly landed the prestigious GP2 title in style ahead of Stoffel Vandoorne. His highlight was undoubtedly pole position, fastest lap and victory at Monaco, a combination that's most attractive to future sponsors.

Alongside his GP2 title in 2014, Jolyon also had his first taste of F1, testing for Force India. He did a very professional job and was invited to perform a similar role with the Lotus team in 2015.

So, with Jolyon managing to clinch his graduation to an F1 race seat with Renault for 2016, younger brother Will will now have a target to aim for, and the teenager started well by winning last year's British Formula Four title.

A YEAR SPENT LEARNING THE ROPES

Landing the GP2 title is supposed to be the final step before F1. Yet, as with F3000 before it, this isn't always the case as F1 vacancies are so rare. So it was that Jolyon spent last year going to grands prix, but only as the Lotus team's reserve driver. He was allowed to run in several practice sessions late in the year, but otherwise it was a case of this Englishman spending time learning every facet of life in the paddock as well as in the pitlane. This will have been both enlightening and frustrating, for no racer likes to be left on the sidelines while their contemporaries are out on track proving their credentials. Yet, his perseverance and positive approach clearly worked and so Jolyon finds himself on the brink of his F1 career at what is now the relatively advanced age of 25, albeit this is almost two years younger than his father Jonathan was when he stepped up from F2 in 1983 back when teenaged F1 drivers were very much a rarity.

TRACK NOTES

Nationality:	BRITISH
Born:	20 JANUARY 1991, HORSHAM, ENGLAND
Website:	www.jolyonpalmer.com
Teams:	RENAULT 2016

CAREER RECORD

First Grand Prix:	2016 AUSTRALIAN GP
Grand Prix starts:	0
Grand Prix wins:	0
Poles:	0
Fastest laps:	0
Points:	0
Honours:	2014 GP2 CHAMPION, 2010 FORMULA TWO RUNNER-UP

SCUDERIA TORO ROSSO

There was no gain in championship position for Toro Rosso last year, as it remained seventh in the rankings, but there was definitely a change in perception as its pair of rookies shone, Max Verstappen in particular. Expect even more from them in 2016.

Max Verstappen propelled Scuderia Toro Rosso higher up the race order than it is accustomed to in 2015 and will be out to go better still.

Minardi was a much-loved little team from its step up from F2 to F1 in 1985 until the end of 2005. It was very Italian, but it wasn't Ferrari. Money was tight, points were scarce, but it kept on plugging away. There were highlights, like Pierluigi Martini leading the Portuguese GP in 1989 and qualifying on the front row for the 1990 United States GP. However, a glance down the list of drivers run by Minardi shows how this was a team that was prepared to blood new talent. Among the ranks of its F1 debutants were Alessandro Nannini, Giancarlo Fisichella, Jarno Trulli, Fernando Alonso and Mark Webber, with the last named stealing onto the podium at the 2002 season-opener in Melbourne to celebrate, despite finishing fifth.

So, when Helmut Marko convinced Red Bull magnate Dietrich Mateschitz that he needed a junior outfit to augment his newly set up Red Bull Racing team, to bring on future drivers for that, Giancarlo Minardi was bought out and the team from Faenza renamed for 2006. Thus Scuderia Toro Rosso was formed and it kicked off in 2006 with Vitantonio Liuzzi, who had contested four grands prix for Red Bull in 2005, and American rookie Scott Speed. The Italian scored the team's lone point, for eighth, in the United States GP. Using the previous year's Red Bull chassis in 2007, Toro Rosso advanced, especially when Sebastian Vettel

THE POWER AND THE GLORY

JAMES KEY
James was sponsored through university by Lotus and got to work on its GT programme. He moved to F1 in 1998 with Jordan. His talents were recognised there, with James rising through the ranks from data engineer to become the team's technical director in 2005. After five years in the post, he accepted a similar position with Sauber before taking over from Giorgio Ascanelli at the end of 2012 to run Scuderia Toro Rosso's technical programme.

MEETING ITS MISSION IN SHAPING TALENT
Despite its declared aim of going racing to bring on talent for Red Bull Racing, 2015 was the first year that Scuderia Toro Rosso has entered a season with two rookies. In Verstappen, it had one who was still 17, for goodness sake. Yet, he and Carlos Sainz Jr picked up points wherever possible, with the only obvious mistakes coming from Verstappen's overenthusiasm. What stood out, though, is that the team has unearthed a real star. On the flip side, there were worries about which engines would be used in 2016, and this was unsettling.

2015 DRIVERS & RESULTS

Driver	Nationality	Races	Wins	Pts	Pos
Carlos Sainz Jr	Spanish	19	0	18	15th
Max Verstappen	Dutch	19	0	49	12th

FOR THE RECORD

Country of origin:	Italy
Team base:	Faenza, Italy
Telephone:	(39) 546 696111
Website:	www.scuderiatororosso.com
Active in Formula One:	As Minardi
	1985-2005; Toro Rosso 2006 on
Grands Prix contested:	526
Wins:	1
Pole positions:	0
Fastest laps:	0

THE TEAM

Team owner:	Dietrich Mateschitz
Team principal:	Franz Tost
Technical director:	James Key
Deputy technical director:	
	Ben Waterhouse
Chief designers:	Paolo Marabini
	& Matteo Piraccini
Head of aerodynamics:	Brendan Gilhome
Team manager:	Graham Watson
Technical co-ordinator:	Sandro Parrini
Chief engineer:	Phil Charles
Test driver:	tba
Chassis:	Toro Rosso STR11
Engine:	Ferrari V6
Tyres:	Pirelli

replaced Speed late in the season and finished fourth in the Chinese GP. This hiring and firing approach, with Marko taking the roll of henchman, has been a feature of the team and, in Vettel's case, the decision to cast aside drivers worked to his benefit. For others, though, this constant threat of being ejected, possibly with terminal effect for their F1 career, has been an oft-distracting pressure that is hard to live with.

In 2008, Toro Rosso did something it was never supposed to do: it beat Red Bull Racing to become an F1 winner. This was all down to an astonishing performance by Vettel at a wet Monza, where he qualified on pole and stormed to victory. Small wonder he was promoted to Red Bull for 2009. This result boosted Toro Rosso to sixth in the rankings.

Since Vettel, there have been no wins, but Toro Rosso highlights have been provided by a run of top-ten finishes from Sebastien Buemi in 2009 and 2010, Jaime Alguersuari in 2011, then Jean-Eric Vergne from 2012 to 2014. However, not one of these drivers has been promoted to Red Bull Racing. Indeed, the only two who have since Vettel's elevation have been Daniel Ricciardo, who made the move in 2014, and Daniil Kvyat, who followed a year later. Perhaps proving this sifting of drivers has been fair, both have shone with Red Bull Racing, most notably the Australian who won three grands prix to Vettel's none when they were paired together in 2014.

Those drivers who found no way to move up when Vettel and Webber were paired together at Red Bull Racing from 2009 to 2013 have had to make careers in other branches of the sport, with Buemi going on to win the World Endurance Championship title with Toyota in 2014.

Last year, with Red Bull Racing's Marko criticizing the performance of the Renault engines both teams were using, and Renault looking to take over the Lotus F1 team, there was uncertainty about which engines Toro Rosso would be using, but they hope their extended association with Renault will provide a better power unit in 2016.

"I really enjoyed my rookie season and I think we delivered some strong performances. This team has already become like a second family."
Max Verstappen

Sebastian Vettel races towards Toro Rosso's first and so far only victory in the 2008 Italian GP.

MAX VERSTAPPEN

This Dutch teenager was a revelation through his first year of F1. People said that, at 17, he'd be too young, but he proved them wrong and produced drives of pure class. He will go better still at the second time of asking, adding experience to raw speed.

Max has racing heritage from both of his parents. Father Jos contested more than 100 grands prix for Benetton, Simtek, Footwork, Tyrrell, Stewart, Arrows and Minardi, while mother Sophie (Kumpen) was Belgian kart champion. So, it was inevitable that Max would become a second-generation racer. What people didn't expect, though, was just how good he would be, as few second-generation drivers have the attacking natures their parents did.

Max's stellar karting record is clear proof that he wasn't simply along for the ride, not just out there for the vicarious pleasure of his parents. Max won title after title, culminating in the World KZ title in 2013.

So, that was that, and Max stepped directly to Formula Three when he was 16. Most would have contested a season of Formula Renault first, but world champions in the making don't need to do that.

Any thoughts that his 2014 campaign in the European F3 Championship would be a learning one were dismissed immediately as Max was straight onto the pace for the Van Amersfoort team, taking a second place at the opening meeting. At the trio of races held at the second round at

Max displayed enough dash and panache in 2015 to worry the sport's biggest names.

Hockenheim, Max grabbed two poles and one win. Showing that this was no fluke, Max then won all six races at the fifth and sixth rounds at Spa-Francorchamps and the Norisring. There were retirements too, and so Max ended the year ranked third behind

Esteban Ocon and Tom Blomqvist.

With Red Bull already backing his career, Max pushed to bypass either Formula Renault 3.5 or GP2, hoping to jump straight to F1. His wish was granted, as Red Bull's talent spotter Helmut Marko was happy to make Max the youngest F1 driver in history, signing him up to race for Scuderia Toro Rosso last year when he made his F1 debut at the age of just 17 and a half.

TRACK NOTES

Nationality:	DUTCH
Born:	30 SEPTEMBER 1997, HASSELT, BELGIUM
Website:	www.verstappen.nl
Teams:	TORO ROSSO 2015-16

CAREER RECORD

First Grand Prix:	2015 AUSTRALIAN GP
Grand Prix starts:	19
Grand Prix wins:	0
	(best result: 4th, 2015 Hungarian GP, 2015 United States GP)
Poles:	0
Fastest laps:	0
Points:	49
Honours:	2014 EUROPEAN FORMULA 3 RUNNER-UP, 2013 WORLD & EUROPEAN KZ KART CHAMPION & EUROPEAN KF KART CHAMPION, 2012 WSK MASTER SERIES KF2 CHAMPION, 2011 WSK EURO SERIES CHAMPION, 2010 WSK WORLD SERIES CHAMPION, 2009 BELGIAN KF5 CHAMPION, 2008 DUTCH CADET KART CHAMPION, 2007 & 2008 DUTCH MINIMAX CHAMPION, 2006 BELGIAN ROTAX MINIMAX CHAMPION

IS MAX A CHAMPION IN THE MAKING?

Many throughout the sport said that being just 17-and-a-half years' old was way too young to be at the outset of a career in F1, but Max more than proved his detractors wrong last year. His hallmark was dazzling overtaking, often diving in where rivals expected no attack to come. Call it the impetuosity of youth, if you will, but it worked. He made mistakes, of course, such as clattering into Romain Grosjean's Lotus at Monaco's Ste Devote, but he also showed uncanny speed and was intrepid as he set about trying to advance up the race order. He didn't always do things according to the book and, intriguingly, said that he gained the idea for his best move of the year - around the outside of Marcus Ericsson's Sauber at Spa's 190mph Blanchimont corner - through playing video games... Seventh place in the second round at Sepang was Max's early-season reward, but he matured to the point that he was able to claim fourth place with a superb drive at the Hungaroring and another at the United States GP.

CARLOS SAINZ JR

Toro Rosso team-mate Max Verstappen took all the plaudits last year, but Carlos was often not that far behind, albeit racing with a less spectacular style. This year, the 21-year-old Spaniard knows precisely what he must do: beat his team-mate.

It's a crazy fact of life that Carlos Jr started to feel in 2014 that he was getting too old and might miss the boat for Red Bull to promote him to F1. After all, he was 19 turning 20 at the time. What madness, yet such is the trend that younger is better that he had some reason to worry.

History relates, of course, that he was given his break with Scuderia Toro Rosso, but the fact that his 2015 team-mate Max Verstappen was 17 proved that his concerns weren't without foundation.

Carlos Jr has motor sport in his blood, as his father, also Carlos, was World Rally Champion in 1990 and 1992. It was circuit racing that appealed to Carlos Jr though. He tried karts and liked them, but didn't start racing until he was 11. Carlos Jr then enjoyed highlights that included winning the Asia/Pacific junior title in 2008 and the Monaco Kart Cup the following year.

Red Bull signed Carlos Jr to be one of the many young drivers it backs, and so he moved into car racing in 2010 at just 15, starting in Formula BMW and finishing fourth in the European series.

Stepping up to Formula Renault for his second season, Carlos Jr was runner-up in

Carlos Jr knows that he's the driver for young Red Bull-backed drivers to aim for.

the European championship and won the regional Northern Europe championship.

Formula Three was next, in 2012, and Carlos Jr placed fifth in the European series with Carlin and sixth overall in the British championship in a packed season.

Aware that Red Bull wants its scholars to win titles or face being dropped from its scholarship scheme, he moved on to GP3 for 2013, but could only finish tenth. Fortunately, Carlos Jr also tried the more powerful Formula Renault 3.5 series that same year and showed impressively in that.

So, for 2014, feeling increased pressure to deliver, Carlos Jr returned to Formula Renault 3.5 with the crack DAMS outfit and seven wins helped him to achieve his a im, winning the title with 227 points to runner-up Pierre Gasly's tally of 192. This was enough to earn him his F1 break.

TRACK NOTES

Nationality:	SPANISH
Born:	1 SEPTEMBER 1994, MADRID, SPAIN
Website:	www.carlossainz.es
Teams:	TORO ROSSO 2015-16

CAREER RECORD	
First Grand Prix:	2015 AUSTRALIAN GP
Grand Prix starts:	19
Grand Prix wins:	0
(best result: 7th, 2015 United States GP)	
Poles:	0
Fastest laps:	0
Points:	18
Honours:	2014 FORMULA RENAULT 3.5 CHAMPION, 2011 EUROPEAN FORMULA RENAULT RUNNER-UP & NORTHERN EUROPEAN FORMULA RENAULT CHAMPION, 2009 MONACO KART CUP WINNER, 2008 ASIA-PACIFIC JUNIOR KART CHAMPION, 2006 MADRID CADET KART CHAMPION

KICKING OFF WITH POINTS

Carlos Jr didn't draw the spotlight like his "bad boy" Toro Rosso team-mate Max Verstappen did, but it won't have escaped people's attention that he was good enough to score points on his debut. Certainly, that opening round in Australia was a shambles, with only 15 cars starting, but ninth place at flagfall was still impressive. To show that it was no fluke, Carlos Jr then scored again next time out, taking eighth at Sepang against a full field of 20 cars. Through the rest of the season, Toro Rosso gave him a car that was good enough to snipe for occasional points finishes, but a run of four retirements through the summer cost him momentum. That said, Carlos Jr was still able to collect points on seven occasions and so did a very respectable job in his maiden season in the World Championship. In terms of speed and bravado, he was bettered by Verstappen, but that shouldn't mask the fact he showed good race craft and seldom put a wheel wrong.

SAUBER

Sauber changed hue from grey to blue and yellow last year, but it remains a team that fails to catch the eye, and its retention of two drivers picked mainly for their sponsorship money suggests it will be the same old story again in 2016.

Felipe Nasr impressed through 2015 and ought to improve second time around for Sauber, with Marcus Ericsson to keep him on his toes.

From small acorns, great oak trees can grow. Certainly, this has been the story of many of today's top F1 teams. In fact, any of the top teams that weren't started by a manufacturer can claim such a story. Those started by racing drivers who had already been successful, like Jack Brabham or Bruce McLaren, had a greater likelihood of succeeding, such was their bloodline. Yet, Swiss sportscar racer Peter Sauber made it to the sport's top table through his own, low-profile pursuit of a dream.

Certainly, Sauber has won but one grand prix in 23 years of F1, through Robert Kubica in the 2008 Canadian GP, but it has remained in the World Championship while other, often better financed, teams have come and gone.

Sauber was a competent racer who marked himself out by building his own racing cars. Having attracted Mercedes' attention by how well his sports-prototypes went with their engines under his engine covers, they offered some works support in 1988. For 1989, the cars were turned out in

silver, running as latter-day Silver Arrows in the livery of Mercedes' great racers of the 1930s and mid-1950s. Toppling Jaguar and Porsche to win the 1989 Le Mans 24 Hours

was a highlight and put him in such favour, backed up by Sauber-Mercedes taking the World Sports-Prototype Championship title both that year and the next, that Mercedes

THE POWER AND THE GLORY

MARK SMITH
Sauber's Birmingham-born technical director got his motorsport grounding working with Comtec then Reynard before joining Jordan for its F1 debut in 1991. He rose to become chief designer in 1998, then took a similar post with Renault in 2002 before returning to Jordan in 2004 as technical director. The same role at Red Bull Racing followed from 2005 to 2008, then Mark moved to Force India. After three years there, Mark spent three years with Caterham. When that folded, he was snapped up by Sauber midway through 2015.

STARTING WITH A BANG
Sauber won't have had high hopes going into 2015, but points finishes in fifth for Nasr and eighth for Ericsson in the first round exceeded its 2014 tally in one go. Thereafter, with its Ferrari engines proving strong, the drivers picked up points in the bottom few of the top ten whenever they could, but were often just outside that. Finding itself ahead of McLaren will have felt surreal for the Swiss team, but Monisha Kaltenborn's troops won't expect to stay ahead in 2016.

2015 DRIVERS & RESULTS

Driver	Nationality	Races	Wins	Pts	Pos
Marcus Ericsson	Swedish	19	0	9	18th
Felipe Nasr	Brazilian	19	0	27	9th

FOR THE RECORD

Country of origin:	Switzerland
Team base:	Hinwil, Switzerland
Telephone:	(41) 44 937 9000
Website:	www.sauberf1team.com
Active in Formula One:	From 1993
	(as BMW Sauber 2006-10)
Grands Prix contested:	402
Wins:	1
Pole positions:	1
Fastest laps:	5

THE TEAM

President:	Peter Sauber
Team principal:	Monisha Kaltenborn
Operations director:	Axel Kruse
Technical director:	Mark Smith
Chief designer:	Eric Gandelin
Head of aerodynamics:	Willem Toet
Head of engineering:	Giampaolo Dall'ara
Head of vehicle performance:	
	Elliot Dason-Barber
Team manager:	Beat Zehnder
Head of track operations:	Timothy Guerin
Test driver:	tba
Chassis:	Sauber C35
Engine:	Ferrari V6
Tyres:	Pirelli

listened when Sauber said that he wanted to graduate to F1.

Sauber made its F1 debut in 1993, but Mercedes had pulled out of any involvement. Yet, with Sauber ranking sixth, thanks to JJ Lehto peaking with fourth at Imola and Karl Wendlinger matching that at Monza, it came on board with engines for 1994.

Never, though, were the cars run as silver arrows, and Mercedes transferred its engines to McLaren in 1995, cutting Sauber adrift to fend for itself.

From here on, Sauber has been a midfield team. Some years, things have gone better for them, such as in 2001 when it gave Kimi Raikkonen his F1 break and he and Nick Heidfeld guided it to fourth overall, albeit far behind Ferrari, McLaren and Williams.

Heinz-Harald Frentzen raced for Sauber from 1994 to 1996 and then again in 2003 when he claimed third in the wet at the US GP at Indianapolis. After he retired, Giancarlo Fisichella and Felipe Massa proved to be Sauber's leading lights. However, it was the arrival of BMW that boosted the team to its greatest heights.

Coming on board in 2006, the German manufacturer provided not only increasingly competitive engines, but also welcome

financial backing. Heidfeld was brought back for his second spell with the team and fifth in 2006 was followed by the team's best-ever ranking, second in 2007, when Heidfeld and Robert Kubica ended the year fifth and sixth in the driver standings. Better was to follow in 2008, when they not only did Kubica give Sauber its one and only win, but Heidfeld chased him home in second in the Canadian GP. McLaren edged Sauber back to third that year, but the team dropped to sixth in 2009 and things have never been as good again.

Ferrari engines replaced BMW units and since then the team has dropped to its more traditional ranking of sixth or seventh. Sergio Perez's second place behind Fernando Alonso's Ferrari in the 2012 Malaysian GP stands out, but many felt that he was held back from attacking, as Sauber didn't want to upset his engine supplier.

A long-time problem for Sauber has been in attracting, then keeping, top technical staff, with many not wanting to leave their

homes in England. The signing of Mark Smith midway through last year should give the team a bit more direction, and the fruits of this much-travelled technical chief's input ought to be seen in full this year.

"It was a demanding and eventful 2015 season. Despite a difficult and challenging environment, we achieved our objective to have a significantly improved performance compared to 2014."

Monisha Kaltenborn

JJ Lehto gave Sauber its first points on its F1 debut by finishing fifth in South Africa in 1993.

⊕ MARCUS ERICSSON

Marcus's first season of F1 was cut short when Caterham stumbled in late 2014, but last year the Swede showed marked improvement as he settled into life with Sauber, and he was able to bring his car home in the championship points on five occasions.

Like almost all of his rivals in F1, Marcus was racing competitively in karts before his age hit double figures. Talent-spotted at an early age by Swedish touring car star Fredrik Ekblom, he advanced to single-seater racing as soon as he was old enough to do so.

Offering guidance at this stage was another Swede, former IndyCar star Kenny Brack, who suggested that Marcus race for a team that had run him a couple of decades before: Fortec Motorsport. This British outfit ran Marcus in the British Formula BMW Championship in 2007 and seven wins meant that he walked away with the title. Staying with Fortec, Marcus was a frequent podium visitor but never a winner as he placed fifth in the 2008 British F3 Championship, as Jaime Alguersuari took the crown.

What followed next was a brave career move, as Marcus was advised to head to Japan in his quest to land another car racing title. He did so with the best team in the Japanese F3 series: TOM'S. It paid off too, as Marcus claimed five wins and the title. And so it was that he gained his

Marcus continues to impress on his good days, but will seek greater consistency.

graduation to GP2, joining Super Nova at Brack's recommendation. Despite winning a race in Valencia, Marcus was too erratic to rank higher than 17th in a campaign littered with retirements.

Back for a second season of GP2 in 2011, Marcus transferred to iSport and advanced to tenth, then eighth position overall in 2012, winning at Spa-Francorchamps.

It was then a brave decision to come back for an almost unheard of fourth year of GP2. Racing for DAMS, Marcus won at the Nurburgring, but could rank only sixth. So, it was with a healthy budget rather than title-winning talent that he lined up his graduation to F1 for 2014.

Life with Caterham in F1 wasn't a dream start to Marcus's grand prix career, as the team was in major financial difficulties, but he progressed to outperform Kamui Kobayashi and displayed improved form until the team's funds ran dry and he was forced to miss the final three rounds.

MAKING SCORING POINTS A HABIT

To say that Marcus's first year of F1, in 2014 with financially beleaguered Caterham, was troubled is to put it mildly. So, it was with much relief that the well-connected Swede settled into his second year at the sport's top level last year, this time with Sauber. With Felipe Nasr also being new to the Swiss team, there was no hierarchy, except Marcus expected to finish ahead in their intra-team battle due to his 16 outings in 2014. When he achieved his best finish to date, eighth, in the opening round, he ought to have been pleased, but F1 rookie Nasr finished three places higher. So, it was vital that Marcus worked his way back in front, which he did in the second half of the season, with a three-race run in the points cementing his growing reputation. As in previous seasons, and most especially when he raced in GP2, there were flashes of ill discipline, such as at Monza where he was penalized for blocking Nico Hulkenberg in qualifying and then triggered a first-corner collision, but the general trend was one of improvement.

TRACK NOTES

Nationality:	SWEDISH
Born:	2 SEPTEMBER 1990, KUMLA, SWEDEN
Website:	www.marcusericssonracing.com
Teams:	CATERHAM 2014, SAUBER 2015-16

CAREER RECORD

First Grand Prix:	2014 AUSTRALIAN GP
Grand Prix starts:	35
Grand Prix wins:	0
	(best result: 8th, 2015 Australian GP)
Poles:	0
Fastest laps:	0
Points:	9
Honours:	2009 JAPANESE FORMULA 3 CHAMPION, 2007 BRITISH FORMULA BMW CHAMPION

In the points on his debut last March in Australia, Felipe was given an early contract to stay on with Sauber for 2016, which gave him the chance to focus on refining his craft rather than worry about Sauber having its traditional drop-off in form.

Second generation drivers with racing blood coursing through their veins are no rarity in the upper echelons of the sport. After all, can you imagine a driver suggesting that his son or daughter become a doctor, lawyer or accountant? In Felipe's case, it was his uncle Amir who did the racing then turned to running one of the leading teams on the South American F3 scene in the 1990s.

From karting, in which he was Brazilian champion in 2007, when he was 15, Felipe had a one-off race in Formula BMW at Interlagos in 2008 before heading to Europe for a full Formula BMW campaign in 2009. It was a worthwhile journey, as Felipe landed the title in dominant fashion.

Felipe's first year in the British F3 Championship, in which he ranked fifth overall for Raikkonen Robertson Racing as Jean-Eric Vergne took the title, he realized that you needed to race for the category's top team, Carlin. So he did just that in 2011, won seven races on his way to landing the title, beating Kevin Magnussen.

F1's immediate feeder formula, GP2, was next, but Felipe found it harder than he had expected and he ranked tenth with DAMS.

Felipe will be looking to build on what turned into a highly promising rookie year for Sauber.

Moving back to the Carlin operation for 2013, he again failed to take a win, but was consistently in the points, so placed fourth overall at season's end as Fabio Leimer landed the coveted title.

Few drivers want to do a third year of GP2, but Felipe had no choice in the matter if he wanted to prove that he was good enough to graduate to F1.

This time there were wins, four of them – at Barcelona, Red Bull Ring, Silverstone and Spa-Francorchamps – but it still wasn't enough to make him champion, so Felipe ended the year behind Jolyon Palmer and Stoffel Vandoorne. However, a sizeable budget from Banco do Brasil bought him a seat with Sauber for 2015.

Felipe arrived in F1 with experience, too, having been the Friday test driver for Williams at two late-season grands prix in 2014 and, with a good group of advisors, he was able to carry momentum into 2015.

TRACK NOTES

Nationality:	BRAZILIAN
Born:	21 AUGUST 1992, BRASILIA, BRAZIL
Website:	www.felipenasr.com
Teams:	SAUBER 2015-16

CAREER RECORD

First Grand Prix:	2015 AUSTRALIAN GP
Grand Prix starts:	19
Grand Prix wins:	0
	(best result: 5th, 2015 Australian GP)
Poles:	0
Fastest laps:	0
Points:	27
Honours:	2014 GP2 RUNNER-UP, 2011 BRITISH FORMULA 3 CHAMPION, 2009 FORMULA BMW EUROPE CHAMPION, 2007 BRAZILIAN KARTING CHAMPION

STARTED WELL, THEN TAILED OFF

Felipe had been angling for his F1 break for several seasons, so he must have been delighted after the season-opening round in Melbourne, for not only had he finished but done so in fifth place, to give Sauber more points than it scored in all of 2014. In truth, it was an extraordinary race in which many teams were struck by power-unit problems, but Felipe also had the boost of beating team-mate Marcus Ericsson, a driver with a year's F1 experience. When Felipe added an eighth-place finish at the third round, in Shanghai, it seemed as though the season would continue to exceed expectations. However, as with so many Sauber seasons, it shone only to deceive and the team's form ebbed away. It then seemed in the second half of the season that Felipe was cursed to always finish just outside the point-scoring positions, with a run of three 11th-place finishes in four races before he finished sixth in Sochi and then ninth next time out in Austin.

McLAREN

This was the darkest of seasons for one of F1's great teams. It was expected to be a year of development as it welcomed Honda back as a partner, but Honda was a year behind its rivals and couldn't catch up. For 2016, McLaren must save its credibility.

Fernando Alonso and Jenson Button had to grin and bear it through 2015 and will have prayed that there will be a huge upswing in 2016.

The tally of 181 grand prix victories tells you that McLaren is a winning team. Its roll call of World Champions, from Emerson Fittipaldi in 1974 to Lewis Hamilton in 2008 with Ayrton Senna the brightest of its stars in between, tells you that McLaren is a truly great team. Yet, first-time F1 viewers in 2015 could have been excused for not noticing that, as the dark grey cars never featured in qualifying or race, lapping embarrassingly far off the pace of teams that it used to beat easily just a few short years ago.

Team founder Bruce McLaren was a shooting star from New Zealand, who became a grand prix winner with Cooper at the age of just 22. That was in 1959, at Sebring, and he soon followed the lead set by his then team-mate Jack Brabham in building cars bearing his name. This satisfied not only his strong engineering interests, but his racing sportscars helped him put money into the bank.

Single-seaters followed, and Bruce entered his first F1 car in the 1966 Monaco GP.

What really made McLaren take off was the success of its cars in the lucrative CanAm sportscar series in North America and then the introduction of the Ford Cosworth DFV.

At a stroke, the team's engine troubles were sorted and Bruce claimed McLaren's first grand prix win in the 1968 Belgian GP. Two years later, though, he was killed testing

THE POWER AND THE GLORY

ERIC BOULLIER
The ability to work almost every weekend from spring to winter, across several categories, was what marked Eric out when he was an engineer with DAMS. Gravity Sport Management then took him from running DAMS' teams in GP2 and A1GP into F1 in 2010 to be principal of the Lotus Renault team. Having shown an ability to take charge of an English-speaking team, McLaren signed him for the same role in 2014 and he has been a steady hand on the tiller.

AN EMBARRASSMENT FOR BOTH PARTIES
Honda was a year behind its rival engine manufacturers when it rejoined McLaren for last year. Of course, Honda and McLaren had achieved great things together in the late 1980s and early 1990s, but this time was always going to be different. In short, it was a disaster for Fernando Alonso and Jenson Button as Honda's all-new turbocharged V6 engine was way down on power and reliability too, hindered in no small part by the lack on in-season testing. Alonso and Button did well to keep going with such uncompetitive equipment.

2015 DRIVERS & RESULTS

Driver	Nationality	Races	Wins	Pts	Pos
Fernando Alonso	Spanish	18	0	11	17th
Jenson Button	British	19	0	16	16th
Kevin Magnussen	Danish	1	0	0	n/a

FOR THE RECORD

Country of origin:	England
Team base:	Woking, England
Telephone:	(44) 01483 261000
Website:	www.mclaren.com
Active in Formula One:	From 1966
Grands Prix contested:	781
Wins:	181
Pole positions:	154
Fastest laps:	152

THE TEAM

Chairman:	Ron Dennis
Racing director:	Eric Boullier
Chief executive officer:	Jost Capito
Director of design & development:	Neil Oatley
Technical director:	Tim Goss
Operations director:	Simon Roberts
Director of engineering:	Matt Morris
Team manager:	David Redding
Chief engineer:	Peter Prodromou
Test drivers:	Oliver Turvey & Stoffel Vandoorne
Chassis:	McLaren MP4-31
Engine:	Honda V6
Tyres:	Pirelli

one of his CanAm cars at Goodwood and the team teetered, but team manager Teddy Mayer kept it going.

Great times followed, with Bruce's fellow Kiwi Denny Hulme doing most of the team's winning. It took until Fittipaldi's arrival in 1974 for its first title challenge, and the Brazilian came out on top, beating Ferrari's Clay Regazzoni to the title, with the team also claiming the constructors' championship. McLaren landed its second drivers' title in 1976, when James Hunt edged out Ferrari's Niki Lauda.

The team then lost ground by failing to get to grips with ground-effects and it took the arrival of Ron Dennis at the helm to put it back onto course. Lauda and Alain Prost won three titles in the mid-1980s, with TAG Porsche power. However, its greatest spell came between 1988 and 1991, when McLaren-Hondas were the cars to have and Prost added another title, in 1989, with Senna champion in 1988, 1990 and 1991. Williams then harnessed Renault power best to dominate, but it wasn't until the late 1990s that McLaren rose to the top again, this time with Mercedes engines, with Mika Hakkinen champion in 1998 and 1999.

In a manner that Bruce would have approved of, McLaren also started building road-going sportscars and a racing version of these won the Le Mans 24 Hours at the first attempt in 1995. Sales of these road cars usefully boosted the team's coffers.

Dennis is an exceedingly ambitious man and he pioneered the building of the remarkable McLaren Technology Centre outside Woking for the team, its supercar programme and other projects. This could not have been more of a far cry from the team's original building under the end of Heathrow's runways at Colnbrook.

Kimi Raikkonen came close to beating Michael Schumacher to the 2003 crown, then Hamilton and Fernando Alonso were both usurped at the final round of 2007 by Raikkonen, now a Ferrari driver. Hamilton did at least atone, racing to the 2008 title, but since then, McLaren has been a strong force but not a title-winning one.

In the hope of finding an advantage over long-time engine suppler Mercedes now that it had its own F1 team, McLaren turned to Honda for engines for 2015. It knew that rival engine builders had a one-year head start with the latest turbocharged V6s, but surely couldn't have imagined just how very poor the Honda V6s would be, making 2015 a near pointless write-off.

"The Abu Dhabi GP marked the end of a long and challenging year for the whole team. That said, the mood at MTC is upbeat and everyone has been working very hard for 2016."
Jenson Button

Denny Hulme scored five wins with McLaren. This was his first, at Monza in the 1968 Italian GP.

Seldom has one of F1's top drivers had to endure such a fall in competitiveness as Fernando did last year, slowed by Honda's awful V6 turbo engines, but he deserves better in 2016, as he remained dignified amid the team's crushing fall from grace.

Winning the World Kart title ought to be a sure-fire way of identifying yourself as a grand prix winner of the future, but Fernando is one of only three of them who have done that, along with Riccardo Patrese and Jarno Trulli. He's also the only one to go on to become World Champion.

That world title was won in 1996. As he was only 15, he had to wait two more years before being old enough to graduate to car racing. It was what followed that marked him out, as Fernando made it to F1 from there after just two years. The first, 1999, yielded the Formula Nissan title, then he became a race winner in the FIA Formula 3000 Championship in his rookie year, dominating at Spa-Francorchamps.

Minardi gave him his break in 2001 and Fernando gained further experience by testing for Benetton, something he continued to do in 2002. Back with a race ride in 2003, when Benetton had been renamed as Renault, Fernando raced to his first win, in Hungary, and ranked sixth.

Fourth overall in 2004 was followed by two titles for Renault, taking seven wins each year, ending Michael Schumacher's five-year run of titles with Ferrari.

Fernando knows his talents deserve more than the two F1 titles he has to his name.

Then came a move to McLaren that ought to have yielded the 2007 title, but he and team-mate Lewis Hamilton were pipped by Ferrari's Kimi Raikkonen. So he returned to Renault and in 2010 joined Ferrari. Yet, titles have eluded him since as drivers from McLaren, Brawn GP, Red Bull and Mercedes have had superior machinery. His best season in the nine years since his 2006 title was in 2013 when he finished as runner-up to Red Bull's Sebastian Vettel, but well clear of Mark Webber in the second Red Bull.

TRACK NOTES

Nationality:	SPANISH
Born:	29 JULY 1981, OVIEDO, SPAIN
Website:	www.fernandoalonso.com
Teams:	MINARDI 2001, RENAULT 2003-06, McLAREN 2007, RENAULT 2008-09, FERRARI 2010-14, McLAREN 2015-16

CAREER RECORD

First Grand Prix:	2001 AUSTRALIAN GP
Grand Prix starts:	254
Grand Prix wins:	32
	2003 Hungarian GP, 2005 Malaysian GP, Bahrain GP, San Marino GP, European GP, French GP, German GP, Chinese GP, 2006 Bahrain GP, Australian GP, Spanish GP, Monaco GP, British GP, Canadian GP, Japanese GP, 2007 Malaysian GP, Monaco GP, European GP, Italian GP, 2008 Singapore GP, Japanese GP, 2010 Australian GP, German GP, Italian GP, Singapore GP, Korean GP, 2011 British GP, 2012 Malaysian GP, European GP, German GP, 2013 Chinese GP, Spanish GP
Poles:	22
Fastest laps:	21
Points:	1778
Honours:	2005 & 2006 FORMULA ONE WORLD CHAMPION, 2010, 2012 & 2013 FORMULA ONE RUNNER-UP, 1999 FORMULA NISSAN CHAMPION, 1997 ITALIAN & SPANISH KART CHAMPION, 1996 WORLD & SPANISH KART CHAMPION, 1994 & 1995 SPANISH JUNIOR KART CHAMPION

ATTEMPTING TO STAY UPBEAT

There were almost too many low points to select one, but the worst moment of 2015 for McLaren must have come at the Belgian GP, when its drivers were hit with major grid penalties for using way beyond their apportioned season's supply of power units. That Jenson Button was hit with a 55-place penalty and Fernando demoted 50 places mattered for little, as this once-great team was so far from the pace that its MP4-30s were due to line up towards the tail of the grid anyway. Honda's turbocharged V6 was so far down on power that the drivers could do nothing and simply had to keep their dignity, hoping that matters would improve drastically for 2016. It would have been easy for the drivers to let rip and criticize the Japanese engine supplier, but they didn't and Fernando finally gave Honda and McLaren welcome respite when he finished fifth in the Hungarian GP. The year was a write-off, but Fernando is a fighter, although any thoughts of more of the same in 2016 will drive him away.

JENSON BUTTON

Last year was a major struggle as Honda's underdeveloped engines held McLaren back. Yet, despite being tempted to follow Mark Webber's lead and go sportscar racing instead, Jenson is staying on for his 17th season at the sport's top level.

Assisted by his father John, who was one of Britain's top rallycross drivers, Jenson carved his way through the karting scene, gathering titles from cadet level all the way to European Super As. So, it came as little surprise that he hit the ground running when he stepped up to car racing in 1998. Formula Ford is notoriously tough, but he won the British title at his first attempt, and the Formula Ford Festival too. So, it was just reward when he was named as that year's recipient of the McLaren *Autosport* BRDC Young Driver award.

Formula Three followed and Jenson adapted immediately to the slicks and wings, ranking third. Formula 3000 was expected to be the next step, providing he could raise the budget. Things happened fast when he tested for the Ligier F1 team and impressed enough to be selected for a shoot-out for the second Williams seat. Beating the far more experienced Bruno Junqueira in this, he found himself an F1 driver just after his 20th birthday.

Having ranked eighth in his first year, Jenson moved to Benetton in 2001 and finished seventh in 2002. For 2003, though, he moved on to BAR and would remain there

Jenson thought long and hard about whether to stay on in F1 for a 17th season.

until 2008. His 2004 campaign, when he ranked third to Ferrari's Schumacher and Barrichello, and then victory in the 2006 Hungarian GP (once the team had been renamed Honda Racing) were the highlights.

Then, with Honda pulling out, there was no drive for 2009, until the 11th hour, when the team was revived as Brawn GP. Amazingly, it found a technical break and Jenson won six races to become champion.

Since moving to McLaren in 2010, Jenson has won eight grands prix, including three in 2011 when he was runner-up to Red Bull Racing's Sebastian Vettel.

TRACK NOTES

Nationality:	BRITISH
Born:	19 JANUARY 1980, FROME, ENGLAND
Website:	www.jensonbutton.com
Teams:	WILLIAMS 2000, BENETTON/RENAULT 2001-02, BAR/HONDA 2003-08, BRAWN 2009, McLAREN 2010-16

CAREER RECORD

First Grand Prix:	2000 AUSTRALIAN GP
Grand Prix starts:	285
Grand Prix wins:	15
	2006 Hungarian GP, 2009 Australian GP, Malaysian GP, Bahrain GP, Spanish GP, Monaco GP, Turkish GP, 2010 Australian GP, Chinese GP, 2011 Canadian GP, Hungarian GP, Japanese GP, 2012 Australian GP, Belgian GP, Brazilian GP
Poles:	8
Fastest laps:	8
Points:	1214
Honours:	2009 FORMULA ONE WORLD CHAMPION, 1999 MACAU FORMULA THREE RUNNER-UP, 1998 FORMULA FORD FESTIVAL WINNER, BRITISH FORMULA FORD CHAMPION & MCLAREN AUTOSPORT BRDC YOUNG DRIVER, 1997 EUROPEAN SUPER A KART CHAMPION, 1991 BRITISH CADET KART CHAMPION

WAITING FOR MORE HORSEPOWER

Jenson and team-mate Fernando Alonso knew that last year was going to have to be written off as a development year as Honda came back into F1 with the other engine suppliers having a headstart. What they couldn't have predicted was that they would be so far off target. It was an embarrassment to have two world champions trailing around near the tail. Jenson started the year with 11th place, last, at the Australian GP, running two laps down with an engine that had been detuned to ensure that he finished. It took until the sixth round, Monaco – where power isn't such an issue – for him to score. He also picked up minor points in Hungary. Jenson said at the Japanese GP that their speed shortfall was a danger against their faster rivals. Small wonder, then, that there was still debate that he would continue in F1. With Mark Webber loving his new life in the World Endurance Championship, many thought that he would be tempted to follow, and few would have blamed him.

MANOR

An F1 minnow for all of its existence, Manor survived a season of financial restructuring and the death of its 2014 star Jules Bianchi, but it has landed a deal to race with Mercedes engines and has strong ambitions to work its way up the grid.

Will Stevens gave his all last year as the team chased after elusive championship points after its 11th-hour salvation to start the season.

The World Championship invited four new teams to join F1 for the start of 2010, and three made it, with USF1 failing to get off the ground. Virgin Racing was one of these, bringing Richard Branson's global corporation into F1. The outfit was run by Manor Grand Prix, a development of John Booth's team that had started life in Formula Renault and worked its way up through the single-seater categories. Under the guidance of Nick Wirth, the team went for a digital-only car design, with all design done on CFD. Sadly, it didn't work, with neither Timo Glock nor Lucas di Grassi able to score, and so the standard approach of using a wind tunnel was used for 2011.

The team's second year of F1 was also pointless, with di Grassi's replacement Jerome d'Ambrosio peaking with a pair of 14th-place finishes. For 2012, Russian supercar manufacturer Marussia brought sponsorship and so the team's cars became known as Marussias. A further push in the right direction came from McLaren providing aerodynamic input and the use of its wind tunnel. However, for the third year running, 14th was their best showing.

Jules Bianchi looked the team's most potent tool when he joined for 2013 and raced to 13th at Sepang. Yet, with nine of their ten rival teams entering superior cars, points continued to prove out of reach.

THE POWER AND THE GLORY

JOHN MCQUILLIAM
John reached F1 when he joined Williams in 1986, but he left to complete a masters degree in composite materials before having his second shot with Arrows. A spell at Jordan followed, where he pioneered the use of composite suspension. John then advanced through the team ranks to become chief designer, responsible for their occasional winning cars in the late 1990s. After quitting F1 at the end of 2007 to work for Wirth Research, John came back in 2010 when the company produced Manor's first F1 car.

CONSOLIDATING ITSELF FROM A LOW BASE
To say that the team didn't have the best preparation for last season is an understatement. Indeed, simply getting the cars to Melbourne for the opening race was a triumph. Neither car was able to qualify, but they progressed and Will Stevens and Roberto Mehri gave their all, albeit to little avail and no points. Alexander Rossi starred when he stepped up from GP2 and focused the team on chasing the best drivers it could for 2016 to chase points.

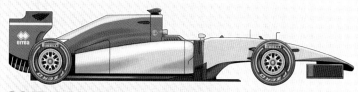

2015 DRIVERS & RESULTS

Driver	Nationality	Races	Wins	Pts	Pos
Roberto Mehrl	Spanish	14	0	0	19th
Alexander Rossi	American	5	0	0	20th
Will Stevens	British	19	0	0	21st

The fifth year brought a major change, with the Cosworth engines being replaced by Ferrari V8s as F1 adopted 1.6-litre V6 turbos. Max Chilton raced to 13th at 2014's opening round, but the team's day of days came at the Monaco GP, when Bianchi scooped a near priceless ninth-place finish, a result that would elevate the team to ninth in the final table and earn it valuable prize money for the first time.

Tragically, Bianchi crashed into a rescue tractor at Suzuka and fell into a coma from which he never recovered, dying without regaining consciousness in July 2015.

Then, it was all up as the team's money had run out, and the team went into administration. However, by February last year, it was back in action, bought out by energy entrepreneur Stephen Fitzpatrick. With former Sainsbury's boss Justin King brought in to firm up the business side, the team - with a name change to Manor Marussia F1 Team - was given next to no time to prepare for the season ahead. It was still alive, though, and that was all that counted. Although it failed to get its cars out to qualify for the first race of 2015 in Australia, as they couldn't get its engine software to work, it got going from there and raced through the entire season.

As expected, points remained a step too far, even with regular scorers McLaren in the doldrums, so the team's best result came at the British GP at Silverstone, when Roberto Mehri and Will Stevens finished 12th and 13th, albeit three laps down on winner Lewis Hamilton's Mercedes.

It appears that good, real-world management practices have been employed, and the team enlarged its staff through 2015, also kitting out a new factory in Banbury, next door to Prodrive. Booth has always been one for practical over fancy, but he and sporting director Graeme Lowdon walked out before last year's Mexican GP after disagreeing with Fitzpatrick over the best way for the team to go forward. McLaren veteran Davey Ryan has been tipped to take the helm.

"The biggest sentiment I take away from the team is incredible pride at just how much we have punched above our weight for such a small team. It was a greater challenge than we ever anticipated."

John Booth

FOR THE RECORD

Country of origin:	England
Team base:	Banbury, England
Telephone:	(44) 01295 225910
Website:	www.manorf1team.com
Active in Formula One:	As Virgin Racing 2010-11, Marussia 2012-14, Manor 2015 on
Grands Prix contested:	112
Wins:	0
Pole positions:	0
Fastest laps:	0

THE TEAM

Owner:	Stephen Fitzpatrick
Chairman:	tba
Sporting director:	tba
Team principal:	John Booth
Technical director:	John McQuilliam
Chief designer:	Rob Taylor
Chief aerodynamicist:	Nikolas Tombazis
Head of R&D:	Richard Connell
Head of vehicle performance:	Paul Davison
Team manager:	Dave O'Neill
Chief engineer:	Dave Greenwood
Test driver:	Jordan King
Chassis:	Manor MR05
Engine:	Mercedes V6
Tyres:	Pirelli

The team's greatest result came at Monaco in 2014, but sadly Jules Bianchi died last year

ALEXANDER ROSSI*

In only a few grands prix at the end of last year, Alexander showed that he can really deliver on motor sport's biggest stage. In 2016, America's best rising star must cement his place, and Manor looks a good environment in which to do just that.

Alexander Rossi deserves his F1 drive as he worked long and hard to reach this stage. There was no pot of family gold for the Californian, just a lot of graft.

His burning desire to race in F1 was given a fillip when he ranked fifth out of 2000 applicants in Red Bull's F1 American Driver Search. He was 14 at the time and impressed judges at the Skip Barber Racing School enough to land a scholarship to race in its single-seater series in 2006.

Stepping up to Formula BMW in 2007, Alexander finished third, just behind 2016 rival Esteban Gutierrez, then returned to claim the title in 2008, winning ten of the 15 races. Alexander also won Formula BMW's shoot-out at season's end and part of the prize was an F1 test with BMW Sauber.

Realizing his best route to F1 was to race in Europe, Alexander competed in Formula Master in 2009. Then, with the USF1 Team being set up, his timing seemed spot-on to take a test driver role, but the team never got off the ground, so Alexander contested GP3 in 2010 instead and ranked fourth. He then moved up to Formula Renault 3.5 in 2011 and won twice at Motorland Aragon

Alexander has waited a long time for a chance and his few 2015 outings suggested promise.

and Paul Ricard to rank third. A second season in Formula Renault 3.5 was less good, as he ranked only 11th, but more F1 experience was gained by driving in first practice in Spain for Caterham.

Racing for Caterham's GP2 team in 2013, Alexander won at Yas Marina to rank ninth. He also ran the first F1 practice session in Canada. In 2014, he was again test driver for Caterham and again had a run-out at Montreal. Then he moved across to Manor Marussia, being promised his race debut in the Belgian GP, but Max Chilton was put back into the car after first practice.

A GP2 programme was lined up for 2015 and Alexander was best of the rest behind Stoffel Vandoorne, winning at Spa-Francorchamps, Monza and Sochi. More importantly, he finally got a proper break.

TRACK NOTES

Nationality:	AMERICAN
Born:	25 SEPTEMBER 1991, AUBURN, USA
Website:	www.alexanderrossi.com
Teams:	MANOR 2015-16

CAREER RECORD

First Grand Prix:	2015 SINGAPORE GP
Grand Prix starts:	5
Grand Prix wins:	0
(best result: 12th, 2015 United States GP)	
Poles:	0
Fastest laps:	0
Points:	0
Honours:	2015 GP2 RUNNER-UP;
	2008 AMERICAS FORMULA BMW CHAMPION &
	FORMULA BMW WORLD CUP WINNER;
	2006 SKIP BARBER WESTERN REGIONAL
	CHAMPION; 2005 IKF GRAND
	NATIONAL CHAMPION

MAKING THE MOST OF HIS CHANCE

Drafted into the Manor Marussia F1 Team for the Singapore GP last September, in place of Roberto Mehri, Alexander had the worst possible start when he shunted his car in the first practice session. This was just what he didn't want to do on a circuit that he needed to learn. However, thereafter, he outperformed the team's other driver, Will Stevens, and raced to 14th place on the bumpy street circuit, albeit two laps down on race winner Sebastian Vettel's Ferrari. Showing that this was no fluke, Alexander went to Japan and produced another strong performance at Suzuka and was gifted a place when Stevens spun ahead of him. The knowledge that he had five grands prix in which to show his skills, rather than a single race, was a relief for a driver who had spent three years within touching distance of an F1 ride, only to be denied. He duly settled down to the task in hand of learning five circuits new to him and yet impressed the team with both his speed and his feedback. His undoubted highlight was racing at his home race at the Circuit of the Americas.

* Not confirmed at the time of going to press.

WILL STEVENS*

Will looked to be doing a solid job last year, but then the arrival of Alexander Rossi towards the end of the season showed that there was room for improvement from the diminutive English racer. This year is his chance to prove he has what it takes.

Great Britain has a hugely competitive kart racing scene and Will was one of the stars of this fierce melting pot from the age of 12 onwards, even travelling far from home in his quest for titles, such as going to the Far East to win the Asia/Pacific Kart Championship in 2007.

At the start of 2009, when he was still 17, Will stepped up from karts to car racing and headed down under to New Zealand to contest the Toyota Racing Series. Carrying the experience gained in this forward into a full campaign in British Formula Renault, he ranked seventh. Returning for a second crack at the British series in 2010, Will rose to fourth with Manor Competition, winning a race at Thruxton and two at Brands Hatch as Tom Blomqvist landed the title. In 2011, Will transferred to Fortec Motorsports and raced in European Formula Renault and again ranked fourth behind Robin Frijns, Carlos Sainz Jr and Daniil Kvyat.

Then came a big step as, in 2012, Will advanced straight past Formula Three to the infinitely more powerful Formula Renault 3.5 series. Like Formula Renault, this looked set to be a two-year project for the racer from Essex, with one podium at

Will concentrated on finishing races last year. Now, he must set his sights on scoring points.

the Hungaroring in the first year as Frijns was crowned champion. This was then followed by five podiums in 2013 when he moved from Carlin to P1 by Strakka Racing. These boosted him from 12th overall to fourth as Kevin Magnussen cleaned up.

No driver wants to do a third year in a category, but Will returned to Formula Renault 3.5 with the same team in 2014, desperate to win the title. Although he claimed his first wins at this level, in the opening race at Monza and at Jerez, Will slipped to fourth overall, with Sainz Jr landing the title ahead of Stoffel Vandoorne and Antonio Felix da Costa.

Will's year had a treat at the end of it, though, as he got to make his F1 debut, buying a ride with Caterham when the team was revived for the final round in Abu Dhabi after having to sit on the sidelines for two rounds when it ran out of money.

When the Caterham team then folded over the winter, Will brought finance to help the Manor Marussia F1 Team get back onto its feet, and thus had his F1 break for 2015.

51

MAKING THE MOST OF THE TOOLS

Everyone understood that even the world's greatest driver wasn't going to win races or even score points in last year's Marussia. So Will could only hope that the struggling team that started the year on the back foot after its 11th-hour reprieve could make progress. To gauge his performance, all one could do was to check how he was getting on against his team-mate Roberto Mehri. Will came out on top in that battle more often than not, but then fared less well when Alexander Rossi came in late in the year. However, Will got to the end of every race bar the Austrian GP, when he lost oil due to a punctured oil radiator, and the US GP, when hit by Rossi. The result books will show that Will scored no points and had a best finish of 13th at Silverstone. What they won't show is the blood, sweat and tears that were spent behind the scenes as the team fought not only to close the gap to the nine other teams, but also to work towards a stronger future.

TRACK NOTES

Nationality:	ENGLISH
Born:	28 JUNE 1991, ROCHFORD, ENGLAND
Website:	www.willstevens.co.uk
Teams:	CATERHAM 2014, MANOR 2015-16

CAREER RECORD

First Grand Prix:	2014 ABU DHABI GP
Grand Prix starts:	20
Grand Prix wins:	0
	(best result: 13th, 2015 British GP)
Poles:	0
Fastest laps:	0
Points:	0
Honours:	2007 ASIA/PACIFIC KART CHAMPION

* Not confirmed at the time of going to press.

HAAS F1

Attempts to enter an American team in the World Championship have been many and varied over the decades since the 1950s, but at last we have a new American F1 attack led by a team with a firm base from its NASCAR activities. Welcome Haas F1.

Team principal Gunther Steiner spent much of last year walking the F1 paddock with team owner Gene Haas as they got their eye in for 2016.

American Formula One teams have won a handful of grands prix across the decades, but never enough to challenge for a constructors' championship title. It has always been a missing part of the F1 puzzle. Thus all eyes are on Haas F1 as it makes a bold entry to the World Championship in 2016 (see Talking Point on pages 58-59).

The key ingredients are chassis built by Dallara, a team principal with F1 experience in Gunther Steiner, engines and a technical partnership with Ferrari and, uniquely, a partnership with a NASCAR stock car team. Of course, it will all be branded as an American team, as any team financed by American money set up by an American industrialist and based in the USA should be. However, in addition to its base in the building next door to the Stewart-Haas NASCAR team at Kannapolis in North Carolina, the F1 squad has a base in Europe too, in the old Manor Marussia F1 Team building at Banbury in England. In time, the plan is for more and more of the work to be

done in the USA, albeit always with a base in Europe for logistical reasons, but Haas is aware that European know-how is critical for the first year at least.

Steiner, no stranger to crossing the Atlantic, will oversee the whole show. He reports, though, that a lot of American engineers and designers are keen to get

THE POWER AND THE GLORY

GENE HAAS
At the age of 25, Gene opened a machine shop with two employees. That was in 1978 and CNC tool manufacturer Haas Automation has since grown into a company with 1500 employees, its turnover topping $1bn in 2008. He set up a NASCAR team in 2002 and went into partnership with former champion Tony Stewart who gave Haas-Stewart Racing its first title in 2011, with Kevin Harvick adding another in 2014. Haas also owns the Wind Shear wind tunnel.

GUNTHER STEINER
This Italian-born engineer is already well known to people in the F1 paddock, as he has been here before. Gunther became involved with motor sport by working for Mazda in the World Rally Championship in 1986. His next move was to join the Jolly club team and he transferred to Prodrive in 1996 then M-Sport, as technical director in 1997. Brought from the rally world into F1 in 2001 by Niki Lauda, Gunther oversaw Jaguar Racing's F1 efforts, but left after a year to join Opel in the DTM before retuning to F1 again in 2006 to join Red Bull Racing.

in on the act and have a crack at proving themselves in F1.

Established by the ambitious Gene Haas, the team is in the incredibly unusual situation of running alongside a sister team in a wholly different branch of motor sport. Indeed, Matt Borland has been appointed as a liaison between the F1 team and Stewart-Haas Racing, overseeing the transfer of technology to the NASCAR outfit and the flow of engineering resources in the opposite direction. Haas's NASCAR team, Stewart-Haas Racing, continues to be at the sharp end in NASCAR, with its lead drivers Kevin Harvick and Kurt Busch sharing eight wins between them last year as they fought each other in the heart of NASCAR's Sprint Cup title battle.

One of the greatest elements of the Haas F1 team going into 2016 is its lead driver, with Romain Grosjean being coaxed across from failing Lotus to lead its attack. A proven racer, the French ace brings not just speed but experience too. More than that, the team signed Romain as he clearly has hunger for more, hunger to chase a dream after being caught up in the Lotus team's perpetual struggles to stay afloat through 2015.

Naturally, Haas F1 is not going to get to the front overnight, so all involved must be prepared to push in the long term, ruling out any driver in the twilight of their career. Likewise, an F1 rookie wasn't on the team's list of considerations, as any races ruined by a rookie's inexperience leading to a non-finish will limit their progress.

"With our aim of scoring points, we're going to depend heavily on Romain to help us with our strategies," Haas explained last autumn, "as well as to learn the car, the race tracks and the learning of the whole operation of an F1 team."

For Grosjean, many thought his decision to leave a seat at Lotus just as Renault was taking over the team was a strange one, especially for a French driver. However, he is optimistic that Haas F1 is "not just like any other team new to F1", as it already has a competition background. This is in NASCAR, he acknowledges, but he feels confident that many operational elements can be transferred, and some are already in place. Should Haas F1 struggle, he has the confidence-inducing thought that he is favourite to fill the second Ferrari seat in 2017 after Kimi Raikkonen's departure.

Former Sauber racer Esteban Gutierrez has been picked as Haas F1's second driver.

So, after years in and out of F1, America now has a grand prix of its own again in Texas, an F1 team in Haas F1 and now it needs to look at finding an American driver who can go on to win.

53

"We always said that we wanted an experienced driver to lead us in 2016. F1 is a tricky business and the best way to learn it is to learn it from other people, so we signed Romain."
Gene Haas

Alan Jones raced for the American-financed Beatrice team in 1985 and 1986, and he's shown here at Brands Hatch in the second of these years.

More and more people took notice of Romain's obvious talents last year when he shone as the Lotus team struggled. This flying Frenchman is just the sort of driver required to guide Haas F1 through its inaugural year in the World Championship.

Some might see Romain's move to an all-new team as a step back from the team for whom he has raced throughout his F1 career. Yet, look at his career history and you'll see that this isn't the first of these decisions that he has had to make.

Having worked his way through the junior formulae with considerable success, winning titles at every level from Formula Renault through Formula Three and GP2, Romain made it to F1 in 2009, stepping up late in the season when Nelson Piquet Jr was dropped. It wasn't a move that worked, though, in a season in which the team was less than competitive.

At this point, with no F1 ride lined up for 2010, Romain found himself at a crossroads. He did what he could to get his career back on track, stepped back to the lesser Auto GP series and won the title. For 2011, he returned to GP2 and did the only thing that he could do to rebuild his credibility: he became champion.

Back in F1 in 2012 with the same team he'd raced for in 2009, albeit now racing as Lotus, Romain was better prepared than he had been for his first attempt, and

Romain is taking another step backwards in his quest to move his F1 career forwards.

appeared on the podium three times through the season to rank eighth. He wasn't everybody's friend, though, as Romain was wild in traffic, most notably at the start of the Belgian GP, when he vaulted over Fernando Alonso's Ferrari at the first corner. Since then, though, Romain has tidied up his act and the progress that he has made has been clear for all to see. Lotus might not have provided him with a car to match the best from Red Bull and, more recently, Mercedes, but he added six podium finishes in 2013, weathered the team's slump in 2014 and continued to shine to the extent that he's now talked of as a future Ferrari driver.

TRACK NOTES

Nationality:	FRENCH
Born:	17 APRIL 1986, GENEVA, SWITZERLAND
Website:	www.romaingrosjean.com
Teams:	RENAULT 2009, LOTUS 2012-15, HAAS F1 2016

CAREER RECORD	
First Grand Prix:	2009 EUROPEAN GP
Grand Prix starts:	83
Grand Prix wins:	0
	(best result: 2nd, 2012 Canadian GP, 2013 United States GP)
Poles:	0
Fastest laps:	1
Points:	287
Honours:	2012 RACE OF CHAMPIONS CHAMPION; 2011 GP2 CHAMPION & GP2 ASIA CHAMPION, 2010 AUTO GP CHAMPION, 2008 GP2 ASIA CHAMPION, 2007 FORMULA THREE EUSOSERIES CHAMPION, 2005 FRENCH FORMULA RENAULT CHAMPION, 2003 SWISS FORMULA RENAULT 1600 CHAMPION

HE KEPT ON PUSHING REGARDLESS

Romain might not have won any grands prix in 2015, but he was one of the season's star drivers. His final ranking in the lower reaches of F1's top ten doesn't make this clear, but the flashes of speed that he showed with financially-troubled Lotus were clear proof of the sheer pace that he has always possessed throughout his career. After a weak start by the team, Romain collected points whenever they were possible. Peaking with third place in the Belgian GP at Spa-Francorchamps behind the two Mercedes drivers was timely indeed, for the bailiffs were circling the team, wanting bills paid, and Romain offered hope through such a credible performance. The take-over of Lotus by Renault came too late to convince Romain to stay but, as he has signed just a one-year deal with Haas F1, he leaves himself free of contract for 2017, when Kimi Raikkonen ought to have left Ferrari, leaving the way clear for him to move across. After all, he will have been racing with a Ferrari engine behind his shoulders through 2016.

ESTEBAN GUTIERREZ

Sergio Perez is Mexico's lead F1 driver, but for 2016 Esteban is back in the show after a year as one of Ferrari's test drivers and he has the ability to deliver well as soon as all-new Haas F1 team can get its cars into a state of competitiveness.

With Mexico returning to the F1 calendar last November, hosting a triumphant return to racing's top table, Esteban's return to the sport's top category after a two-year spell on the sidelines is timely indeed. He has yet to race for a top team, and knows that he won't be this year either, as his return is with Haas F1 as it makes its F1 debut, but his career pedigree is enough to suggest that he will be able to make a good fist of it.

Esteban was a star of Mexico's karting championships, but moved up to car racing as soon as he turned 16, impressively finishing as the runner-up to Daniel Morad in the 2007 US Formula BMW series. Moving to Europe the following year, Esteban won the European Formula BMW title, but was beaten in the BMW World finals by Alexander Rossi.

After a year spent contesting the European Formula Three Championship, ranking ninth as Jules Bianchi cleaned up, Esteban moved on to GP3 in 2010 and won the inaugural title for this equivalent series with ART Grand Prix.

For 2011 and 2012, Esteban raced in GP2, ranking third for ART-run Lotus GP team

Esteban will be especially excited at the thought of contesting a Mexican GP.

behind Davide Valsecchi and Luiz Razia at his second attempt after winning races at Valencia, Silverstone and the Hungaroring.

By this stage, though, Esteban had a fair degree of F1 experience, as he had become Sauber's test driver in 2011 after earlier run-outs in 2009 and 2010. So he landed a race seat with the Swiss team for 2013. Although his best result was seventh place at Japanese GP and team-mate Nico Hulkenberg outscored him 51 to six, Esteban was kept on for 2014.

Esteban's second season was a real setback as he failed to score, his best result being 12th place in the opening round in Melbourne, but more experienced team-mate Adrian Sutil also failed to score as both were held back not only by Sauber's perennial lack of money for development, but also by the new-generation turbocharged Ferrari V6 engine simply not being a match for those from Mercedes and Renault.

TRACK NOTES

Nationality:	MEXICAN
Born:	25 AUGUST 1991, MONTERREY, MEXICO
Website:	www.estebanracing.com
Teams:	SAUBER 2013-14, HAAS F1 2016

CAREER RECORD	
First Grand Prix:	2013 AUSTRALIAN GP
Grand Prix starts:	38
Grand Prix wins:	0
	(best result: 7th, 2013 Japanese GP)
Poles:	0
Fastest laps:	1
Points:	6
Honours:	2010 GP3 CHAMPION, 2008 EUROPEAN FORMULA BMW CHAMPION, 2007 UNITED STATES FORMULA BMW RUNNER-UP, 2005 MEXICAN ROTAX MAX KART CHAMPION

A YEAR SPENT ON THE SIDELINES

No driver likes to be idle. This isn't just because they love racing, but because they fear a loss of career momentum, and Esteban found himself out of the running in 2015, surplus to the requirements of any of the F1 teams, for a race seat, at least. Instead, after two years racing for Sauber, and two years of testing for the Swiss team before that, he had to content himself with being a test driver, an activity restricted last year by a lack of in-season testing. That said, he was at least on Ferrari's books, and so was able to bask in the associated glory. Not that it made him busy, as he was used for only two days of testing all year, covering just 1030km. Being part of Ferrari's broader plans had its benefits, as it elected to place him with another team for 2016 so that he could continue to hone his craft. For the year ahead, it will be with Ferrari-powered Haas F1 that he goes into action, no doubt looking forward to contesting a Mexican GP for the first time.

McLaren's team work was as excellent as ever in the pitstops, but its poor 2015 season is one it will want to put behind it.

TALKING POINT: FORMULA ONE WELCOMES NEW AMERICAN INVOLVEMENT

Haas F1's arrival for 2016 is a considerable boost to the World Championship, as the lack of American teams has long been a problem for Formula 1. It may well be years before the team is able to challenge for wins, but it is a welcome addition.

Although the Indianapolis 500 was a round of the World Championship from 1950 to 1960, American involvement really began when it hosted its first grand prix at Sebring, Florida, in 1959. There had been a few American drivers involved to that point, including Harry Schell, Phil Hill and Dan Gurney, who came across to Europe to pursue their road racing dreams, but hosting a race showed that the US was interested in racing beyond its own Indycar and NASCAR categories.

Yet, as the race was shunted to Riverside, California, then Watkins Glen, New York, what F1 needed to keep the USA's interest beyond its annual race was year-round involvement by an American team.

The first to try was Lance Reventlow's team, but its 1960 Scarab was already outdated because its engine was at the front while F1 teams were putting it behind the driver's shoulders. The next abortive attempt came in 1963, when the Scirocco-Powell team built its own car.

In 1966, American fans finally had a team to cheer for. This was Eagle, Gurney's team. That it was based both in England as well as in California showed the logistical problems of running an F1 operation from the USA. Gurney won the Belgian GP in 1967, but the team didn't last beyond 1968, as he diverted his attention to more lucrative American racing series.

Don Nichols' Shadow concern had built cars for the CanAm sportscar series, then set up a base in Britain and entered F1 in 1973. It would race on until 1979 before being bought by Teddy Yip for the 1980 season. Shadow's best result was Alan Jones' win in the 1977 Austrian GP.

In 1974, two more American teams joined Shadow on the F1 grid. Parnelli, headed by Vel Miletich and Indycar racer Parnelli Jones, was run from California and Norfolk and peaked with fourth in the 1975 Swedish GP, thanks to American ace Mario Andretti.

Penske started its involvement at that same 1974 North American double-header. Run by racer turned industrial mogul Roger Penske, it had a European base at Poole, along with its HQ in Pennsylvania. Penske raced on until the penultimate round of 1977, matching Eagle and Shadow in taking victory when John Watson won the 1976 Austrian GP.

In the mid-1980s, Team Haas (USA) entered F1, with racer turned Indycar entrant Carl Haas running Lolas driven by Alan Jones and Patrick Tambay from a base near Heathrow, but they quit in 1986.

Then there was nothing, until USF1 was mooted for 2010 when F1 invited four teams to boost the size of the grids in the World Championship. This was to be an American team, based in the USA, but it looked likely to happen only when Argentinian driver Jose Maria Lopez brought money. However, the team failed to get off the ground.

In Haas F1, there are more serious ingredients. Firstly, Gene Haas - no relation to Carl - has a leading NASCAR team, next to which it will base itself at Kannapolis in North Carolina.

Secondly, in team principal Gunther Steiner, the team has a man with F1 experience, having held the same position for Jaguar Racing then Red Bull Racing in 2005. Thirdly, it struck a deal with Dallara to help produce its first chassis under the guidance of former Ferrari, Jaguar, McLaren and Marussia designer Rob Taylor, backed by aerodynamicist Ben Agathangelou, who has just upgraded Ferrari's wind tunnel.

Gene Haas always planned to hire the best people, but realized he needed partners with F1 experience, thus adding Ferrari to the mix. "We soon learned just how much there was to learn," he explained. "To say you can build a car on your own is foolish."

So Haas F1 will run Ferrari engines and some were vexed that Haas F1 had unlimited time in Ferrari's wind tunnel last year, while the teams racing in the World Championship were limited to 30 hours. Ferrari will also be involved in the design of the gearbox, electronics and suspension while keeping a protective wing over the fledgling team.

Although proudly being based in the USA, Haas is wise enough to have added a base in England, taking over the former Marussia factory at Banbury. "When we started," he said, "we planned to do everything out of Kannapolis, but that changed. The Banbury facility is more about logistics."

Haas is unusual among team owners in that he has business reasons for this leap into the F1 pond, as he also wants to promote his Haas Automation machine tool business. What better way to do that than have a plainly American team, preferably piloted by at least one American rising star on the international stage? For its first year at least, though, American hot shots will have to wait, as Romain Grosjean brings speed and experience to lead the team, joined by Esteban Gutierrez, a veteran of two full F1 campaigns.

Formula 1 has waited too long for an American team of substance, so let's see whether Haas F1 can get stuck in.

Top: The sleek-looking Haas F1 Team headquarters is in North Carolina, but it will have a base in Banbury, England, from which to run its team logistics.

Above left: Parnelli was one of three American teams that contested the World Championship in the 1970s. This is Mario Andretti at Watkins Glen in 1975.

Above right: Stewart-Haas Racing has become one of America's top NASCAR teams, with Kevin Harvick leading the way, along with team-mate Kurt Busch.

TALKING POINT: FORMULA ONE IS LOSING ITS EUROPEAN FLAVOUR

Although Italy, Britain, Germany and France used to be staples of the World Championship, their influence is declining rapidly as the Formula 1 calendar continues to expand, with an ever more global spread, and many don't consider this to be a wholly good thing.

The French invented Grand Prix racing, way back in 1906 at Le Mans. Yet, such has been the recent reshaping of the World Championship calendar that we have already become accustomed to its annual race no longer being on the calendar. Indeed, the most recent French GP was back in 2008, since when it hasn't been able to afford the fee for hosting a grand prix. Long-time F1 fans say its loss is at the expense of F1's soul.

Franz Tost, Scuderia Toro Rosso team principal, is adamant that this is sufficient reason not to let France back onboard: "We must go to countries that can afford F1, it's as simple as that. If they can't afford it, we don't go there." Others feel slightly more sentimental on the matter.

It's great that the German GP is back for 2016 after a year off the agenda – this despite the title-chasing form of a pair of German drivers, Nico Rosberg and Sebastian Vettel – but the country's long-term place in a sport in which it has played a major part is still far from assured. It could be pointed out that attendance figures were disappointing when Hockenheim last hosted a grand prix, in 2014, but F1 has to be aware that it appears to be cutting the roots of the tree it is trying to climb.

Britain now has the comfort of a long-term deal, but only after Silverstone updated its facilities. Late in 2015, though, its managing director Patrick Allen said that, with an escalation clause, he couldn't be sure Silverstone could afford its fee until the end of its contract in 2026.

However, perhaps most unthinkable of all, Italy's tenure of a date was again being questioned last year. Had you told F1 fans of the possibility of these four classic grands prix being off the calendar as recently as 20 years ago, they would have thought us crazy. This quartet of race-mad nations have, after all, been the backbone of F1 since the World Championship began in 1950. Monaco has always been the icing, but they have been the cake, home to the teams, drivers and constructors.

Pirelli's Paul Hembery is a keen supporter of the Italian GP, saying: "Maybe I'm a little bit old fashioned, but there are a few events I've always looked to since I started watching F1, and Monza is one of them, as are Spa and Silverstone. We try to support the race at Monza by taking lots of guests to the event."

Manor boss Graeme Lowdon feels that the calendar should be made to work as a whole, rather than on a race-by-race basis. "If Monza or any of the iconic venues are at threat, perhaps something could be done in a more optimum way somewhere else. If we do nothing but chase income, the sport will just eat itself up."

For now, though, we have to accept that their tenure is far from assured as F1 continues to chase pastures new, even to the extent that it has gone one beyond the teams' proposed maximum of 20 races for 2016. Indeed, there is a record of seven sets of back-to-back grands prix simply to squeeze this number into the calendar and still fit in a break for the teams in August.

With new host nations, such as the latest addition, Azerbaijan, tending to be the ones that have made the largest bids to host grands prix, F1 has moved beyond the more obvious pattern of expansion that led to the establishment of rounds in the nations with the two largest populations: China and India. Azerbaijan can make no such claim, with a population of under 10 million.

What worries the purists is that not only does Azerbaijan have no history of motorsport – other than a couple of imported races for GT cars – but also that it has been given the title of European GP, when it's beyond the Caucasus mountains, thus in Asia. That would mean little, except that it might now be lined up to fill one of the eight places in the calendar reserved for races in Europe. This isn't the case in 2016, but it could be a bargaining point held over one of the current F1 venues in Europe.

Not all the new venues have worked out well. Take the Turkish GP, which made its entrance in 2005, at the excellent Istanbul Park circuit, yet disappeared after seven years as Turkish sports fans failed to find F1 attractive so left the grandstands empty.

Of course, Formula One Management and the FIA have to decide what they seek. Global awareness is one thing, but having sustainable races in front of large crowds aware of F1's rich history – such as the sell-out British GP at Silverstone – are ingredients that are essential for the sport's soul and image. It's not a case of wanting to stand in the way of global expansion and, of course, it would be great to have a race in Africa again, but to lose a firm footing in Europe would be to the detriment of F1's history as well as its future.

Above left:
The Chinese
GP at Shanghai
International Circuit
is now a firm fixture
on the F1 calendar.

Above: The most
recent French GP,
held at Magny-Cours
back in 2008, was
won by Felipe Massa
for Ferrari.

Left: Baku, capital
of Azerbaijan, will
receive a global
focus like never
before when F1
comes to town.

While F1 adds grands prix in new venues, the long-standing race around Monaco's harbour remains a much-loved constant.

KNOW THE TRACKS 2016

It's a case of another year, another change to the World Championship. This year, for the first time since Sochi made its bow in 2014, there is a brand new venue for F1 teams to tackle: the circuit in the heart of the Azerbaijani capital Baku joining the show. Other than this, the championship calendar has, once again, been shuffled into a new order.

The World Championship calendar never stands still. Last year, F1 made a triumphant return to its old stamping ground in Mexico City, with huge crowds filling the grandstands to shout their support, not just for countryman Sergio Perez but for F1 as a whole, making it a feel-good occasion all round. That this took place in the largest city in Latin America, which also happened to be one with a rich F1 history, was considered a major plus for the World Championship.

This year, it's not a case of returning to a favoured venue of old but, instead, heading to pastures new to augment its global spread. It's more than safe to say that when the teams and drivers considered where F1 might take them in the future, they wouldn't have picked Azerbaijan as a likely destination. Still, that is what this oil-rich nation's government has financed in its quest to make the country stand out on the global stage, continuing its policy of building a name for itself through hosting international cultural and sporting events.

Unusually, the new race has taken the title of European GP, somewhat stretching the limits of the continent, perhaps to give Formula One Management more leverage when it negotiates future contracts with the established grands prix across Europe (*see* Talking Point on pages 58-59).

The new grand prix brings the season's tally up to 21, one more than teams said they would like, as they attempt to balance increased revenue against the exhaustion of their personnel through the course of an increasingly busy year. The race, on a temporary street circuit in capital city Baku, slots into the schedule between the Canadian and Austrian GPs in June.

Other than this, the 2016 World Championship calendar has been shuffled a little from its traditional pattern by moving the Malaysian GP from its previous slot as the second race of the year to be part of a more logical double-header with the Japanese GP at Suzuka, although it would have made more sense to be partnered with the race in neighbouring Singapore.

This means the order of the early-season flyaway races in 2016 is: Australia, Bahrain, China and, moving forward from autumn, Russia. This means the mountainous backdrop to the Sochi Autodrom should be even more spectacular, with the peaks still capped with snow. More than that, the weekend marks the start of a ten-day national holiday in Russia and so more local fans ought to be able to attend their home race.

One of the best pieces of news is the return of the German GP, this time slotting into the calendar after rather than before the Hungarian GP, after a year out of circulation following financial difficulties. F1 needs races in the countries that have long been integral to its history, and hopefully the financial problems that beset its pattern of alternation between Hockenheim and the Nurburgring are now behind us. For 2016, the race will be back at Hockenheim.

The teams are relieved that the four-week summer break in August has been kept, even with extra round, so teams still ought to feel refreshed when they turn up for the Belgian GP at Spa-Francorchamps at the end of the month.

This has been achieved by continuing last year's policy of having double-headers, that's to say grand prix meetings on consecutive weekends. With next to no testing between races now, this is possible, although it proves quite a challenge for those in charge of the teams' logistics.

The final four flyaway races hold the pattern they adopted last year, with the Circuit of the Americas, the Autodromo Hermanos Rodriguez in Mexico City, Interlagos and then the Yas Marina Circuit in Abu Dhabi offering four incredibly different challenges as the season reaches its climax.

The mixture is great throughout 2016, so let's hope that the teams can cope with the increase from 19 races in 2015 to 21 this time around. F1 continues to spread its message around the globe and we must also hope the race in Baku is both well run and well attended, and goes on to enjoy a longer run than recent grands prix in Turkey and South Korea, two other countries with minimal or no racing history.

MELBOURNE

Australia's grand prix holds onto the honour of being the first of the season. This imbues the Albert Park circuit with an extra level of excitement as F1 kicks off.

Melbourne is a brilliant location to start 2016's World Championship action but, in truth, the Albert Park circuit isn't one of the greatest tracks on the calendar, offering a handful of interesting corners but no truly great ones.

The lap starts with a right/left esse, and the first part has often been the scene of plenty of action at the start of a race. It takes on a feel that it maintains for much of the lap, with temporary concrete walls lining either flank.

Turn 3 is probably the most exciting place to be on lap 1. Drivers are torn between what might be their best passing opportunity all race, and the consequences of either being too bold and getting it wrong, coming out worse off, or being caught out by another driver's excess of ambition.

Thanks to the walls, there's precious little space for evasive action on the way in to the corner, but there's a large gravel bed straight ahead. Bent wings tend to be the punishment, as well as the spectre of lost places.

Turn 4 is more open and feels doubly so, as there's space on either side of the track. A fast right flick then takes the track into its second run through trees, down to a right kink, followed by a left swerve out onto the open run around the far side of the park's lake.

Apart from tight Turn 9, there's a chance for drivers to find some flow, all the way to Turn 13. The next three corners are also near 90-degree turns, before the highest speed of the lap is achieved on the run past the pits and the approach to Turn 1.

INSIDE TRACK
AUSTRALIAN GRAND PRIX

Date:	**20 March**
Circuit name:	**Albert Park**
Circuit length:	**3.295 miles/5.300km**
Number of laps:	**58**
Email:	**enquiries@grandprix.com.au**
Website:	**www.grandprix.com.au**

PREVIOUS WINNERS

2006	**Fernando Alonso** RENAULT
2007	**Kimi Raikkonen** FERRARI
2008	**Lewis Hamilton** McLAREN
2009	**Jenson Button** BRAWN
2010	**Jenson Button** McLAREN
2011	**Sebastian Vettel** RED BULL
2012	**Jenson Button** McLAREN
2013	**Kimi Raikkonen** LOTUS
2014	**Nico Rosberg** MERCEDES
2015	**Lewis Hamilton** MERCEDES

Location: Albert Park is one mile south of the centre of Melbourne, with access by the city's numerous tram routes, meaning that the circuit doesn't have to find parking space for tens of thousands of cars.

Where to stay: Melbourne is packed with hotels, with some visitors favouring those along the River Yarra, others the ones out on the beach at St Kilda.

How it started: Sports-mad Melbourne added to its staples of cricket, tennis and Australian Rules Football in 1996 when it wrested the Australian GP from Adelaide. The circuit, laid out around a lake in Albert Park, saw Damon Hill the first to triumph for Williams after team-mate Jacques Villeneuve suffered falling oil pressure late in his F1 debut.

Best race: Mika Hakkinen should have won for McLaren in 1999, but was denied by throttle problems and retired. The race started with both Stewarts catching fire on the grid. Jacques Villeneuve crashed out and Eddie Irvine came through to win for Ferrari.

Local aces: After years of supporting Mark Webber, Australian fans wave their flags for Daniel Ricciardo, hoping that he will become their first world champion since Alan Jones in 1980. With three F1 titles, Jack Brabham remains Australia's most successful F1 ace.

Marina
Clark
Lauda
Hill
Whiteford
Waite
Ascari
Jones Chicane
Senna
Pit Lane
START
Prost

Gear 111 Km/h 1 Timing sector ⚠ DRS detection ⚠ DRS activation

2015 POLE TIME: **HAMILTON (MERCEDES), 1M26.327S, 137.413MPH/221.145KPH**
2015 WINNER'S AVERAGE SPEED: **124.775MPH/200.807KPH**

2015 FASTEST LAP: **HAMILTON (MERCEDES), 1M30.945S, 130.435MPH/209.915KPH**
LAP RECORD: **M SCHUMACHER (FERRARI), 1M24.125S, 141.016MPH/226.944KPH, 2004**

SAKHIR

Run as a double-header with the Russian GP, but providing quite a contrast with Sochi, Bahrain's circuit is one of two on the Arabian peninsula, but the only one that feels as though it's in a desert.

Like so many of the F1 circuits that Hermann Tilke has designed, this one starts its lap with the start/finish straight being brought to an end by a tight right-hander followed by a couple of twisting corners. This means that if a driver is on the optimal line out of the first corner, they won't necessarily be in the right position for the next one. This makes the corner something of a lottery, and so adds to the circuit's appeal. Whether in the opening lap melee, or at any other point during the grand prix, Turn 1 remains the best overtaking spot.

Unusually, the Sakhir International Circuit's lap was built with two clear sections, and it's as the cars power out of Turn 3 that they leave the "oasis" section with its much-watered grass verges and heads out into the desert. The location's natural rocky backdrop then prevails

all the way out to the Turn 4 right-hand hairpin and then back through the sweepers of Turns 5 to 7 before twisting back on itself in an even sharper hairpin at Turn 8. Now running parallel to the start/finish straight, the track runs first one way behind the paddock, then doubles back through a lefthand hairpin at Turn 10 and goes in the opposite direction.

Good exit speed from Turn 11 is then vital for the gentle climb to Turn 13, with the sweep through Turn 12 perhaps the greatest challenge of the 3.363-mile lap for the drivers. From Turn 13, it's then a flat-out blast back down the gradual slope to 90-degree Turn 14 and more open Turn 15 to re-enter the oasis section again.

As at Melbourne, the circuit's fastest point, at 187mph, is just before the braking point for Turn 1.

INSIDE TRACK
BAHRAIN GRAND PRIX

Date:	**3 April**
Circuit name:	**Bahrain International Circuit**
Circuit length:	**3.363 miles/5.412km**
Number of laps:	**57**
Email:	**info@bic.com.bh**
Website:	**www.bahraingp.com.bh**

PREVIOUS WINNERS

2006	**Fernando Alonso** RENAULT
2007	**Felipe Massa** FERRARI
2008	**Felipe Massa** FERRARI
2009	**Jenson Button** BRAWN
2010	**Fernando Alonso** FERRARI
2012	**Sebastian Vettel** RED BULL
2013	**Sebastian Vettel** RED BULL
2014	**Lewis Hamilton** MERCEDES
2015	**Lewis Hamilton** MERCEDES

Location: The circuit is found in the rocky desert at Sakhir, to the south of Bahrain's capital city, Manama.

Where to stay: Downtown Manama is the best place to be, with interesting souks to add to the experience of being in this part of the world.

How it started: Dubai had become the Gulf's leading sporting venue, hosting high-profile events, but Bahrain struck first to land F1. It made its F1 bow in 2004 when Michael Schumacher won for Ferrari and, apart from missing out in 2011, when political unrest kept F1 away, it has been a constant since then.

Best race: For offering something different, the 2009 Bahrain GP stands out, as Toyota ran its cars with light fuel loads to fill the front row of the grid. But you had to start with what fuel you had left back then and they soon had to pit and fell down the order as Jenson Button came through to win for Brawn GP ahead of Red Bull's Sebastian Vettel.

Local aces: Bahrain is still waiting for a breakthrough from one of its young drivers, with Hamad Al Fardan winning the 2009 Asian FV6 title but retiring. Ali Al Khalifa spent last year racing in Italian F4.

Gear ⚙ 111 Km/h ❶ Timing sector ⚠ DRS detection △ DRS activation

2015 POLE TIME: HAMILTON (MERCEDES), 1M32.571S, 130.778MPH/210.467KPH
2015 WINNER'S AVERAGE SPEED: 120.843MPH/194.478KPH

2015 FASTEST LAP: RAIKKONEN (FERRARI), 1M36.311S, 125.699MPH/202.294KPH
LAP RECORD: M SCHUMACHER (FERRARI), 1M30.252S, 134.262MPH/216.074KPH, 2004

SHANGHAI

Moved forward to be the second part of the season-opening double-header, the Shanghai International Circuit offers plenty of scope for overtaking and close racing beneath its giant grandstands.

If the Shanghai International Circuit looks huge on television, it feels even larger if you go there. Stand on the pit straight and you will be dwarfed by the towering grandstands opposite the pits.

You then you realize that the wing-shaped bridges that cross the track at either end of the pit straight start at the ninth storey. The scale of the place comes even more into perspective should you walk to the far end of the circuit.

Indeed, on the none too infrequent smoggy days, you can feel cut off from the rest of the track if out at Turns 11 to 13, unable to see anything else as the massively long return straight feeds back into the gloom.

The flow of the track is one of the best visited by F1, even if the atmosphere can be lacking, as Chinese fans have yet to truly embrace the sport.

From the first sequence of bends, you can feel that F1 circuit designer Hermann Tilke thoroughly enjoyed shaping the place, with the track rising as it sweeps right, then flattening out at Turn 2 before dipping as it turns sharply left through Turn 3 and flattening out again.

The approach to Turn 6 is a clear spot for trying an overtaking manoeuvre before the signature high-speed sweep through Turns 7 and 8. Accelerating hard out of Turn 10, there's a short straight before Turns 11 to 13, which are almost a reverse of Turns 1 to 3, albeit on the level. Then comes the longest straight, with a maximum of just over 200mph hit before the Turn 14 hairpin.

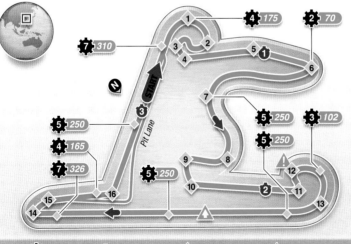

Gear ①⟨111⟩ Km/h ① Timing sector ⚠ DRS detection ⚠ DRS activation

2015 POLE TIME: HAMILTON (MERCEDES), 1M35.782S, 127.304MPH/204.877KPHH
2015 WINNER'S AVERAGE SPEED: 114.077MPH/183.590KPH

2015 FASTEST LAP: HAMILTON (MERCEDES), 1M42.208S, 119.301MPH/191.996KPH
LAP RECORD: M SCHUMACHER (FERRARI), 1M32.238S 132.202MPH/212.759KPH, 2004

INSIDE TRACK
CHINESE GRAND PRIX

Date:	**17 April**
Circuit name:	**Shanghai International Circuit**
Circuit length:	**3.390 miles/5.450km**
Number of laps:	**56**
Email:	**f1@china-sss.com**
Website:	**www.f1china.com.cn**

PREVIOUS WINNERS	
2006	**Michael Schumacher** FERRARI
2007	**Kimi Raikkonen** FERRARI
2008	**Lewis Hamilton** McLAREN
2009	**Sebastian Vettel** RED BULL
2010	**Jenson Button** McLAREN
2011	**Lewis Hamilton** McLAREN
2012	**Nico Rosberg** MERCEDES
2013	**Fernando Alonso** FERRARI
2014	**Lewis Hamilton** MERCEDES
2015	**Lewis Hamilton** MERCEDES

Location: Shanghai is expanding rapidly, but there's still open land between the city centre and the circuit, which is 20 miles to the north.

Where to stay: The towns near the circuit are somewhat dull, so travelling fans tend to stay in downtown Shanghai and travel out either by taxi or Metro.

How it started: Built with government backing, the circuit was placed on marshy land that had little other use and was ready for racing in 2004, at a time when F1 and its sponsors were desperate to go racing in this burgeoning economy. Ferrari's Rubens Barrichello won the first race.

Best race: Lewis Hamilton won't like remembering this, but the 2007 Chinese GP, in which he could have wrapped up the title in his rookie year, was the most exciting yet. Weather conditions were changing and McLaren waited too long to call him in on worn tyres and he slid off into a gravel trap at pit entry, handing victory to Ferrari's Kimi Raikkonen, who went on to be champion.

Local aces: China is still waiting to have an F1 driver of its own, although Franky Cheng, Ho-Pin Tung and Ma Qing Hua have all tested F1 cars.

SOCHI

A new date in spring, as the championship's fourth round, ought to make Sochi feel very different from its first two renditions, with the scenic setting again most likely to steal the show.

Unusually, the opening corner of the Sochi Autodrom is a fast kink, much like Imola's Tamburello used to be, albeit turning the cars to the right rather than to the left. With the following corner being a 90-degree right, there is inevitably overtaking action, or at least attempted overtaking action here, particularly on the opening lap.

This potential for providing dramatic moments was demonstrated by Nico Rosberg on F1's first visit, when he dived up the inside of his Mercedes team-mate Lewis Hamilton to take the lead of the race, only to lock up and sail straight on, thus handing the lead back to the British driver.

The loop from here, through Turn 3 to Turn 4, is one of the longest arcs in F1, seemingly turning left forever as it runs through a lengthy semi-circle. Then the lap is divided into a series of short straights interspersed with tight corners, making it all a bit point-and-squirt and overtaking extremely unlikely.

The lap's flow only returns after the tight righthander at Turn 10, with the back section of the lap enjoying a snaking sweep down to Turn 13. This ought to be a good spot for overtaking as Turn 13 is a sharp right, but it has yet to offer as many passing opportunities as Turn 2, possibly because, as perhaps the lap's trickiest corner, it offers plenty of scope for getting things wrong.

The flow of the lap is then very much broken up as the final six corners, running around the back of the F1 paddock, are slow ones. Yet, good exit speed from the final turn onto the start/finish straight can enable a driver to get a good run all the way to Turn 2 at the start of the following lap, reaching a peak of 200mph before having to hit the brakes there.

INSIDE TRACK
RUSSIAN GRAND PRIX

Date:	**1 May**
Circuit name:	**Sochi Autodrom**
Circuit length:	**3.634 miles/5.848km**
Number of laps:	**53**
Email:	**info@sochiautodrom.ru**
Website:	**www.sochiautodrom.ru/en**

PREVIOUS WINNER

2014	**Lewis Hamilton** MERCEDES
2015	**Lewis Hamilton** MERCEDES

Location: The circuit is in the centre of Sochi on Russia's coastline along the north-east corner of the Black Sea. Backed by the Caucasus mountains, it is a multi-season resort, offering skiing in winter and a semi-tropical climate in the summer.

Where to stay: Being a resort city, there is a wide choice of hotels to suit all budgets.

How it started: Russia had long wanted to host a grand prix, but numerous bids had failed, with attempts to host a grand prix both in Moscow and on new, purpose-built circuits outside it coming to nought. There was talk of St Petersburg landing a World Championship round, but, with President Putin's express intervention, a deal was done for Sochi to host the first Russian GP, with a circuit using some of the infrastructure of a sporting complex used for the Winter Olympic Games in 2014.

Best race: Sochi's first grand prix was exciting from the outset, with Nico Rosberg outbraking Mercedes team-mate Lewis Hamilton into Turn 2. However, he outbraked himself and flatspotted his tyres. This meant that he had to pit for new rubber and Hamilton won as he pleased.

Local aces: Russia had an F3 series from 1997, but Italian drivers dominated that and its first F1 driver, Vitaly Petrov, cut his teeth instead in Formula Renault around Europe before trying GP2. His best result before losing his F1 ride was third for Renault at the 2011 Australian GP. Daniil Kvyat took a more conventional route through junior single-seaters, being GP3 champion in 2013 before getting his F1 break with Toro Rosso in 2014.

175   6   4   187   8   146
6   270
250   7   254
5   8   314
3
9
4   7   305   2   168   6   264
119   109   153
2
10
3   152   11
273   12   14   15   200
233   13   Pit Lane
4   163   START
3   128   321   1   8   16   3   128
1   111

Km/h (simulated speeds)

2015 POLE TIME: **ROSBERG (MERCEDES),** 1M37.113S, 134.704MPH/216.786KPH

2015 WINNER'S AVERAGE SPEED: **118.826MPH/191.232KPH**

2015 FASTEST LAP: **VETTEL (FERRARI),** 1M40.071S, 130.723MPH/210.378KPH

LAP RECORD: **VETTEL (FERRARI), 1M40.071S 130.723MPH/210.378KPH, 2015**

BARCELONA

Spanish fans have flocked here in droves for years to see if Fernando Alonso might give them a home win. Hopefully McLaren will have advanced sufficiently to at least offer them some hope.

Spring weather has always been an attraction to encourage people to attend the Spanish GP, bolstered by the fact that it's traditionally the first F1 race in Europe, and it's a place where teams tend to bring their first development parts after the season-opening flyway races. The city of Barcelona is another attraction. Yet, strip away these points of interest, and the Circuit de Catalunya struggles to match F1's great circuits, like Suzuka, Spa-Francorchamps and Silverstone.

The downhill sprint to the first corner offers a good chance for overtaking on lap 1, and remains the best opportunity for the remainder of the race, but the lapchart seldom lies and it's still pitstops that lead to more changes of position than on-track action.

There is a welcome gradient change here, with the long Renault right-hander climbing constantly, with further altitude gain out of Repsol. From SEAT, it's downhill all the way to tight Turn 7 before the track rears up for the climb to Campsa.

A downhill straight follows, into the hairpin at Turn 10, but it fails to produce much in the way of overtaking. Going upwards again, the track kinks through Turn 11, then doubles back through 12, before flattening out and dropping out of 13.

Last year's race was lacklustre and there were calls for the final section of the lap to be changed back to how it used to be, without the Turn 14/15 chicane, so that cars could sweep onto the start/finish straight, as they did until circuit modifications in 2007, and so have more hope of getting close enough to the car they're chasing to try a passing move into the first corner.

INSIDE TRACK
SPANISH GRAND PRIX

Date:	**15 May**
Circuit name:	**Circuit de Catalunya**
Circuit length:	**2.892 miles/4.654km**
Number of laps:	**66**
Email:	**info@circuitcat.com**
Website:	**www.circuitcat.com**

PREVIOUS WINNERS

2006	**Fernando Alonso** RENAULT
2007	**Felipe Massa** FERRARI
2008	**Kimi Raikkonen** FERRARI
2009	**Jenson Button** BRAWN
2010	**Mark Webber** RED BULL
2011	**Sebastian Vettel** RED BULL
2012	**Pastor Maldonado** WILLIAMS
2013	**Fernando Alonso** FERRARI
2014	**Lewis Hamilton** MERCEDES
2015	**Nico Rosberg** MERCEDES

Location: The circuit nestles in rolling hills 15 miles north of Barcelona, near Montmelo.

Where to stay: With Barcelona being such a vibrant city, you ought to stay there, close enough to the Ramblas or port for fun in the evenings. The circuit can even be reached by taking a train to Montmelo.

How it started: Barcelona had hosted grands prix on a street circuit in its Pedralbes suburb in the 1950s, then on a track in its Montjuich Park between 1969 and 1975. Its third shot came with this circuit when it opened in 1991.

Best race: With overtaking rare here, it has only been since the advent of DRS that the racing has livened up. The race in 2014 came to a climax when Nico Rosberg attacked Lewis Hamilton in the final two laps but failed to find a way past.

Local aces: Until Fernando Alonso came along, Spain had never produced a grand prix winner. He put that right in 2003 and became its first world champion two years later. No other Spanish driver has looked likely to become a grand prix winner, with Pedro de la Rosa falling short, Jaime Alguersuari being dropped by Red Bull then quitting the sport last year and Roberto Mehri still trying to become an F1 regular.

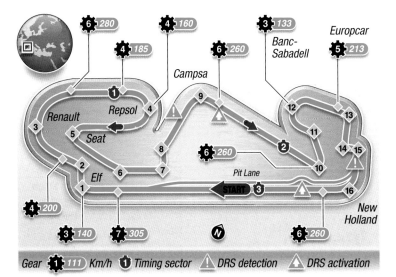

Gear 🔧 **111** Km/h ➊ Timing sector ⚠ DRS detection 🔺 DRS activation

2015 POLE TIME: **ROSBERG (MERCEDES)**, 1M24.681S, 122.966MPH/197.895KPH	2015 FASTEST LAP: **HAMILTON (MERCEDES)**, 1M28.270S, 117.966MPH/189.849KPH
2015 WINNER'S AVERAGE SPEED: **113.127MPH/182.060KPH**	LAP RECORD: **RAIKKONEN (FERRARI)**, 1M21.670S, 127.500MPH/205.192KPH, 2008

MONACO

F1 fans know how wide an average F1 track is. Well, Monaco's street circuit is far from average. It's a narrow, bumpy, rising and falling stretch of tarmac like no other, but enjoyed by all.

This ancient grand prix circuit is so hemmed in and restricted by the buildings and streetware of Monte Carlo that it has next to no space for expansion, which explains why its shape has changed little since it opened for racing in 1929.

Starting on a start/finish straight just in from the harbour that isn't even straight, as it arcs gently to the right, the lap starts on the level, then begins to climb almost as soon as it has turned right at Ste Devote.

The ascent goes over a slight brow at Eau Rivage, then treats the drivers to a fast lefthander, Massenet. This spits them out from being enclosed by barriers for a moment as it enters Casino Square before getting the barriers hard alongside its passage again for the descent past the Tip Top Bar on the drop to the righthand Mirabeau hairpin.

The drop then increases as the track goes down to the Grand Hotel hairpin, then yet more through Mirabeau Bas and Portier where it reaches the seafront.

The drivers can't see over the barriers, though, and have to focus instead on the curving tunnel that follows. Back into the daylight at its far end, they then lose a little more height before reaching the harbourside at the Nouvelle Chicane.

Blasting past the yachts, drivers negotiate the fast left, Tabac, before going left/right, then almost immediately right/left around Piscine. The end of the lap is typically tight, with the Rascasse hairpin then the right flick over a brow at Antony Noghes.

Racing at Monaco isn't physical, as lap speeds are low, but the threat of clipping a barrier keeps the drivers alert.

INSIDE TRACK
MONACO GRAND PRIX

Date:	**29 May**
Circuit name:	**Monte Carlo Circuit**
Circuit length:	**2.075 miles/3.339km**
Number of laps:	**78**
Email:	**info@acm.mc**
Website:	**www.acm.mc**

PREVIOUS WINNERS	
2006	**Fernando Alonso** RENAULT
2007	**Fernando Alonso** McLAREN
2008	**Lewis Hamilton** McLAREN
2009	**Jenson Button** BRAWN
2010	**Mark Webber** RED BULL
2011	**Sebastian Vettel** RED BULL
2012	**Mark Webber** RED BULL
2013	**Nico Rosberg** MERCEDES
2014	**Nico Rosberg** MERCEDES
2015	**Nico Rosberg** MERCEDES

Location: The circuit snakes around the heart of Monte Carlo, from the harbourside up the steeply-sloping hill behind to Casino Square and then back down again.

Where to stay: This depends wholly on your budget, as hotels in Monaco can vary from the expensive to the astronomical. To keep your expenditure in check, stay in nearby Menton and travel in by train.

How it started: Cigarette manufacturer Antony Noghes came up with the idea of racing on the streets of the principality and the original layout that was first used in 1929 has changed remarkably little since.

Best race: There have been super close finishes, but no race can challenge the bizarre one in 1982 when there were two new leaders in the final two and a bit laps after Alain Prost crashed his Renault out of the lead. Riccardo Patrese took over, then spun and stalled, The next three rivals all hit trouble at the same time, allowing Patrese to recover to clinch it for Brabham.

Local aces: Many drivers live in Monaco for the great weather and for its generous tax benefits. However, Louis Chiron was a true Monegasque and, as yet, remains its most successful F1 racer, having finished third in his home race in 1950 for Maserati.

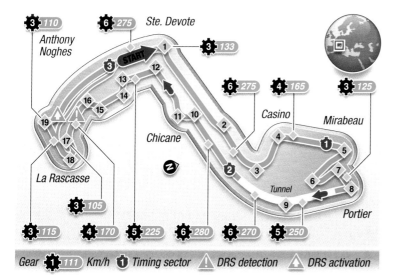

Gear — Km/h — Timing sector — DRS detection — DRS activation

2015 POLE TIME: **HAMILTON (MERCEDES)**, 1M15.098S, 99.398MPH/159.966KPH
2015 WINNER'S AVERAGE SPEED: 88.778MPH/142.874KPH

2015 FASTEST LAP: **RICCIARDO (RED BULL)**, 1M18.063S, 95.623MPH/153.891KPH
LAP RECORD: **M SCHUMACHER (FERRARI)**, 1M14.439S, 100.369MPH/161.528KPH, 2004

Something extraordinary happened last year: the Circuit Gilles Villeneuve produced a less than enthralling grand prix. Hopefully, it will return to its traditional offering of thrills and spills this June.

History relates that this circuit, on an island on the far side of the St Lawrence Seaway from Montreal, has been the scene of dramatic racing moments ever since it first hosted F1 back in 1978.

There's something about its layout, with its long straights and sections of heavy braking that leads to great racing, risky moves and occasional contact. Drama never seems far away.

Mechanically, the Circuit Gilles Villeneuve is a car breaker, and the concrete walls that surround the track make it trickier than most, but Turn 1 seems to invite drivers to have a go and so does the final chicane.

From the grid, drivers have to kink to the right just after the start, then jockey to get into position not only to turn left for Virage Senna, but for the second corner too, as the Island Hairpin follows almost immediately after it. Getting it right through the first part is no guarantee that a driver can complete the move by the righthand hairpin that follows.

From Island Hairpin, the track enters the "far side", the stretch of this island track that runs alongside the river. There's a series of quick esses, bound by walls, then a more open sweeper at Pont de la Concorde, out of which a good exit might enable a driver to try a passing move into the L'Epingle hairpin.

Yet, most of the passing moves are attempted just after the fastest point of the lap, where drivers almost hit 200mph before braking and changing down to third for the chicane. The turn-in is all but blind, then the walls beyond beckon and it has been where many drivers' races ended.

72

INSIDE TRACK
CANADIAN GRAND PRIX

Date:	12 June
Circuit name:	Circuit Gilles Villeneuve
Circuit length:	2.710 miles/4.361km
Number of laps:	70
Email:	info@circuitgillesvilleneuve.ca
Website:	www.circuitgillesvilleneuve.ca

PREVIOUS WINNERS	
2005	**Kimi Raikkonen** McLAREN
2006	**Fernando Alonso** RENAULT
2007	**Lewis Hamilton** McLAREN
2008	**Robert Kubica** BMW SAUBER
2010	**Lewis Hamilton** McLAREN
2011	**Jenson Button** McLAREN
2012	**Lewis Hamilton** McLAREN
2013	**Sebastian Vettel** RED BULL
2014	**Daniel Ricciardo** RED BULL
2015	**Lewis Hamilton** MERCEDES

Location: The circuit is just across the river from downtown Montreal, on the Ile de Notre Dame, and can be reached by road or, better still, by metro.

Where to stay: Montreal has a wide range of hotels and it's worth being as close to the centre as possible, as the nightlife is excellent.

How it started: The Canadian GP had been held at Mosport Park since 1961, when it was a sportscar race, save for a two outings at St Jovite. However, the circuit had fallen behind F1 safety standards and so this circuit was built for the 1978 Canadian GP when, fittingly, local ace Gilles Villeneuve won for Ferrari.

Best race: The one in 2011, when Jenson Button came through to win for McLaren stands out. He survived contact with teammate Lewis Hamilton, a drive-through penalty for going too fast behind the safety car, a two-hour stoppage because of standing water and a puncture before catching and passing Sebastian Vettel on the final lap.

Local aces: Gilles Villeneuve won six grands prix and the hearts of fans worldwide for his bravado, but never the F1 title, which is what his son Jacques managed in 1997 with Williams. Lance Stroll is being lined up as Canada's next F1 racer.

Gear 🔧 111 Km/h   ⬤ 1 Timing sector   ⚠ DRS detection   🔺 DRS activation

2015 POLE TIME: **HAMILTON (MERCEDES), 1M14.393S, 131.131MPH/211.035KPH**
2015 WINNER'S AVERAGE SPEED: **123.861MPH/199.336KPH**

2015 FASTEST LAP: **RAIKKONEN (FERRARI), 1M16.987S, 126.713MPH/203.925KPH**
LAP RECORD: **BARRICHELLO (FERRARI), 1M13.622S, 132.511MPH/213.256KPH, 2004**

BAKU

The Baku Street Circuit is a temporary facility that offers something really different to F1's usual venues, as it offers gradient change and passes some of Baku's key buildings.

F1 circuit architect Hermann Tilke doesn't involve himself only with all-new, purpose-built circuits on parcels of virgin land, but street circuits too. And this circuit, is centred on Baku Boulevard, the most prestigious thoroughfare in Azerbaijan's capital. It has been designed not only to take racing to Azerbaijan's people but also to show off the capital's top buildings on F1's global stage.

Street circuits in F1 have been few far between, other than the sport's staple, Monaco. The one in Sochi couldn't be more different to that, and is equally at odds with the one around Valencia's docks that was used until 2012. This new track, in the heart of Baku, is very different again, its buildings rich in Asian culture, as you would expect from a country on the Caspian Sea.

Running in an anti-clockwise direction, it starts its lengthy lap with a short dash to a 90-degree lefthander, then a short straight to another and a longer straight along the back of the Government Building to a third.

The stretch that heads west from there snakes through an esse, then passes ancient Maiden Tower to reach the old city, and arcs all the way around it, running around the old city wall. This is narrow, but it all changes when the drivers exit Turn 16 and accelerate hard, carrying that speed through a series of kinks along a 1.367-mile long stretch along the capital's promenade, Neftchilar Avenue, with their peak speed being recorded as they pass the pits before they have to brake hard for Turn 1. Inevitably, this will also be the favoured place for overtaking.

INSIDE TRACK
EUROPEAN GRAND PRIX

Date:	19 June
Circuit name:	Baku Street Circuit
Circuit length:	3.753 miles/6.006km
Number of laps:	51
Email:	info.bakugp.az
Website:	www.bakugp.az

PREVIOUS WINNERS
Not applicable

Location: The circuit is in Azerbaijan's capital, Baku, on the shore of the Absheron Peninsula that juts into the Caspian Sea.

Where to stay: The government has financed the construction of numerous international brand hotels to host visitors and competitors attending the prestige events that it has hosted in recent years, including the Eurovision Song Contest and the European Games. Many Soviet-era buildings were cleared to enable the building of parks along the city's foreshore.

How it started: Azerbaijan has long wanted to promote itself on the world stage and has used its oil wealth to do so. There has been motor racing in the capital before, with a couple of races for GT cars in recent years. Yet, these were only in preparation for its real goal: F1. Bernie Ecclestone had talked of awarding Azerbaijan with a race in 2015, in place of the Korean GP with whom Formula One Management was having contractual difficulties. However, it was later moved back to 2016.

Best race: With no F1 held there to date, the best race has to be picked from the trio of races for GT3 sportscars that were run on a street circuit at the foot of the Baku Flame Towers as a standalone race in 2012, then rounds of the FIA GT championship in 2013 and the Blancpain Sprint series in 2014, with Laurens Vanthoor being in the winning Belgian Audi Club Team WRT R8 in 2013 and 2014, pipping Rob Bell and Kevin Estre's Hexis Racing McLaren in 2013.

Local aces: There are none yet and, until the county builds a permanent circuit, it will be hard for any to get going.

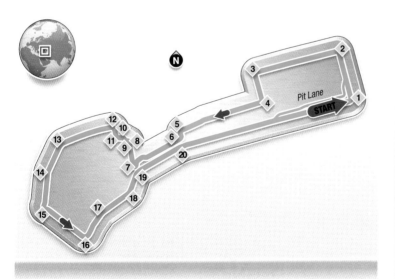

"I am pleased that Azerbaijan has designed an innovative new street circuit that will definitely help to create a world class event when we race there in 2016."
Bernie Ecclestone

RED BULL RING

Many people think an F1 circuit looks beautiful, even when standing still, but to make it look even better still simply add mountain scenery, and nowhere achieves this like Austria.

Like many a circuit that has had to be modified over the decades, as ever faster cars have required changes to protect the drivers, this gem of an Austrian circuit has clear evidence of its earlier days, when it used to range more widely cross the mountainside in its days as the Osterreichring.

Yet, today's curtailed version, now known as the Red Bull Ring, is still a circuit to make your heart soar. There can be no denying that no F1 venue can match it for its scenic backdrop as it nestles in mountainside meadows beneath the forests of the higher slopes and the fields of the broad valley below.

As with Spa-Francorchamps and the Nurburgring, the old circuit offered a greater number of high-speed sweeping bends, but the Red Bull Ring is still something to behold. For starters, it has a steeply climbing rise to the first corner, Castrol Edge. Then it continues to climb from there all the way to the lap's best passing spot, the uphill sharp right known as Remus.

The track climbs a little more and then dips towards Schlossgold, and then a whole lot more as it doubles back and swerves its way across to Rauch, turns left there then left again through Wurth Kurve. Both are open bends, as is the kink at Turn 7, where the track rises up again behind the paddock, before dipping again through the final pair of corners, Rindt, then Red Bull Mobile, with the last corner made all the more difficult as drivers have to wait to pass the dip on its apex before they dare to go hard on the throttle to accelerate past the pits to start another lap.

74

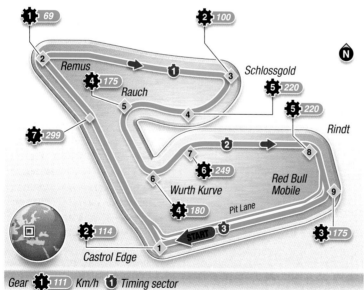

Gear 🔧 111 Km/h ❶ Timing sector

»

INSIDE TRACK
AUSTRIAN GRAND PRIX

Date:	**3 July**
Circuit name:	**Red Bull Ring**
Circuit length:	**2.688 miles/4.326km**
Number of laps:	**71**
Email:	**information@projekt-spielberg.at**
Website:	**www.projekt-spielberg.at**

PREVIOUS WINNERS

1987	**Nigel Mansell** WILLIAMS
1997	**Jacques Villeneuve** WILLIAMS
1998	**Mika Hakkinen** McLAREN
1999	**Eddie Irvine** FERRARI
2000	**Mika Hakkinen** McLAREN
2001	**David Coulthard** McLAREN
2002	**Michael Schumacher** FERRARI
2003	**Michael Schumacher** FERRARI
2014	**Nico Rosberg** MERCEDES
2015	**Nico Rosberg** MERCEDES

Location: The circuit's setting is rural, in the Styrian mountains, 44 miles north-west of Graz, just above the village of Zeltweg.

Where to stay: This has always been a problem, as the local guest houses are soon filled, so many commute from Graz.

How it started: Austria's first grand prix was held just down the hill on a circuit laid out on the runways of Zeltweg's military airfield in 1963, earning it a World Championship round for 1964. However, this was downgraded to sportscar events until 1969, the year in which it moved up the hill to the Osterreichring. People liked the new track and F1 came back in 1970, and continued to come until 1987. Then they returned when it became the A1 Ring, from 1997 to 2003.

Best race: The 1982 season was extraordinary as no driver dominated, with 11 drivers sharing the 16 grands prix. The Austrian GP produced a first-time winner in Elio de Angelis, and the Lotus driver had to resist a fierce charge from Williams' Keke Rosberg, holding on to win by 0.05s.

Local aces: Austria has produced some great drivers, with Jochen Rindt and Niki Lauda both becoming World Champions and Gerhard Berger winning ten grands prix.

2015 POLE TIME: **HAMILTON (MERCEDES)**, 1M08.455S, 141.362MPH/227.501KPH
2015 WINNER'S AVERAGE SPEED: **126.784MPH/204.040KPH**

2015 FASTEST LAP: **ROSBERG (MERCEDES)**, 1M11.235S, 135.845MPH/218.622KPH
LAP RECORD: **M SCHUMACHER (FERRARI)**, 1M08.337S, 141.606MPH/227.894KPH, 2003

SILVERSTONE

It's open, it's fast and it's lined from the start of the lap to the end by banks of spectators, making this well-attended grand prix one of the high points of any World Championship season.

Some circuits can be a bit stop-start in their lay-out, with rare corners that can be taken at high speed to show off an F1 car's capabilities followed by slow corners. Silverstone is no such venue. It's a track on which drivers can find a flow through a series of high-speed turns and enjoy stretching their car's capabilities.

Built to utilize the perimeter roads of a World War Two airfield, its shape has been modified this way and that since its early days, but its essence remains as a largely flat track, peppered with fast, open corners.

The righthand kink that starts the lap, Abbey, is a seventh-gear sweeper, as is Farm that follows. Then drivers have to be hard on the anchors to slow for the Village hairpin. With The Loop also being a second-gear corner, there's much jostling for position and the pair of corners act as a complex when considered together, with many a passing move starting at Village and only finally being concluded as the cars accelerate hard out of Aintree.

Overtaking is possible at the end of the Wellington Straight before the drivers double back through Luffield and accelerate hard past the old pits, through Copse all the way to their arrival at Becketts. This is the hardest corner of the lap, as it snakes right, left, right.

The approach to Stowe at the end of the Hangar Straight matches that to Becketts, as drivers get close to 190mph. Then the flow continues into the Vale and drivers have to drop to as low as third gear for the first time since The Loop, before accelerating through lengthy righthander Club to complete the lap.

INSIDE TRACK
BRITISH GRAND PRIX

Date:	**10 July**
Circuit name:	**Silverstone**
Circuit length:	**3.659 miles/5.900km**
Number of laps:	**52**
Email:	**sales@silverstone-circuit.co.uk**
Website:	**www.silverstone-circuit.co.uk**

PREVIOUS WINNERS

2006	**Fernando Alonso** RENAULT
2007	**Kimi Raikkonen** FERRARI
2008	**Lewis Hamilton** McLAREN
2009	**Sebastian Vettel** RED BULL
2010	**Mark Webber** RED BULL
2011	**Fernando Alonso** FERRARI
2012	**Mark Webber** RED BULL
2013	**Nico Rosberg** MERCEDES
2014	**Lewis Hamilton** MERCEDES
2015	**Lewis Hamilton** MERCEDES

Location: Silverstone is 16 miles south-west of Northampton, near Towcester, on the county border with Buckinghamshire.

Where to stay: Northampton, Milton Keynes, Buckingham and Oxford all offer hotels, with bed and breakfasts in the villages closer in.

How it started: Silverstone was an airfield left with little reason to exist after the end of World War Two and its perimeter roads and runways were used for racing for the first time in 1948. Two years later, it hosted the first World Championship race.

Best race: Few who were there in 1987, at the height of Mansellmania, will forget the excitement of the battle between Nigel Mansell and his Williams team-mate Nelson Piquet. Less than good friends, Mansell's desire to get past was two-fold, as he really wanted to win at home and put one over Piquet for assorted insults. He was forced to make an unplanned pitstop, and make up a 28s deficit. Having caught the Brazilian, his move to get past into Stowe with less than three laps to go was magnificent.

Local aces: Britain has produced ten World Champions, with Lewis Hamilton the most recent in 2015. There is a crop of rising talent in GP2 waiting to make the step up whenever an F1 ride becomes available.

Luffield — 3 140   Woodcote — 6 280
6 295   6 295
Club
5 215   18   3 START   1   Brooklands   Wellington Straight — 6 275
17   16   Abbey   9
Vale   3 105   Farm   Copse
5 240   The Loop   Maggots — 1 305
Stowe   15   Chapel   14   12   11
7 300   Hangar Straight   13   5 220   Becketts

Gear **1** **111** Km/h **1** Timing sector ⚠ DRS detection ⚠ DRS activation

2015 POLE TIME: HAMILTON (MERCEDES), 1M32.248S, 142.851MPH/229.897KPH
2015 WINNER'S AVERAGE SPEED: 124.813MPH/200.868KPH

2015 FASTEST LAP: HAMILTON (MERCEDES), 1M37.093S, 135.723MPH/218.425KPH
LAP RECORD: ALONSO (FERRARI), 1M30.874S, 145.011MPH/233.373KPH, 2011

One of the best attended weekends on the Formula 1 calendar every year, Silverstone, the home of the British Grand Prix, is where it all started, more than 65 years ago.

HUNGARORING

The current format of the cars, with DRS, has transformed racing here, as it has brought to an end the processions that used to be held at the Hungaroring when overtaking was all but possible.

For years, F1 fans were less than excited at the thought of the Hungarian GP, as races at the twisty circuit were rarely exciting. Indeed, after the dash to Turn 1 on the opening lap and the continuation of tussling through this righthander with a downhill exit all the way to Turn 2, the layout's tight nature made overtaking very difficult indeed.

Fortunately, the latest technology has given the chasing car more than a fighting chance of overtaking, thanks to DRS, and the place has been transformed, even though the entry to Turn 1 remains the best place for overtaking.

Built from scratch across a valley near the capital Budapest, the Hungaroring is predominantly a medium-speed circuit as it wanders around one side of the valley, dips down then up to the other side and does the same in reverse.

The first corner is approached down a gentle slope and drops away from its entry to its exit. Doubling back behind the paddock, the track continues to fall away through Turn 2 and on down through more open Turn 3 to cross the stream at its foot before rearing up and snapping left at Turn 4.

From here, the track doubles back through Turn 5 to start a swerving run across the far side of the valley before it drops to the right at Turn 11, dips into the valley and then climbs again through Turns 12 and 13 before reaching its final turn, a long right onto the start/finish straight. This is, in many ways, the most important corner of the lap, as good exit speed for the blast past the pits is vital, with 185mph the target before the drivers start braking.

INSIDE TRACK
HUNGARIAN GRAND PRIX

Date:	**24 July**
Circuit name:	**Hungaroring**
Circuit length:	**2.722 miles/4.381km**
Number of laps:	**70**
Email:	**office@hungaroring.hu**
Website:	**www.hungaroring.hu**

PREVIOUS WINNERS

2006	**Jenson Button** HONDA
2007	**Lewis Hamilton** McLAREN
2008	**Heikki Kovalainen** McLAREN
2009	**Lewis Hamilton** McLARFN
2010	**Mark Webber** RED BULL
2011	**Jenson Button** McLAREN
2012	**Lewis Hamilton** McLAREN
2013	**Lewis Hamilton** MERCEDES
2014	**Daniel Ricciardo** RED BULL
2015	**Sebastian Vettel** FERRARI

Location: The Hungaroring is located in rolling hills 12 miles north-east of capital city Budapest, near the village of Mogyorod.

Where to stay: Budapest is close and a stimulating city in which to stay, in Buda, on the far side of the Danube, or Pest, on its near side; either way, it's the place to stay.

How it started: The circuit was opened in 1986, when Hungary was still behind the Iron Curtain. With 200,000 fans turning out to watch Nelson Piquet win, it cemented its place on the F1 calendar.

Best race: The 1989 Hungarian GP was a cracker as Nigel Mansell jumped Ayrton Senna in traffic to win for Ferrari, but Daniel Ricciardo's win in 2014 topped it. The Red Bull racer was fortunate when a safety car deployment enabled him to pit when the first four had just passed the pitlane entrance., but late in the race, he fought with Fernando Alonso's Ferrari and Lewis Hamilton's Mercedes, and beat them both.

Local aces: Due to Hungary being made communist in 1949, it hasn't a long history of providing top racing drivers. Ferenc Szisz won the first grand prix, at Le Mans in 1906, but none since has managed the feat. Zsolt Baumgartner started 20 grands prix in 2003 and 2004.

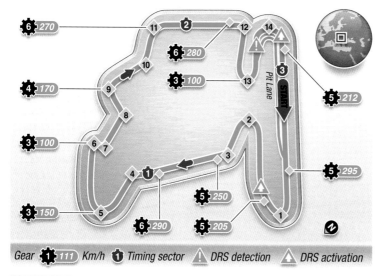

Gear 🔧 Km/h 🔧 Timing sector ⚠️ DRS detection ⚠️ DRS activation

---

2015 POLE TIME: HAMILTON (MERCEDES), 1M22.020S, 119.473MPH/192.274KPH
2015 WINNER'S AVERAGE SPEED: 106.140MPH/170.816KPH

2015 FASTEST LAP: RICCIARDO (RED BULL), 1M24.821S, 115.537MPH/185.939KPH
LAP RECORD: M SCHUMACHER (FERRARI), 1M19.071S, 123.828MPH/199.282KPH, 2004

It's great to have a German Grand Prix back on the world championship calendar, and hopefully Hockenheim's policy of cutting ticket prices will swell the crowd in 2016.

Hockenheim is another circuit that has been curtailed over the years to make it safer. Yet, few of today's historic circuits' nature have changed as much as the one at Hockenheim.

The changes were made for the 2002 season and much of the famed loop through the forest was lost. Certainly the fans in the grandstands that tower over the stadium section at the end start and finish of the lap get to see the cars go past more times during a grand prix, but the daunting nature of the flat-out blast between the trees, interspersed with a trio of chicanes, are much missed.

The first corner is a fast righthander and the bulk of the passing happens at the second turn, a righthand hairpin. This is the lap's most challenging corner as, snaking left out of there, the drivers are immediately presented with the circuit's longest straight. It's actually not straight, but a long arc with the forest some way off to their left.

The fastest point of the lap is at the braking point before the far hairpin, Spitzkehre, with drivers having to haul their cars down from 190mph to 40mph for the sharp righthander. There's always a chance of overtaking into here.

Turn 7 is a seventh-gear kink and the low-speed entry to the Mercedes Arena means that it's possible to try a move in front of the grandstand here.

However, it's only when drivers turn right at Turn 12 that they get to race in the presence of the fans as they enter the stadium section, where the lap is completed with a series of loops in front of the grandstands.

INSIDE TRACK
GERMAN GRAND PRIX

Date:	31 July
Circuit name:	Hockenheim
Circuit length:	2.842 miles/4.574km
Number of laps:	67
Email:	Info@hockenheimring.de
Website:	www.hockenheimring.de

PREVIOUS WINNERS

2001	**Ralf Schumacher** WILLIAMS
2002	**Michael Schumacher** FERRARI
2003	**Juan Pablo Montoya** WILLIAMS
2004	**Michael Schumacher** FERRARI
2005	**Fernando Alonso** RENAULT
2006	**Michael Schumacher** FERRARI
2008	**Lewis Hamilton** McLAREN
2010	**Fernando Alonso** FERRARI
2012	**Fernando Alonso** FERRARI
2014	**Nico Rosberg** MERCEDES

Location: Hockenheim is located outside the town of the same name, some 55 miles due south of Frankfurt.

Where to stay: Speyer is the closest town of note, but many prefer to stay in the more dynamic university city of Heidelberg.

How it started: Built in 1929, at a time when Germany was seeking to show its engineering excellence through racing, it was used as a test circuit by Mercedes. It played second fiddle to the Nurburgring, until Niki Lauda's fiery crash there in 1976. From then on, Hockenheim was home to the German GP, until alternation began in 2011.

Best race: Rubens Barrichello's first F1 win, in 2000, was a dramatic one, as the race ought to have belonged to McLaren, but a Mercedes employee made a protest by invading the track, bringing out the safety car, which bunched the field and brought the Brazilian's Ferrari back into the mix.

Local aces: For all its pre-war excellence, Germany failed to produce an F1 winner until Wolfgang von Trips won the 1961 Dutch GP. It took even longer to get a World Champion, with German fans having to wait until 1994 when Michael Schumacher took the title with Benetton. He would add six more before Sebastian Vettel rattled off four in a row.

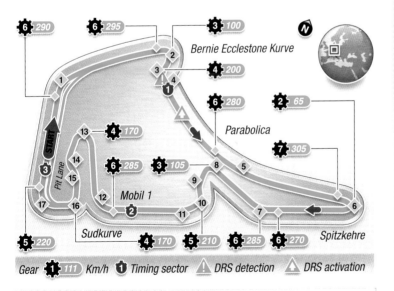

Bernie Ecclestone Kurve
Parabolica
Mobil 1
Sudkurve
Spitzkehre

Gear ⚙ 111 Km/h ❶ Timing sector ⚠ DRS detection 🔺 DRS activation

2014 POLE TIME: **ROSBERG (MERCEDES),** 1M16.540S, 133.671MPH/215.123KPH
2014 WINNER'S AVERAGE SPEED: 121.922MPH/196.215KPH

2014 FASTEST LAP: **HAMILTON (MERCEDES),** 1M19.908S, 128.049MPH/206.075KPH
LAP RECORD: **RAIKKONEN (McLAREN),** 1M14.917S, 136.567MPH/219.784KPH, 2004

SPA-FRANCORCHAMPS

This is a circuit that has it all, from steep inclines to high-speed sweepers, an uphill hairpin and a never less than exciting chicane. Oh, and it has weather too, changeable weather.

The Red Bull Ring in Austria has the most stunning mountain scenery as its backdrop, but there are sections of Spa-Francorchamps that perhaps outstrip even this. The view from the banking on the infield section of the track by the Les Combes chicane looks across the valley to Blanchimont, with sections of the track appearing in breaks between the trees. It has an obvious majesty and it is made all the more special because Spa-Francorchamps has thrilled fans and, in days gone by, even scared drivers. It is, make no mistake, a proper racing circuit.

The essence of the track is the way in which it is part of the Ardennes landscape, rising and falling with the terrain and carving its passage across the wooded slopes.

The lap starts with a short blast to the highest point at the first corner, the La Source hairpin. Diving back down the slope past the old pits, the track then rears up sharply through the left/right sweep at Eau Rouge, flicks left at Raidillon, then climbs and climbs, with drivers reaching 200mph, on the lengthy ascent to Les Combes. A good exit from Eau Rouge should give a driver the tow required to go for a move into this right/left chicane, the circuit's best passing spot.

Leaving here, the track keeps dropping through its hardest corner – the double-apex Pouhon – and on down to its 15th turn, Curve Paul Frere. From here, it climbs, with drivers flat-out until they have to brake heavily for the Bus Stop, a scratchy end to a magnificent lap.

Just to make it trickier still, Spa-Francorchamps is famed for sudden changes in weather, with rain no stranger.

INSIDE TRACK
BELGIAN GRAND PRIX

Date:	**28 August**
Circuit name:	**Spa-Francorchamps**
Circuit length:	**4.352 miles/7.004km**
Number of laps:	**44**
Email:	**secretariat@spa-francorchamps.be**
Website:	**www.spa-francorchamps.be**

PREVIOUS WINNERS

2005	**Kimi Raikkonen** McLAREN
2007	**Kimi Raikkonen** FERRARI
2008	**Felipe Massa** FERRARI
2009	**Kimi Raikkonen** FERRARI
2010	**Lewis Hamilton** McLAREN
2011	**Sebastian Vettel** RED BULL
2012	**Jenson Button** McLAREN
2013	**Sebastian Vettel** RED BULL
2014	**Daniel Ricciardo** RED BULL
2015	**Lewis Hamilton** MERCEDES

Location: Thirty miles south-east of Liege, the circuit is in a valley leading down from the village of Francorchamps.

Where to stay: The resort town of Spa is popular, with more hotels in Malmedy and Stavelot, while many fans camp in the fields near Franorchamps.

How it started: A track layout using public roads from Francorchamps into the neighbouring valley for a blast from Malmedy to Stavelot before returning up the slope was opened in 1924. That was 9.236 miles long. It was cut back to 4.317 miles in 1979 to be given its current form. Antonio Ascari won the first grand prix at Spa for Ferrari in 1925.

Best race: Michael Schumacher spotted changing conditions in 1992 and was rewarded with his first F1 win. Nigel Mansell could have won, but his Williams was down on power. Ayrton Senna's gamble of staying on slicks failed and Schumacher brought his Benetton in at just the right time.

Local aces: Jacky Ickx, world championship runner-up to Jochen Rindt in 1970 when racing for Ferrari, remains Belgium's most successful F1 racer, also winning the Le Mans 24 Hours six times. McLaren test driver GP2 champion Stoffel Vandoorne looks to be its best rising star and is on McLaren's books.

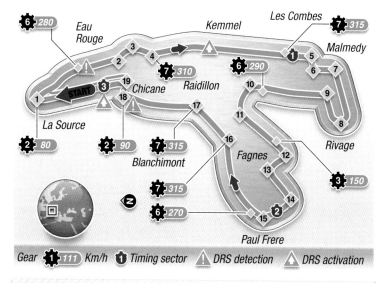

Gear ⚙ 111 Km/h ❶ Timing sector ⚠ DRS detection ◭ DRS activation

2015 POLE TIME: HAMILTON (MERCEDES),
1M47.197S, 146.156MPH/235.215KPH
2015 WINNER'S AVERAGE SPEED:
134.138MPH/215.874KPH

2015 FASTEST LAP: ROSBERG (MERCEDES),
1M52.416S, 139.370MPH/224.295KPH
LAP RECORD: VETTEL (RED BULL), 1M47.263S
146.065MPH/235.069KPH, 2009

⬤ MONZA

For decades, this high-speed venue was one of F1's toughest challenges. Now, it's thought of more as an historic circuit, with its long straights dotted with chicanes, reducing the challenge.

The basic outline of the circuit at Monza has changed little since it was built in the 1920s. Yes, there was once a racing oval that could be included as part of its lap, but that was last used by F1 in 1961. The main change since then was the insertion of three chicanes for 1972. They were included to cut fast-rising speeds and break up the groups of slipstreaming cars that hunted in packs and were extremely spectacular but considered to be an accident waiting to happen.

The first chicane, Variante del Rettifilo, has been many shapes, but its current format is a simple right/left sequence. Because this has cut speeds, the long right that follows, now called Curva Biassono after starting life as Curva Grande, is nothing like the challenge it once was.

The Roggia chicane is the other way around, going left then right, before drivers run through the two Lesmo righthanders in a clearing in the trees at the point of the track furthest from the pits. Exit speed from the second is vital as there's a long, kinked straight that follows, sloping up at its end before feeding the cars into the third chicane. This one, Ascari, is longer and more open in shape, going left, right and left. Again, exit speed is crucial as it's followed by a straight.

The entry to Parabolica is taken as drivers brake from almost 210mph and it's probably the trickiest corner of all, but fortunately it opens out in angle before joining the start/finish straight. A good run out of here is crucial for a chasing driver and, especially with DRS activated, many a passing manoeuvre is attempted into the first chicane.

INSIDE TRACK
ITALIAN GRAND PRIX

Date:	**4 September**
Circuit name:	**Autodromo Monza**
Circuit length:	**3.600 miles/5.793km**
Number of laps:	**53**
Email:	**infoautodromo@monzanet.it**
Website:	**www.monzanet.it**

PREVIOUS WINNERS	
2006	**Michael Schumacher** FERRARI
2007	**Fernando Alonso** McLAREN
2008	**Sebastian Vettel** TORO ROSSO
2009	**Rubens Barrichello** BRAWN
2010	**Fernando Alonso** FERRARI
2011	**Sebastian Vettel** RED BULL
2012	**Lewis Hamilton** McLAREN
2013	**Sebastian Vettel** RED BULL
2014	**Lewis Hamilton** MERCEDES
2015	**Lewis Hamilton** MERCEDES

Location: This legendary circuit is a royal park on the northern edge of the town of Monza, 10 miles to the north-west of Milan.

Where to stay: There are small hotels in and around Monza, but most prefer to stay in vibrant Milan, and the very well-heeled further to the north in the hotels on the southern shore of Lake Como.

How it started: Built in just 100 days, the circuit opened in 1922, offering both a high-speed road circuit and a banked oval that could be incorporated into the lap. Pietro Bordino won that year's Italian GP in a Fiat at an average speed of 86.905mph.

Best race: The 1971 Italian GP remains the best ever, with five drivers in a bunch racing to the finish line, through which BRM's Peter Gethin burst to pip Ronnie Peterson's March by 0.01s. All five were covered by 0.61s.

Local aces: Italian drivers stole the show in the early years of the world championship, with Giuseppe Farina, for Alfa Romeo, the inaugural champion in 1950, and Ferrari's Alberto Ascari champion in 1952 and 1953. Then Juan Manuel Fangio dominated the decade and there hasn't been an Italian world champion since. Indeed, there have been no Italians racing in F1 since Jarno Trulli in 2011.

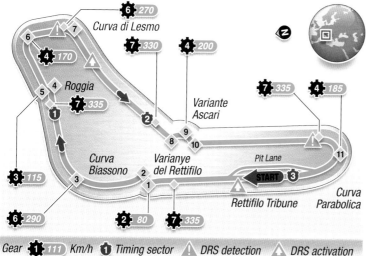

Curva di Lesmo · Roggia · Variante Ascari · Curva Biassono · Varianye del Rettifilo · Pit Lane · START · Rettifilo Tribune · Curva Parabolica

Gear 🔧 111 Km/h ❶ Timing sector ⚠ DRS detection ⚠ DRS activation

2015 POLE TIME: **HAMILTON (MERCEDES), 1M23.397S, 155.384MPH/250.066KPH**
2015 WINNER'S AVERAGE SPEED: **146.583MPH/235.903KPH**

2015 FASTEST LAP: **HAMILTON (MERCEDES), 1M26.672S, 149.512MPH/240.617KPH**
LAP RECORD: **BARRICHELLO (FERRARI), 1M21.046S, 159.909MPH/257.349KPH, 2004**

This street circuit in downtown Singapore couldn't be more different to the one that precedes it, Monza, as it's packed with right-angled turns and bumps. Also, the Singapore GP is held at night.

For a street circuit, Singapore's Marina Bay Circuit offers a fair degree of flow, as it has a decent number of straights of note. However, it also has more than its share of 90-degree corners, making overtaking something of a challenge, and sometimes breaking up good battles.

The first corner is entered under a city flyover and is a sharp left that feeds through an arcing right, almost directly into a lefthand hairpin. Overtaking action is always frantic through this complex of corners on the opening lap of a grand prix and also when cars emerge from the pit exit after midrace stops.

The race order then tends to settle down along the straight to Turn 5 and the longer straight that follows, Raffles Boulevard, past the towering office blocks to a 90-degree lefthander at Turn 7.

Overtaking ought to be possible into here, but is trickier than it looks as drivers brake hard from hitting the greatest speed they'll manage, 185mph.

Having run around the Padang playing fields, including a great sweep through Turns 11 and 12, plus a run across steel-framed Anderson Bridge, the track then starts its homeward leg with a decently long straight before cars have to be slowed for tight Turn 14.

The most critical corner of the twisting section that follows under a huge grandstand is the right/left Turn 20/21 combination. Better exit speed than a rival is vital as it can be built upon, past the giant Ferris Wheel and all the way through a pair of fast left kinks onto the start/finish straight. This sets up the possibility of a passing move into Turn 1.

INSIDE TRACK
SINGAPORE GRAND PRIX

Date:	**18 September**
Circuit name:	**Marina Bay Circuit**
Circuit length:	**3.152 miles/5.073km**
Number of laps:	**61**
Email:	**info@singaporegp.sg**
Website:	**www.singaporegp.sg**

PREVIOUS WINNERS

2008	**Fernando Alonso** RENAULT
2009	**Lewis Hamilton** McLAREN
2010	**Fernando Alonso** FERRARI
2011	**Sebastian Vettel** RED BULL
2012	**Sebastian Vettel** RED BULL
2013	**Sebastian Vettel** RED BULL
2014	**Lewis Hamilton** MERCEDES
2015	**Sebastian Vettel** FERRARI

Location: Only Monaco and the new circuit in Baku take racing right to the people to this extent, with Singapore's circuit right in the heart of the city.

Where to stay: Singapore offers a range of top-rank hotels, with many visitors combining their visit with a stay at beach resorts.

How it started: Singapore had held races on its streets in the 1960s and 1970s, but the desire was to take racing right into the heart of the metropolis. This was realized in 2008, with Singapore's first world championship round being an instant hit.

Best race: It's ironic, but the Singapore GP that's most talked about from the eight held so far is the first, the one won in 2008 by Renault's Fernando Alonso. He started 15th after mechanical problems, and rose to 11th before pitting. However, his race was transformed almost immediately, as his team-mate Nelson Piquet Jr spun and ended up against a wall, bringing out the safety car. His rivals had to wait to pit, and Nico Rosberg and Robert Kubica had so little fuel left that they had to come in when the pits were closed, earning a penalty. Thus, Alonso rose from last to first.

Local aces: Singaporean drivers have yet to star at the top. Dennis Lian tried Formula V6 Asia and A1GP, but shone in neither. Singapore-born British driver Richard Bradley is starring in the World Endurance Championship.

Gear **1 111** Km/h **1** Timing sector ⚠ DRS detection ⚠ DRS activation

2015 POLE TIME: VETTEL (FERRARI),
1M43.885S, 109.063MPH/175.521KPH
2015 WINNER'S AVERAGE SPEED:
94.866MPH/152.672KPH

2015 FASTEST LAP: RICCIARDO (RED BULL),
1M50.041S, 102.962MPH/165.701KPH
LAP RECORD: RAIKKONEN (FERRARI),
1M45.599S, 107.358MPH/172.776KPH, 2008

SEPANG

The Malaysian GP will have a different feel in 2016 as it has been moved back towards the end of the calendar to form part of a double-header with the Japanese GP in early October.

Drivers know when they board their flights for Malaysia that they have a real prospect of great racing with plenty of overtaking. Sepang is a circuit that offers plenty of scope for changing places, with one of its defining features being an abundance of track width.

This undoubtedly remains F1 circuit designer Hermann Tilke's signature track. The Circuit of the Americas may now have exceeded it, but Sepang was standard-setting when it opened in 1999, thanks to its wide, sweeping layout, with several high-speed corners adding real challenge to the 3.444-mile lap.

The first corner has always been the main place for overtaking. Its broad entry allows for myriad lines of attack and defence and it's followed immediately by a sharp lefthander, itself a double challenge, because a fast line in doesn't necessarily lead to a fast line out.

The track then dips through an arcing Turn 3 before rising sharply into Turn 4, a corner made tricky as it flattens on apex. The serpentine run through Turns 5 and 6 is a challenge and a good line through Turns 7 and 8 can help a driver line up a possible move into the tight Turn 9.

Rising again through Turn 10, the track reaches its highest point at Turn 11. Then the downward-sloping Turn 12/13 esse is the toughest corner of the lap. After braking hard for the righthand hairpin at Turn 14, the drivers hit the lengthy return straight past the rear face of the giant grandstand. At its end is the final corner, a lefthand hairpin and again its entry and exit facilitate overtaking, as does the even longer straight down to Turn 1.

INSIDE TRACK
MALAYSIAN GRAND PRIX

Date:	2 October
Circuit name:	Sepang Circuit
Circuit length:	3.444 miles/5.542km
Number of laps:	56
Email:	inquiries@sepangcircuit.com.my
Website:	www.malaysiangp.com.my

PREVIOUS WINNERS	
2006	**Giancarlo Fisichella** RENAULT
2007	**Fernando Alonso** McLAREN
2008	**Kimi Raikkonen** FERRARI
2009	**Jenson Button** BRAWN
2010	**Sebastian Vettel** RED BULL
2011	**Sebastian Vettel** RED BULL
2012	**Fernando Alonso** FERRARI
2013	**Sebastian Vettel** RED BULL
2014	**Lewis Hamilton** MERCEDES
2015	**Sebastian Vettel** FERRARI

Location: Built on a palm plantation out near the airport, the circuit is 30 miles south of the centre of the capital city, Kuala Lumpur.

Where to stay: Most people stay in downtown Kuala Lumpur, as the city has a lot to offer, but some stay in the hotels out near the airport, and others in resort hotels on the beach to the west of Sepang.

How it started: Anxious to bring tourists to Malaysia at a time when the economy in South-East Asia was in a dip, Sepang was commissioned and Hermann Tilke handed the job of designing it. It was adjudged a considerable hit and Eddie Irvine was the winner of its inaugural grand prix in 1999, helped by his Ferrari team-mate Michael Schumacher delaying title rival Mika Hakkinen's McLaren.

Best race: The best race at Sepang in recent years was in 2012, when Sauber rookie Sergio Perez put Fernando Alonso's Ferrari under huge pressure in the closing laps, but he slid wide at Turn 13 and had to settle for second.

Local aces: Alex Yoong is the only Malaysian driver to have raced in F1 thus far, struggling with Minardi in 2001 and 2002. Jazeman Jaafar is the best-placed of Malaysia's current hopefuls, ranking eighth overall in Formula Renault 3.5 last year.

Gear ⚙ 111 Km/h ❶ Timing sector ⚠ DRS detection ⚠ DRS activation

2015 POLE TIME: **HAMILTON (MERCEDES),**
1M49.834S, 112.891MPH/181.681KPH
2015 WINNER'S AVERAGE SPEED:
114/471MPH/184.224KPH

2015 FASTEST LAP: **ROSBERG (MERCEDES),**
1M42.062S, 121.488MPH/195.516KPH
LAP RECORD: **MONTOYA (WILLIAMS),**
1M34.223S, 131.991MPH/212.419KPH, 2004

SUZUKA

Suzuka is an old-school circuit, with its use of topography, tricky esses, high-speed bends and limited run-off. In short, it's a challenge that all drivers relish, making a win here doubly desired.

First-time visitors to Suzuka are always astonished by two things: firstly the gradients involved and then just how narrow it is in places.

Built in 1962 and little changed since, it's a real drivers' circuit and its autumn date means that the weather can be more than a little wet and wild to add to the challenge it already offers.

The track slopes down past the pits to the First Curve, then turns back up the slope out of Turn 2. The four-corner esses that follow, running uphill, are undoubtedly one of the trickiest sequences at any track on the planet. Immediately out of the last of these comes the long left, Dunlop Curve. With the gradient flattening out, a fast right then a slow one lead to a most unusual element, an underpass. This is where the track crosses itself.

The hairpin at Turn 11 is a definite overtaking spot on entry and then feeds the cars onto a short straight followed by a long, long right.

Next up is Turn 13, a lefthander over a crest before perhaps the key corner of the lap, Spoon. This is a corner out of which drivers need optimum exit speed for the circuit's longest straight all the way down to high-speed 130R, taken in seventh, after crossing a bridge over the track below at 190mph.

From here, the next time the cars have to slow is for the ultra-tight Casio Triangle chicane. There have been many passing moves into here, not all successful, such as the Prost/Senna collision in 1989, but some show caution and wait to get a good run into the first corner, where there's more space for passing.

84

INSIDE TRACK

JAPANESE GRAND PRIX

Date:	9 October
Circuit name:	Suzuka Circuit
Circuit length:	3.608 miles/5.806km
Number of laps:	53
Email:	info@suzukacircuit.com.jp
Website:	www.suzukacircuit.co.jp

PREVIOUS WINNERS

2004	**Michael Schumacher** FERRARI
2005	**Kimi Raikkonen** McLAREN
2006	**Fernando Alonso** RENAULT
2009	**Sebastian Vettel** RED BULL
2010	**Sebastian Vettel** RED BULL
2011	**Jenson Button** McLAREN
2012	**Sebastian Vettel** RED BULL
2013	**Sebastian Vettel** RED BULL
2014	**Lewis Hamilton** MERCEDES
2015	**Lewis Hamilton** MERCEDES

Location: The circuit is on the main Japanese island, Honshu, situated on a hillside 30 miles south-west of Nagoya.

Where to stay: There is a hotel next to the funfair in the entertainment that includes the circuit, with others in the town of Suzuka. Some stay in the larger cities of Osaka to the west or Nagoya to the north-east, but traffic can be a problem.

How it started: Opened for racing in 1962, Suzuka hosted Japanese national racing, but finally stepped onto the international stage in 1987, when Gerhard Berger won the third-ever Japanese GP for Ferrari.

Best race: Damon Hill's victory in atrociously wet conditions in 1994 stands out as one of Suzuka's most memorable races. Not for wheel-to-wheel battling, but for the way that he attacked in his Williams to hold off rival Michael Schumacher's Benetton to keep the title race open.

Local aces: Despite its standing in the ranks of automotive manufacturers, Japan has yet to produce a World Champion or even a grand prix winner. Three Japanese drivers have stepped onto the podium, with third places claimed by Aguri Suzuki, Takuma Sato and Kamui Kobayashi, in 1990, 2004 and 2012 respectively, with Kobayashi's at Suzuka.

Spoon Curve — 5 230
Hairpin — 6 295 · 2 70 · 2 95 · 6 260
Casino Triangle
13 · 14 · 11 · 10 · 12 · 16 · 17 · 18 · N
1 · 15 · 8 · 9 · 7 · 3 · START · 7 300
2 · Pit Lane
4 185 · 7 305 · 6 260 · 5 210 · 6 · 5 · 4 · 3
Degner Curve
6 285 · 5 210 · 2 · 1
Dunlop "S" Curves
3 140 · 5 240 · 4 160 · First Curve

Gear 🔧 1 111 Km/h · 1 Timing sector · ⚠ DRS detection · ⚠ DRS activation

2015 POLE TIME: ROSBERG (MERCEDES), 1M32.584S, 140.303MPH/225.797KPH
2015 WINNER'S AVERAGE SPEED: 130.103MPH/209.381KPH

2015 FASTEST LAP: HAMILTON (MERCEDES), 1M36.145S, 135.107MPH/217.434KPH
LAP RECORD: RAIKKONEN (McLAREN), 1M31.540S, 141.904MPH/228.373KPH, 2005

CIRCUIT OF THE AMERICAS

Gradient change is the key feature of this circuit in Texas, and the venue is now part of a three-country sweep down on through Mexico to Brazil to take the season towards its conclusion.

Like the Red Bull Ring, the Circuit of Americas treats the drivers to a steep ascent to the first corner. The drivers then turn sharply left at the crest of the slope and dive back down the incline to a fast right at Turn 2, where they can, on quiet laps, enjoy the view over the infield and the observation tower. Not so on the opening lap, though, when the pack will still be jockeying for position.

Turns 3 and 4 are a left/right chicane. Then comes the trickiest and most impressive stretch of track, a series of esses from lefthand Turn 5 to lefthand Turn 9. Running along the level, they are a real challenge. Then, after a fast kink at Turn 10, there's a short straight to the far hairpin at Turn 11.

Out of here, the drivers can relax a little down the lap's longest straight and the fastest point of the lap is just before Turn 12, the quickest cars will exceed 205mph, before they brake heavily for the sharp left there. Overtaking is a definite possibility into here, but very much not through the twisting eight-corner sequence that takes the drivers all the way to the final corner, Turn 20.

As with so many corners leading onto a straight, good exit speed is crucial for drivers to have a chance of making a passing move, but the use of DRS has made it less critical than in the days before these opening wing slots were introduced.

And, like many grand prix circuits, the first corner is where overtaking moves are pulled off most frequently, and not just on the opening lap of the race, but action into Turn 12 produces almost as many successful changes of position.

INSIDE TRACK
UNITED STATES GRAND PRIX

Date:	23 October
Circuit name:	Circuit of the Americas
Circuit length:	3.400 miles/5.472km
Number of laps:	56
Email:	info@circuitoftheamericas.com
Website:	www.circuitoftheamericas.com

PREVIOUS WINNERS

2012	**Lewis Hamilton** McLAREN
2013	**Sebastian Vettel** RED BULL
2014	**Lewis Hamilton** MERCEDES
2015	**Lewis Hamilton** MERCEDES

Location: The Circuit of the Americas lies on rolling land 10 miles to the south-east of Austin, Texas, just outside the city limits.

Where to stay: Fast-growing Austin has more than enough hotels, restaurants, bars and music venues to keep visitors happy.

How it started: The Circuit of the Americas was built to be the United States' tenth grand prix venue after Sebring, Riverside, Watkins Glen, Long Beach, Caesar's Palace, Detroit, Dallas, Phoenix and Indianapolis all had a go, or goes, at piquing Americans' interest in F1. It opened for business in 2012 after F1 circuit designer Hermann Tilke followed the brief of incorporating the leading corners of the best F1 circuits.

Best race: The inaugural race, in 2012, came down to a fight between Lewis Hamilton and Sebastian Vettel. The German led from pole, with team-mate Mark Webber demoting Hamilton's McLaren to third. Four laps later, Hamilton passed the Australian and set off after Vettel. When the pair came up to lap Narain Karthikeyan's HRT, Hamilton dived past into Turn 12, never to be headed again. Fernando Alonso rose from seventh to third in his Ferrari, to give himself a chance of beating Vettel to the title at the final round.

Local aces: The United States has had two World Champions: Phil Hill, for Ferrari in 1961, and Mario Andretti, for Lotus in 1978. Since Andretti returned to Indycars in 1982, there have been very few American racers, with GP2 ace Alexander Rossi being lined up as the next to take to the sport's top stage.

Gear 🔧 **111** Km/h ① Timing sector ⚠ DRS detection ⚠ DRS activation

2015 POLE TIME: **ROSBERG (MERCEDES),** 1M56.824S, 105.562MPH/169.886KPH
2015 WINNER'S AVERAGE SPEED: **103.699MPH/166.888KPH**

2015 FASTEST LAP: **ROSBERG (MERCEDES),** 1M40.666S, 122.506MPH/197.154KPH
LAP RECORD: **VETTEL (RED BULL), 1M39.347S** 124.132MPH/199.772KPH, 2012

MEXICO CITY

The vibe at last autumn's return of the Mexican GP was fantastic. It's like welcoming an old friend back to the fold in having Mexico onboard again, with its track little changed from its earlier days.

The teams delighted in the new pit and paddock facilities when F1 returned to Mexico City last autumn after a 23-year break. They were a huge improvement on the facilities on F1's previous visit. However, for the drivers accelerating away from the grid, the run to the first corner remains a simple charge between trees in this parkland setting. Turn 1, Espiral, is a 90-degree right approached at 190mph, followed by the left/fight Eses Moises Solana, just as it was before. As has always been the case at the Autodromo Hermanos Rodriguez, this offers the best opportunity for overtaking.

Indeed, the circuit layout is unchanged all the way out through the left/right Ese del Lago to its furthest point from the pits, Horquilla. Watched over by large grandstands there, this tight corner turns the cars back onto a short straight before a wonderful sequence of esses from Turn 9 to Turn 13, the pick of the circuit's corners.

It's after the short straight out of here that the main changes were made for the circuit's 2015 return to F1. The sharp right at Turn 14 feeds the cars in front of the giant grandstands overlooking the park's baseball stadium. Snaking its way though this tight enclosure, the track then pops out midway around what was what was once its most feared corner, the Peraltada. Lightly banked, the drivers are then able to accelerate flat-out through the rest of the righthander to pop out onto the broad start/finish straight, where they know that a good tow and a press of the button to engage the DRS will give them the opportunity they need to challenge, and hopefully pass, the car ahead.

INSIDE TRACK
MEXICAN GRAND PRIX

Date:	30 October
Circuit name:	Autodromo Hermanos Rodriguez
Circuit length:	2.747 miles/4.421km
Number of laps:	70
Email:	rosario@cie.com.mx
Website:	
www.autodromohermanosrodriguez.com.mx	

PREVIOUS WINNERS

1969	**Denny Hulme** McLAREN
1970	**Jacky Ickx** FERRARI
1986	**Gerhard Berger** BENETTON
1987	**Nigel Mansell** WILLIAMS
1988	**Alain Prost** McLAREN
1989	**Ayrton Senna** McLAREN
1990	**Alain Prost** FERRARI
1991	**Riccardo Patrese** WILLIAMS
1992	**Nigel Mansell** WILLIAMS
2015	**Nico Rosberg** MERCEDES

Location: The circuit is situated in Mexico City's eastern suburbs. Altitude is a factor here, as it sits on a plateau at 6,000 feet above sea-level, making breathing harder than usual for the engines.

Where to stay: Many pick the hotels around the airport, which is just up the road, but the hotels in the city centre are more fun.

How it started: With Ricardo and Pedro Rodriguez starting to shine, it was decided to build a circuit so that they might win at home. The circuit opened in 1962, but its maiden F1 event, a non-championship race, was marred when Ricardo was killed in practice.

Best race: The 1964 Mexican GP was the most dramatic, as it was the championship decider between Graham Hill, John Surtees and Jim Clark. Hill had his goggle strap snap and Surtees's Ferrari developed a misfire, but Clark's run to victory ended two laps short with his Lotus leaking oil, leaving Surtees to finish second and lift the title.

Local aces: Ricardo Rodriguez was set to be Mexico's first F1 superstar, until he was killed. Brother Pedro won two grands prix, but he too died in a racing accident. The nation's best hope for F1 glory now is Sergio Perez.

Peraltada

Ese Moises Solana

START · Pit Lane · Recta Principal · Recta del Ovalo · Recta Trasera · Ese del Lago · Hairpin

🏁 Timing sector   ⚠ DRS detection   ⚠ DRS activation

2015 POLE TIME: ROSBERG (MERCEDES), 1M9.480S, 120.668MPH/194.947.620KPH
2015 WINNER'S AVERAGE SPEED: ROSBERG (MERCEDES), 110.975MPH/278.597KPH

2015 FASTEST LAP: ROSBERG (MERCEDES), 1M20.521S, 119.568MPH/192.426KPH
LAP RECORD: ROSBERG (MERCEDES), 1M20.521S, 119.568MPH/192.426KPH, 2015

INTERLAGOS

What's not to like about this Brazilian gem? It's got gradient change, plenty of it, passion from the fans, plenty of that, and its corners link together in a way that produces plenty of overtaking.

After racing on the flat in Mexico City, the drivers ought to appreciate the contrast when they reach Brazil. The first corner of the lap, Descida do Sol, is the trickiest. It's approached at just under 200mph, with the cars feeling dwarfed by the high concrete walls on either side of the track.

Indeed, at points on the ascent from Subida dos Boxes, it must feel as though they're in a canyon. Right at the feet of the fans packing the grandstand, it's made harder still by an all but blind entry, with the exit concealed until deep into the corner by the end of the pitwall.

Then, as the drivers tip over the crest and dive sharply downhill on the exit, it's all change as they can see out over much of the circuit and the suburbs, fields and lakes beyond. The cars plunge into the compression at Senna S, then arc left onto the straight down the hill to Descida do Lago, again exceeding 190mph before tucking their cars into this fourth-gear lefthander.

The track then starts its ascent back up the slope to the rear of the paddock before entering Ferradura, where two open rights are followed by a tighter one, Laranja. Plunging back down the slope from here, drivers must do an about-face at Pinheirinho, climb the slope again to Cotovelo.

Then comes the drop through Mergulho to sweep around to Juncao. This is a critical corner as a good exit is paramount, as it's flat-out from here, constantly turning left under the watch of the packed grandstands all the way up the slope to the first corner, where a good tow makes it the easiest spot for overtaking.

INSIDE TRACK
BRAZILIAN GRAND PRIX

Date:	13 November
Circuit name:	Autodromo Jose Carlos Pace Interlagos
Circuit length:	2.667 miles/4.292km
Number of laps:	71
Email:	info@gpbrazil.com
Website:	www.gpbrazil.com

PREVIOUS WINNERS

2006	**Felipe Massa** FERRARI
2007	**Kimi Raikkonen** FERRARI
2008	**Felipe Massa** FERRARI
2009	**Mark Webber** RED BULL
2010	**Sebastian Vettel** RED BULL
2011	**Mark Webber** RED BULL
2012	**Jenson Button** McLAREN
2013	**Sebastian Vettel** RED BULL
2014	**Nico Rosberg** MERCEDES
2015	**Nico Rosberg** MERCEDES

Location: The circuit is built across a hillside above a chain of lakes - Interlagos means "between the lakes" - 9 miles south of the centre of Sao Paulo.

Where to stay: Sao Paulo offers a wide range of hotels, but traffic can be heavy so the ones in the Cidada Jardim district are preferable.

How it started: Building a circuit on this site was discussed in 1920, but it wasn't until 1940 that the plans came to fruition. It took until 1972 for Interlagos to host its first F1 race, with a round of the world championship in 1973.

Best race: For the passionate local fans, any race that Ayrton Senna won was the best, so 1991 was a special year of celebration. However, the 2008 title-decider was even more dramatic. Lewis Hamilton looked to come up short for the second year in a row for McLaren, but he held his nerve after a late-race slide down the order to claim the fifth place required to pip Ferrari's race winner Felipe Massa.

Local aces: Both Nelson Piquet and Ayrton Senna claimed three F1 titles apiece, after Emerson Fittipaldi was Brazil's trail-blazer, being champion in 1972 and 1974. However, Senna looked set for more before being killed at Imola in 1994.

Senna "S" — Subida dos Boxes — Descida do Lago — Juncao — Curva do Sol — Reta Oposta

Gear — Km/h — Timing sector — DRS detection — DRS activation

2015 POLE TIME: ROSBERG (MERCEDES), 1M11.282S, 135.223MPH/217.620KPH
2015 WINNER'S AVERAGE SPEED: 125.120MPH/201.362KPH

2015 FASTEST LAP: HAMILTON (MERCEDES), 1M14.832S, 128.808MPH/207.296KPH
LAP RECORD: MONTOYA (WILLIAMS), 1M11.473S, 134.837MPH/217.000KPH, 2004

YAS MARINA

This season-concluding venue couldn't be more different to the previous venue, Interlagos, if it tried. Built on an island in Abu Dhabi, it wraps its lap around a marina and under a hotel.

Most circuits built from scratch have a little gradient for the designers to work with or at least have some built in. The Yas Marina circuit has none of that, having been built in an entirely level area that the Abu Dhabi government had put aside as a leisure complex. As a consequence, circuit architect Hermann Tilke had to work a little harder to build some excitement into its 21 turns. Unusually, the only notable gradient change comes from Tilke running the pit exit road under the circuit so that it emerges on the left of the track after the first corner even though the pits are located to the right of the pit straight.

The first corner comes very soon after the starting grid and is a 90-degree left. From here, the track runs through a great, open esse before slowing cars with a tight left/right chicane, then a hairpin. What follows is Hermann Tilke's trademark feature for this circuit, a long straight, approached at 200mph, into a tight corner. It's made for overtaking and seldom disappoints.

After braking hard for the left/right shuffle at the end of this first straight, the drivers then enter another straight down to a similar conclusion at Turn 11, where overtaking moves are also far from unusual.

Then the circuit meets the marina, running past the yachts there before, uniquely, ducking under a spectacular bridge between two parts of the hotel. As the Abu Dhabi GP is run from evening into night, this looks spectacular when lit.

The lap concludes with a left, a short straight, then a pair of rights that feed the cars back onto the start/finish straight.

88

INSIDE TRACK
ABU DHABI GRAND PRIX

Date:	**27 November**
Circuit name:	**Yas Marina Circuit**
Circuit length:	**3.451 miles/5.554km**
Number of laps:	**56**
Email:	
customerservice@yasmarinacircuit.com	
Website:	**www.yasmarinacircuit.com**

PREVIOUS WINNERS	
2009	**Sebastian Vettel** RED BULL
2010	**Sebastian Vettel** RED BULL
2011	**Lewis Hamilton** McLAREN
2012	**Kimi Raikkonen** LOTUS
2013	**Sebastian Vettel** RED BULL
2014	**Lewis Hamilton** MERCEDES
2015	**Nico Rosberg** MERCEDES

Location: The Yas Marina Circuit is part of an upmarket sports complex on Yas Island to the east of Abu Dhabi Island.

Where to stay: Of course, there's the hotel that straddles the circuit, but there's a wider choice on Abu Dhabi Island. Or you could of course rent a yacht in the marina...

How it started: A grand prix in Abu Dhabi had never been under discussion, with brasher neighbour Dubai seen as a far more likely venue. However, even though Dubai built its own circuit, Abu Dhabi bankrolled a far better one and won the race to be the first state on the Arabian Peninsula to host a round of the world championship, in 2009.

Best race: The second grand prix held here, in 2010, remains the best, as Sebastian Vettel had only an outside chance of the title that was largely being fought out between his Red Bull team-mate Mark Webber and Ferrari's Fernando Alonso. Yet, he prevailed to win and the title became his when Alonso's final pitstop was mistimed, and he and Webber came out in traffic.

Local aces: Abu Dhabi has yet to produce a competitive single-seater driver who might race one day in its grand prix. Its top drivers are in sportscars, with Khaled Al Qubaisi racing in the FIA World Endurance Championship, and in rallying, which isn't that surprising considering the local terrain.

Gear **1** 111 Km/h **1** Timing sector ⚠ DRS detection ⚠ DRS activation

2015 POLE TIME: **ROSBERG (MERCEDES),** 1M40.237S, 123.945MPH/199.471KPH

2015 WINNER'S AVERAGE SPEED: **115.573MPH/185.997KPH**

2015 FASTEST LAP: **HAMILTON (MERCEDES),** 1M44.517S, 118.869MPH/191.302KPH

LAP RECORD: **VETTEL (RED BULL),** 1M40.279S, 131.367MPH/211.463KPH, 2009

Nico Rosberg makes a great start from pole as Lewis Hamilton comes under attack from both Kimi Raikkonen and Sergio Perez on the run to Turn 1.

Albert Park in Melbourne, home of the Australian Grand Prix, is a great place for the new Formula 1 season to start, offering not only a city-centre skyline but also beautiful surroundings.

REVIEW OF THE 2015 SEASON

For the second year in a row, Mercedes was in a class of its own, the title battle fought out between its pair of drivers, Lewis Hamilton and Nico Rosberg. Behind them, Ferrari returned to some sort of form and Red Bull Racing struggled with Renault engines, but their slump was nothing next to McLaren's, as its new partnership with Honda left it above only Marussia.

With no major rule changes, after the introduction of 1.6-litre turbocharged V6s in 2014, there wasn't expected to be a change in the order. Indeed, there wasn't at the front, as Mercedes picked up where it had left off and such was the pace of its W06s that the team took pole at every round bar one.

It was clear from the opening round that the title battle was going to be between Mercedes' drivers, with a tetchy atmosphere breaking out between them as they focused only on each other. Despite Lewis Hamilton winning three of the first four rounds, Nico Rosberg came back into the mix at the Spanish GP. Following this up with wins at Monaco and Austria put him on to Hamilton's tail, but the English driver closed the matter with three races still to run for his third title. That he did so in a race in which he forced Rosberg wide to get by emphasized Hamilton's will to win. Rosberg won the final three races fair and square, and so ended the year second overall.

Ferrari had a new lead driver for 2015 as Sebastian Vettel replaced Fernando Alonso. With McLaren having a woeful year, the Spaniard must have spent the season casting envious glances at his old pit as Vettel rediscovered his winning ways as early as the second round, when Ferrari managed its tyres best in Malaysia's soaring temperatures. With further victories in both Hungary and Singapore, Vettel put pressure on Rosberg in the battle to be

runner-up. Team-mate Kimi Raikkonen was seldom in the mix.

Williams' return to form in 2015 was no flash in the pan as it built on its performances of 2014 to see Valtteri Bottas and Felipe Massa gather points on a regular basis. Podium finishes were rarer and required a trip up by Mercedes or Ferrari, although Bottas's third place in Canada and Massa's next time out in Austria were on merit.

That Red Bull Racing tumbled from second in 2014 to fourth last year was not down to having the most competitive engine. The Renault wasn't a match for the Mercedes and Ferrari V6s used by their leading rivals, but the team lost a lot of respect with its public complaints about French-built powerplants. Indeed, there was a spell when it seemed that the team's failed attempts to land different engines for 2016 would leave it without even the option of continuing with Renault. There was improvement through the season, though, with a second place apiece for Daniel Ricciardo and Daniil Kvyat, with the former suffering some bad luck.

With McLaren's awful form with Honda power, Force India took fifth overall, with Sergio Perez and Nico Hulkenberg making the most of Mercedes power. Perez's third place at Sochi was a highlight, with Hulkenberg shining in Brazil.

Lotus made a shrewd choice, changing from Renault to Mercedes engines, and was rewarded with a run of seventh-place finishes as it lived in a hand-to-mouth fashion as its budget was slow in arriving. Romain Grosjean gave it a timely gift: third place in the Belgian GP to keep the bailiffs from the door at least for a few grands prix. Pastor Maldonado continued to get into scrapes.

Toro Rosso isn't a team that has attracted many headlines over the years, except for when Sebastian Vettel gave it its only win, at Monza in 2008. Step forward Max Verstappen to change that. There was huge interest when he made his debut at the Australian GP, becoming the youngest ever F1 driver at just 17 years and 166 days. That he was in the points second time out was proof that he was ready. Then, with a series of audacious moves, he showed that he could really race too, meaning that F1 had a new star.

Like Lotus, Sauber spent the year battling its finances, but it was given a dream start, when both Felipe Nasr and Marcus Ericsson scored points in the opening round in Australia, a boost after the team's pointless campaign in 2014.

Together, McLaren and Honda were the act to beat in the late 1980s, when Ayrton Senna and Alain Prost dominated. Nobody expected Honda's return to yield such glory straight away, with Honda being a year behind its rivals. However, what unfolded was beyond Ron Dennis' worst nightmares as Jenson Button and Alonso, world champions both, found themselves almost stone last. Development was slow to come.

Marussia's miracle was to be revived just in time for the start of the season, but it only had an updated car and rookie drivers, unsurprisingly never scoring.

Mercedes made it plain at Melbourne that they would dominate the World Championship for the second year in a row. Its drivers were in a class of their own, and McLaren were among many who struggled, many not even making it to the start line.

An 11th-hour rescue deal for Marussia made it a field of 20 cars. Yet, in reality, the scrap for victory was only ever going to be fought out between the two Mercedes. In the end, Lewis Hamilton led Nico Rosberg home in a dominant one-two, more than half a minute clear of the best of the rest.

In truth, the rest were in disarray. Neither Marussia qualified and three others failed to make the start, leaving just 15 cars to go racing. The three who missed out were McLaren's Kevin Magnussen – himself standing in for Fernando Alonso who was recovering from an accident in testing – Red Bull's Daniil Kvyat and Williams' Valtteri Bottas. They suffered, respectively, engine and gearbox failure on the way to the grid, and a back injury.

The front row was filled by Mercedes – Hamilton beating Rosberg to pole – with Williams' Felipe Massa next, but 0.797s in arrears. The silver arrows duly controlled the race, with Hamilton leading Rosberg away at the start and heading Rosberg at the finish by 1.36s. More than half a minute back, Sebastian Vettel marked his first start for Ferrari with third place, getting the better of Massa by making his one and only pitstop three laps later than the lone Williams racer.

Sauber failed to score a point at all in 2014, but ended the day at Albert Park with smiles all round as they picked up 14 points as rookie Felipe Nasr and Marcus Ericsson grabbed fifth and eighth, helped in no small part by Lotus duo Romain Grosjean and Pastor Maldonado both retiring on the opening lap, then Kimi Raikkonen relinquishing fifth place late on when his Ferrari's left rear wheel wasn't attached properly after his second pitstop.

To talk of McLaren only as a footnote feels unusual, but its pre-season woes with the new Honda engine continued, and the team had to accept that its pace was quicker only than Marussia – and their cars failed to venture onto the track due to a lack of working software after being brought out of administration

94

Hamilton leads from Mercedes team-mate Rosberg, with Vettel making his first Ferrari start.

MELBOURNE ROUND 1
DATE: **15 MARCH 2015**

Laps: **58** • Distance: **191.110 miles/307.562km** • Weather: **Warm & sunny**

Pos	Driver	Team	Result	Stops	Qualifying Time	Grid
1	**Lewis Hamilton**	Mercedes	1h31m54.067s	1	1m26.327s	1
2	**Nico Rosberg**	Mercedes	1h31m55.427s	1	1m26.921s	2
3	**Sebastian Vettel**	Ferrari	1h32m28.590s	1	1m27.757s	4
4	**Felipe Massa**	Williams	1h32m32.263s	1	1m27.718s	3
5	**Felipe Nasr**	Sauber	1h33m29.216s	1	1m28.800s	11
6	**Daniel Ricciardo**	Red Bull	57 laps	1	1m28.329s	7
7	**Nico Hulkenberg**	Force India	57 laps	2	1m29.208s	14
8	**Marcus Ericsson**	Sauber	57 laps	3	1m31.376s	16
9	**Carlos Sainz Jr**	Toro Rosso	57 laps	1	1m28.510s	8
10	**Sergio Perez**	Force India	57 laps	1	1m29.209s	15
11	**Jenson Button**	McLaren	56 laps	1	1m31.422s	17
R	**Kimi Raikkonen**	Ferrari	40 laps/wheel	2	1m27.790s	5
R	**Max Verstappen**	Toro Rosso	32 laps/power unit	1	1m28.868s	12
R	**Romain Grosjean**	Lotus	0 laps/power unit	0	1m28.560s	9
R	**Pastor Maldonado**	Lotus	0 laps/collision	0	1m29.480s	10
NS	**Daniil Kvyat**	Red Bull	0 laps/gearbox	0	1m29.070s	13
NS	**Kevin Magnussen**	McLaren	0 laps/power unit	0	1m32.037s	18
NS	**Valtteri Bottas**	Williams	0 laps/back injury	0	1m28.087s	6
NS	**Will Stevens**	Marussia	0 laps/software	0	no time	-
NS	**ROBERTO MEHRI**	MARUSSIA	0 LAPS/SOFTWARE	0	no time	-

FASTEST LAP: **HAMILTON, 1M30.945S, 130.945MPH/209.915KPH ON LAP 50** • RACE LEADERS: **HAMILTON 1-24 & 27-58; ROSBERG 25-26**

Such was Mercedes' domination in Melbourne, that nobody predicted anything than another victory for the silver arrows in Malaysia. Yet, thanks to a clever strategy, Ferrari was able to provide Sebastian Vettel with the opportunity to take his first win in red.

Perhaps the first sign came when Mercedes failed to lock out the front row of the grid, with Vettel lapping faster than Nico Rosberg. There had been an element of lottery, though, as rain arrived during Q2 and the track was wetter still for the final session. Lewis Hamilton laid down the marker in the opening moments, on intermediate tyres, and late on Vettel came within 0.074s of matching it on full wet tyres. Yet, with dry weather predicted for race day, Mercedes didn't appear too worried.

What happened on the Sunday, however, left Mercedes in no doubt that its performance advantage had been usurped by superior tyre choice and strategy.

Hamilton stayed in front on the blast to the first corner, with Vettel being more than a little robust in his efforts to keep Rosberg behind him. Then, three laps in, Marcus Ericsson spun his Sauber at Turn 1 when tussling with Nico Hulkenberg's Force India and the safety car had to be deployed. Already feeling that their tyre wear was too high, Mercedes took the opportunity to bring both cars in to change them to a harder compound. Vitally, Vettel stayed out, thus taking the lead, with Hulkenberg and Lotus's Romain Grosjean next up.

Hamilton and Rosberg then had to advance from sixth and ninth, respectively. Vettel continued to lap quickly on his mediums and stayed out for a further 13 laps. Although he rejoined behind both Mercedes, the German lapped 2s per lap faster and passed Rosberg on lap 21, regaining the lead three laps later when Hamilton made his second stop.

Mercedes knew it would have to bring its drivers in for a third stop and so the race was Vettel's by 8.569s, his SF15-T so kind to its tyres that its wear of the faster mediums matched Mercedes on the slower harder tyres. Max Verstappen finished seventh in his Toro Rosso to become F1's youngest point-scorer, at 17 years and 188 days.

SEPANG ROUND 2

DATE: **29 MARCH 2015**

Laps: **56** • Distance: **192.888 miles/310.424km** • Weather: **Very hot & sunny**

Pos	Driver	Team	Result	Stops	Qualifying Time	Grid
1	Sebastian Vettel	Ferrari	1h41m05.793s	2	1m49.908s	2
2	Lewis Hamilton	Mercedes	1h41m14.362s	3	1m49.834s	1
3	Nico Rosberg	Mercedes	1h41m18.103s	3	1m50.299s	3
4	Kimi Raikkonen	Ferrari	1h41m49.615s	3	1m42.173s	11
5	Valtteri Bottas	Williams	1h42m16.202s	3	1m53.179s	8
6	Felipe Massa	Williams	1h42m19.379s	3	1m52.473s	7
7	Max Verstappen	Toro Rosso	1h42m43.555s	3	1m51.980s	6
8	Carlos Sainz Jr	Toro Rosso	55 laps	2	1m43.700s	15
9	Daniil Kvyat	Red Bull	55 laps	3	1m51.590s	5
10	Daniel Ricciardo	Red Bull	55 laps	3	1m51.541s	4
11	Romain Grosjean	Lotus	55 laps	3	1m52.980s	10*
12	Felipe Nasr	Sauber	55 laps	4	1m41.308s	16
13	Sergio Perez	Force India	55 laps	2	1m43.468s	14
14	Nico Hulkenberg	Force India	55 laps	3	1m43.022s	13
15	Roberto Mehri	Marussia	53 laps	3	1m46.677s	19
R	Pastor Maldonado	Lotus	47 laps/brakes	3	1m42.197s	12
R	Jenson Button	McLaren	41 laps/engine	3	1m41.635s	17
R	Fernando Alonso	McLaren	21 laps/engine	1	1m41.745s	18
R	Marcus Ericsson	Sauber	3 laps/spun off	0	1m53.260s	9
W	Will Stevens	Marussia	-	-	-	-

FASTEST LAP: **ROSBERG, 1M42.062S, 121.488MPH/195.516KPH ON LAP 43** • RACE LEADERS: **HAMILTON 1-3, 18-23 & 38; VETTEL 4-17, 24-37 & 39-56;**
* 2-PLACE GRID PENALTY FOR LEAVING PITLANE OUT OF ORDER IN Q2

It took until only his second grand prix for Ferrari for Vettel to rediscover his winning form.

CHINESE GP

After Ferrari's win in Malaysia, Mercedes got back on top in China, but it wasn't all smiles in its camp after the race. As is often the case when a team dominates, its drivers set about each other, and Lewis Hamilton's victory left Nico Rosberg somewhat aggrieved.

There had been a degree of soul-searching at Mercedes since Ferrari had got the better of it in Malaysia and the team achieved a far better set-up to stop its cars from eating their tyres. Thus it was with relief that Hamilton and Rosberg put Sebastian Vettel in the shade in qualifying by almost 1s.

Then, after a less than enthralling race, in which Hamilton controlled proceedings and Rosberg was unable to find a way past, Rosberg accused his team-mate of dropping his pace to "back him up" against Vettel and so make him use his tyres up more than he'd have done if allowed to remain clear of his compatriot's Ferrari.

With Vettel not far behind as the race entered its final laps, a stalemate was brought about when Max Verstappen's Toro Rosso lost eighth place when the gearbox failed and stranded him in a dangerous position, bringing out the safety car.

A rapid getaway propelled Kimi Raikkonen past both Williams into a fourth position that he wasn't to lose, with Felipe Massa leading home Valtteri Bottas. A further 10s back, Romain Grosjean was delighted to score for Lotus, while team-mate Pastor Maldonado could also have scored, but he went off when coming in for his second pitstop. He was then hit from behind by Jenson Button's McLaren and subsequent brake failure forced him out.

Mercedes had improved its engine over the close-season, but Renault had not and there was talk that the V6 in the back of the Red Bull RB11s could be as much as 100bhp down. Not only were the Red Bulls slow, but the engines were proving unreliable, too. Even Daniel Ricciardo's best efforts, using his third engine in three races, got him only to seventh on the grid, and Daniil Kvyat was five places further back. When the Australian made a dreadful start, dropping to 17th, the mountain to climb was even steeper, and he managed only to get to ninth, between the Sauber drivers.

SHANGHAI ROUND 3

DATE: **12 APRIL 2015**

Laps: **56** • Distance: **189.840 miles/305.518km** • Weather: **Warm & sunny**

Pos	Driver	Team	Result	Stops	Qualifying Time	Grid
1	**Lewis Hamilton**	Mercedes	1h39m42.008s	2	1m35.782s	1
2	**Nico Rosberg**	Mercedes	1h39m42.722s	2	1m35.824s	2
3	**Sebastian Vettel**	Ferrari	1h39m44.996s	2	1m36.687s	3
4	**Kimi Raikkonen**	Ferrari	1h39m45.843s	2	1m37.232s	6
5	**Felipe Massa**	Williams	1h39m50.552s	2	1m36.954s	4
6	**Valtteri Bottas**	Williams	1h39m51.893s	2	1m37.143s	5
7	**Romain Grosjean**	Lotus	1h40m01.016s	2	1m37.905s	8
8	**Felipe Nasr**	Sauber	1h40m04.633s	2	1m38.067s	9
9	**Daniel Ricciardo**	Red Bull	1h40m14.125s	2	1m37.540s	7
10	**Marcus Ericsson**	Sauber	55 laps	2	1m38.158s	10
11	**Sergio Perez**	Force India	55 laps	3	1m39.290s	15
12	**Fernando Alonso**	McLaren	55 laps	2	1m39.280s	18
13	**Carlos Sainz Jr**	Toro Rosso	55 laps	2	1m38.538s	14
14	**Jenson Button**	McLaren	55 laps*	2	1m39.276s	17
15	**Will Stevens**	Marussia	54 laps	2	1m42.091s	19
16	**Roberto Mehri**	Marussia	54 laps**	2	1m42.842s	20
17	**Max Verstappen**	Toro Rosso	52 laps/engine	2	1m38.393s	13
R	**Pastor Maldonado**	Lotus	49 laps/collision	2	1m38.134s	11
R	**Daniil Kvyat**	Red Bull	15 laps/engine	0	1m38.209s	12
R	**Nico Hulkenberg**	Force India	9 laps/gearbox	0	1m39.216s	16

FASTEST LAP: HAMILTON, 1M42.208S, 119.301MPH/191.997KPH ON LAP 31 • RACE LEADERS: HAMILTON 1-13, 16-33 & 35-56; ROSBERG 14-15; RAIKKONEN 34
* 5-SECOND PENALTY FOR CAUSING A COLLISION
** 5-SECOND PENALTY FOR SAFETY CAR PERIOD INFRINGEMENT

Hamilton on the podium, flanked by Rosberg and Vettel, after his second win in three starts.

BAHRAIN GP

Lewis Hamilton made it three wins from four starts to open out a 27-point lead, but he was pushed all the way by Ferrari's Kimi Raikkonen, who put on impressive charge in the closing laps as both Mercedes were slowed by brake-by-wire problems.

The Mercedes drivers arrived at Sakhir trying to play down the sour atmosphere that had sprung up between them in China, and Hamilton handled his attack better to maintain his 100 per cent record of pole positions in 2015. Nico Rosberg was 0.558s slower and, vitally, on the second row as Sebastian Vettel qualified his Ferrari second.

Hamilton led away, but matters quickly became worse for Rosberg. Kimi Raikkonen pushed him back to fourth at Turn 2, but he regained third going into Turn 1 on lap 4. In the same place, four laps later, Vettel made a mistake, and this let Rosberg take second. Hamilton, however, had more than 5s in hand, and he was able to call the shots through the remainder of the race.

It was close, though, especially when Hamilton rejoined the circuit after the first pitstop, only just ahead of the scrapping Vettel and Rosberg, both of whom had pitted earlier. Rosberg chose this moment to get back into second place, but was unable to do anything to usurp Hamilton, who then made his second stop earlier than his rivals and was comfortably in front when his car was hit with a brake-by-wire problem on the final lap, but he held on to win.

Rosberg was denied second place on the penultimate lap when he was hunted down by Raikkonen, who had made his tyres work better than Vettel, and the Finn's middle stint on the medium rubber was the key to him keeping the two Mercedes in sight before catching them as the race neared its end. When Rosberg slipped wide at Turn 1, Raikkonen pounced. Vettel fell to fifth behind Valtteri Bottas's Williams after running wide and having to pit for a new wing.

McLaren remained without a point to its name, with Fernando Alonso missing out on tenth place by just 4s behind Felipe Massa's Williams. Team-mate Jenson Button didn't even get to the start, his MP4-30 left in the garage after its fourth electrical problem of the meeting.

Bottas was one of the stars of the race, guiding his Williams through the dark to fourth place.

SAKHIR ROUND 4
DATE: **19 APRIL 2015**

Laps: **57** • Distance: **191.539 miles/308.253km** • Weather: **Hot & dark**

Pos	Driver	Team	Result	Stops	Qualifying Time	Grid
1	**Lewis Hamilton**	Mercedes	1h35m05.809s	2	1m32.571s	1
2	**Kimi Raikkonen**	Ferrari	1h35m09.189s	2	1m33.227s	4
3	**Nico Rosberg**	Mercedes	1h35m11.842s	2	1m33.129s	2
4	**Valtteri Bottas**	Williams	1h35m48.766s	2	1m33.381s	5
5	**Sebastian Vettel**	Ferrari	1h35m49.798s	3	1m32.982s	2
6	**Daniel Ricciardo**	Red Bull	1h36m07.560s	2	1m33.832s	7
7	**Romain Grosjean**	Lotus	1h36m30.572s	2	1m34.484s	10
8	**Sergio Perez**	Force India	56 laps	2	1m34.704s	11
9	**Daniil Kvyat**	Red Bull	56 laps	2	1m35.800s	17
10	**Felipe Massa**	Williams	56 laps	2	1m33.744s	6*
11	**Fernando Alonso**	McLaren	56 laps	2	1m35.039s	14
12	**Felipe Nasr**	Sauber	56 laps	3	1m34.737s	12
13	**Nico Hulkenberg**	Force India	56 laps	3	1m34.450s	8
14	**Marcus Ericsson**	Sauber	56 laps	3	1m35.034s	13
15	**Pastor Maldonado**	Lotus	56 laps	3	1m35.677s	16
16	**Will Stevens**	Marussia	55 laps	2	1m38.713s	18
17	**Roberto Mehri**	Marussia	54 laps	2	1m39.722s	19
R	**Max Verstappen**	Toro Rosso	34 laps/electrical	2	1m35.103s	15
R	**Carlos Sainz Jr**	Toro Rosso	29 laps/wheel	1	1m34.462s	9
R	**Jenson Button**	McLaren	0 laps/electrical	0	No time	20

FASTEST LAP: RAIKKONEN, 1M36.311S, 125.700MPH/202.295KPH ON LAP 42 • RACE LEADERS: HAMILTON 1-15, 18-33, 40-57; RAIKKONEN 16-17, 35-39; ROSBERG 34
* STARTED FROM THE PITLANE

The tally was three wins to his team-mate Lewis Hamilton and one to Ferrari's Sebastian Vettel, but Mercedes' Nico Rosberg struck back in Spain by racing to a dominant victory as Hamilton was slow away at the start and fell to third before fighting back to finish second.

The first step Rosberg took towards claiming his first win of 2015 - and keeping Mercedes team-mate Hamilton in check - came in qualifying, when he secured his first pole position of the year. He proved he had learned the lesson from the previous round, when he had gone slowly in Q2 in an attempt to save his tyres, and had then been unable to get back onto pace in the Q3 shoot-out. This time, he was on the pace, and it worked.

Mercedes' closest challenger - Ferrari's Sebastian Vettel - was 0.777s away from pole, so the race was going to be between the two Mercedes drivers. Except Hamilton failed to make a competitive start and was overtaken by Vettel before the first corner, and Rosberg will surely have smiled when he saw a red car next in line as they turned into the first corner. Valtteri Bottas challenged Hamilton at that first turn, but failed to edge his Williams into third.

With a performance advantage over Vettel, Rosberg then controlled the race. In a bid to push Vettel back to third, Hamilton pitted on lap 13, and Vettel responded by coming in a lap later. Infuriatingly for the British driver, his stop was slow and it left Hamilton still third after the first round of stops. Another roll of the dice by Mercedes midway through the race put Hamilton onto a three-stop strategy. That it worked and moved him ahead of Vettel was a success, but Rosberg was far enough clear to pit just twice and still win by 17s.

No other driver was able to topple Vettel and, as is often the way on the Circuit de Catalunya, overtaking was in short supply. Bottas was able to finish fourth, though he was pushed all the way by Kimi Raikkonen in the second Ferrari.

Fernando Alonso was the race's first retirement, but the Spanish fans at least had Carlos Sainz Jr to cheer on as the Toro Rosso driver claimed more points by finishing ninth.

It all came good for Rosberg at round five, when he started on pole and was always in control.

BARCELONA ROUND 5
DATE: **10 MAY 2015**

Laps: **66** • Distance: **190.904 miles/307.231km** • Weather: **Hot & bright**

Pos	Driver	Team	Result	Stops	Qualifying Time	Grid
1	**Nico Rosberg**	Mercedes	1h41m12.555s	2	1m24.681s	1
2	**Lewis Hamilton**	Mercedes	1h41m30.106s	3	1m24.948s	2
3	**Sebastian Vettel**	Ferrari	1h41m57.897s	2	1m25.458s	3
4	**Valtteri Bottas**	Williams	1h42m11.772s	2	1m25.694s	4
5	**Kimi Raikkonen**	Ferrari	1h42m12.557s	2	1m26.414s	7
6	**Felipe Massa**	Williams	1h42m33.869s	3	1m26.757s	9
7	**Daniel Ricciardo**	Red Bull	65 laps	2	1m26.770s	10
8	**Romain Grosjean**	Lotus	65 laps	2	1m27.375s	11
9	**Carlos Sainz Jr**	Toro Rosso	65 laps	2	1m26.136s	5
10	**Daniil Kvyat**	Red Bull	65 laps	2	1m26.629s	8
11	**Max Verstappen**	Toro Rosso	65 laps	2	1m26.249s	6
12	**Felipe Nasr**	Sauber	65 laps	2	1m28.005s	15
13	**Sergio Perez**	Force India	65 laps	2	1m28.442s	18
14	**Marcus Ericsson**	Sauber	65 laps	2	1m28.112s	16
15	**Nico Hulkenberg**	Force India	65 laps	3	1m28.365s	17
16	**Jenson Button**	McLaren	65 laps	3	1m27.854s	14
17	**Will Stevens**	Marussia	63 laps	3	1m31.200s	19
18	**Roberto Mehri**	Marussia	62 laps	3	1m32.038s	20
R	**Pastor Maldonado**	Lotus	45 laps/called in	3	1m27.450s	12
R	**Fernando Alonso**	McLaren	26 laps/brakes	1	1m27.760s	13

FASTEST LAP: **HAMILTON, 1M28.720S, 117.967MPH/189.849KPH ON LAP 54** • RACE LEADERS: **ROSBERG 1-15, 17-45, 51-66; RAIKKONEN 16; HAMILTON 46-50**

The ebb and flow between Mercedes' pair of drivers swung in Nico Rosberg's favour at home in Monaco when a dominant Lewis Hamilton was defeated by a tactical blunder during a safety car period that dropped him to third place behind Rosberg and Sebastian Vettel.

It's long been said that the key to victory at Monaco rests more heavily on claiming pole position than it does at all other F1 venues. So, with pole bagged, Hamilton had good reason to feel happy with life on Saturday afternoon in the principality.

When he then converted pole into the lead of the race, his smile would have been larger still. Then, having edged clear in the opening stint, it looked as though the battle was all but won, the British driver's second Monaco victory in the bag. Yet, with a lead of 19.349s over Rosberg as they completed their 63rd lap, Max Verstappen's Toro Rosso piled into Romain Grosjean's tenth-placed Lotus at Ste Devote, bringing out the safety car.

It was at this point that the race went away from Hamilton, as Mercedes called him in for a fresh set of tyres and discovered, to its horror, that he hadn't had enough of a margin to do this and return to the track still in the lead. With neither Rosberg nor Vettel being called in, Hamilton rejoined in third and was unable to advance from there in the eight laps after the safety car withdrew.

After the race, Mercedes team boss Toto Wolff said that the team accepted the blame, while pointing out that you have no GPS at Monaco. Regardless of that, you felt that the team's management had a lot of explaining to do.

Thus, Rosberg claimed a third consecutive win in the place in which he was brought up and closed to just ten points behind Hamilton at the top of the championship table. Red Bull Racing collected its best finish to this point of the campaign, with Daniil Kvyat and Daniel Ricciardo fourth and fifth, both ahead of Kimi Raikkonen's Ferrari. Two places further back, in eighth, was Jenson Button. It's been a long time since the 2009 World Champion would have been pleased to steal into the points, but this finishing position brought him and McLaren their first points of a frustrating season.

MONACO ROUND 6

DATE: **24 MAY 2015**

Laps: **78** • Distance: **161.887 miles/260.532km** • Weather: **Warm & sunny**

Pos	Driver	Team	Result	Stops	Qualifying Time	Grid
1	Nico Rosberg	Mercedes	1h49m18.420s	1	1m15.440s	2
2	Sebastian Vettel	Ferrari	1h49m22.906s	1	1m15.849s	3
3	Lewis Hamilton	Mercedes	1h49m24.473s	2	1m15.098s	1
4	Daniil Kvyat	Red Bull	1h49m30.385s	1	1m16.182s	5
5	Daniel Ricciardo	Red Bull	1h49m32.028s	2	1m16.041s	4
6	Kimi Raikkonen	Ferrari	1h49m32.765s	1	1m16.427s	6
7	Sergio Perez	Force India	1h49m33.433s	2	1m16.808s	7
8	Jenson Button	McLaren	1h49m34.483s	2	1m17.093s	10
9	Felipe Nasr	Sauber	1h49m42.046s	2	1m18.101s	14
10	Carlos Sainz Jr	Toro Rosso	1h49m43.476s	1	1m16.931s	20*
11	Nico Hulkenberg	Force India	1h49m44.652s	2	1m17.193s	11
12	Romain Grosjean	Lotus	1h49m46.835s	1	1m17.007s	15**
13	Marcus Ericsson	Sauber	1h49m49.579s	3	1m18.513s	17
14	Valtteri Bottas	Williams	1m50m04.209s	2	1m18.434s	16
15	Felipe Massa	Williams	77 laps	3	1m17.278s	12
16	Roberto Mehri	Marussia	76 laps	1	1m20.904s	19
17	Will Stevens	Marussia	76 laps	1	1m20.655s	18
R	Max Verstappen	Toro Rosso	62 laps/collision	2	1m16.957s	9
R	Fernando Alonso	McLaren	41 laps/gearbox	1	1m26.632s	13
R	Pastor Maldonado	Lotus	5 laps/brakes	0	1m16.946s	8

FASTEST LAP: RICCIARDO, 1M18.063S, 95.623MPH/153.891KPH ON LAP 74 • RACE LEADERS: HAMILTON 1-64; ROSBERG 65-78
* STARTED FROM THE PITLANE FOR FAILING TO STOP FOR WEIGHING
** 5-PLACE GRID PENALTY FOR GEARBOX CHANGE

Rosberg celebrates again, but his rueful smile suggests he knows how fortunate he was.

In the past, Lewis Hamilton has let misfortunes get to him, but he came back strongly after Mercedes' strategic blunder cost him victory at Monaco and triumphed easily in Canada, despite having to reduce his fuel consumption to make it to the finish.

Practice had suggested that pole ought to go to Nico Rosberg, as Hamilton had flat-spotted two sets of his Mercedes' tyres and thus limited his options in qualifying. Yet it went the other way as Rosberg's first run was slower than Hamilton's only run in Q3 and the German overruled his engineers and changed his car's set-up, only to go slower.

Kimi Raikkonen had a strong run for Ferrari to qualify third, while team-mate Sebastian Vettel had a shocker, first being hit with a five-place grid penalty for passing Roberto Mehri's Marussia under red flags, then suffering an ECU problem that left him sidelined at the end of Q1. This allowed Valtteri Bottas to line up fourth for Williams, ahead of an all-Lotus third row.

Hamilton was quickly off the mark and soon put himself out of range for Rosberg to haul him in by using his DRS. With Raikkonen falling back little by little, Rosberg was free to give chase, but he had no answers to the English driver's pace. The gap between them was 3.3s at the time of their first pitstop. This was planned to be their only stop, so Hamilton seemed to have matters under control, which is more than could be said for Raikkonen, who pitted from third, but spun almost immediately after rejoining. He later blamed it not on cold tyres, but on the car's torque map. This handed the position to Bottas and he was to keep it to the finish for Williams' first podium of 2015. Impressively, Vettel advanced from 18th to fifth, just 4s behind his team-mate, with Felipe Massa also passing Maldonado late in the race.

If it all seemed serene for Mercedes, it was far from that in the cockpit, as Hamilton and Rosberg were being asked to slow down, to save fuel and brake life, respectively. With 25 of the 70 laps remaining, Rosberg was just 1s behind, but Hamilton gunned it in the closing laps, just to be sure. McLaren would have dreamed of such limitations, with its cars being the first out of the race.

MONTREAL ROUND 7

DATE: **7 JUNE 2015**

Laps: **70** • Distance: **189.686 miles/305.271km** • Weather: **Warm but cloudy**

Pos	Driver	Team	Result	Stops	Qualifying Time	Grid
1	**Lewis Hamilton**	Mercedes	1h31m53.145s	1	1m14.393s	1
2	**Nico Rosberg**	Mercedes	1h31m55.430s	1	1m14.702s	2
3	**Valtteri Bottas**	Williams	1h32m33.811s	1	1m15.102s	4
4	**Kimi Raikkonen**	Ferrari	1h32m38.770s	2	1m15.014s	3
5	**Sebastian Vettel**	Ferrari	1h32m43.048s	2	1m17.344s	18*
6	**Felipe Massa**	Williams	1h32m49.526s	1	1m17.886s	15
7	**Pastor Maldonado**	Lotus	1h32m59.809s	1	1m15.329s	6
8	**Nico Hulkenberg**	Force India	69 laps	1	1m15.614s	7
9	**Daniil Kvyat**	Red Bull	69 laps	1	1m16.079s	8
10	**Romain Grosjean**	Lotus	69 laps!	2	1m15.194s	5
11	**Sergio Perez**	Force India	69 laps	1	1m16.338s	10
12	**Carlos Sainz Jr**	Toro Rosso	69 laps	1	1m16.042s	11
13	**Daniel Ricciardo**	Red Bull	69 laps	1	1m16.114s	9
14	**Marcus Ericsson**	Sauber	69 laps	1	1m16.262s	12
15	**Max Verstappen**	Toro Rosso	69 laps	1	1m16.245s	19**
16	**Felipe Nasr**	Sauber	68 laps	1	1m16.620s	14
17	**Will Stevens**	Marussia	66 laps	2	1m19.157s	17
R	**Roberto Mehri**	Marussia	57 laps/halfshaft	1	1m19.133s	16
R	**Jenson Button**	McLaren	54 laps/exhaust	2	No time	20**
R	**Fernando Alonso**	McLaren	44 laps/exhaust	1	1m16.276s	13

FASTEST LAP: RAIKKONEN, 1M16.987S, 126.713MPH/203.925KPH ON LAP 42 • RACE LEADERS: HAMILTON 1-28, 30-70; ROSBERG 29
* 5-PLACE GRID PENALTY FOR OVERTAKING UNDER RED FLAGS
** 15-PLACE GRID PENALTY
! 5-SECOND PENALTY FOR CAUSING A COLLISION

Hamilton led Rosberg and Raikkonen into the first corner and never looked back.

AUSTRIAN GP

Taking the lead at the start of the grand prix was all that Nico Rosberg needed to do to get the upper hand on his pole-sitting Mercedes team-mate Lewis Hamilton, then he duly raced to a deserved win. His fans now wanted to know whether he could repeat this feat.

Hamilton claimed pole – gifted to him by Rosberg, who ran off the track at the last corner – and should have fancied his chances of reaching the first corner in front. However, thanks to a throttle problem, Hamilton had to dump the clutch and, suffering from wheelspin, it allowed Rosberg to blast past. Although Hamilton tried at both the second and the third corners to get back in front, his moves were to no avail. By the time the Mercedes duo reached the third turn, Schlossgold, the signal was being given for the safety car to be deployed.

The reason for this was that two former World Champions were out, with Kimi Raikkonen and Fernando Alonso eliminated after coming together. The incident that claimed them occurred after Turn 2, Remus. Raikkonen lost control and hit Alonso, with the McLaren ending up on top of the Ferrari.

The safety car withdrew after six laps and Rosberg enjoyed excellent pace as he executed a one-stop strategy in dominant fashion. Victory reduced Hamilton's championship advantage to just ten points, but it was probably worth more than that to Rosberg, as it suggested that he really did have the pace to challenge his team-mate.

Third place had looked to be going to Sebastian Vettel, but his Ferrari crew struggled to replace his right rear wheel at his midrace pitstop. Felipe Massa took advantage and raced to his first podium finish of 2015, fulfilling his son's pre-race prediction. However, if there had been even a couple more laps, he would probably have been overhauled by the charging German.

Valtteri Bottas finished a distant fifth, his Williams one place ahead of the Force India of Nico Hulkenberg, a driver enjoying new-found fame for being the first current F1 driver to win the Le Mans 24 Hours since Bertrand Gachot and Johnny Herbert achieved the feat in 1991. And, in late drama, Pastor Maldonado took seventh from Max Verstappen on the final lap.

Felipe Massa flashes past the scenic backdrop en route to his first podium finish of 2015.

RED BULL RING ROUND 8
DATE: 21 JUNE 2015

Laps: **71** • Distance: **190.851 miles/307.145km** • Weather: **Cool & cloudy**

Pos	Driver	Team	Result	Stops	Qualifying Time	Grid
1	**Nico Rosberg**	Mercedes	1h30m16.930s	1	1m08.655s	2
2	**Lewis Hamilton**	Mercedes	1h30m25.730s!	1	1m08.455s	1
3	**Felipe Massa**	Williams	1h30m34.503s	1	1m09.192s	4
4	**Sebastian Vettel**	Ferrari	1h30m35.111s	1	1m08.810s	3
5	**Valtteri Bottas**	Williams	1h31m10.534s	1	1m09.319s	6
6	**Nico Hulkenberg**	Force India	1h31m21.005s	1	1m09.278s	5
7	**Pastor Maldonado**	Lotus	70 laps	1	1m10.374s	10
8	**Max Verstappen**	Toro Rosso	70 laps	1	1m09.612s	7
9	**Sergio Perez**	Force India	70 laps	1	1m12.522s	13
10	**Daniel Ricciardo**	Red Bull	70 laps	1	1m10.482s	18*
11	**Felipe Nasr**	Sauber	70 laps	1	1m09.713s	8
12	**Daniil Kvyat**	Red Bull	70 laps	2	1m09.694s	15*
13	**Marcus Ericsson**	Sauber	69 laps	3	1m10.426s	11
14	**Roberto Mehri**	Marussia	68 laps	1	1m14.071s	16
R	**Romain Grosjean**	Lotus	35 laps/gearbox	1	No time	9
R	**Carlos Sainz Jr**	Toro Rosso	35 laps/power unit	1	1m10.465s	12
R	**Jenson Button**	McLaren	8 laps/electrical	2	1m12.632s	20**
R	**Will Stevens**	Marussia	1 lap/oil leak	0	1m15.368s	17
R	**Kimi Raikkonen**	Ferrari	0 laps/collision	0	1m12.867s	14
R	**Fernando Alonso**	McLaren	0 laps/collision	0	1m10.736s	19**

FASTEST LAP: ROSBERG, 1M11.235S, 135.845MPH/218.622KPH ON LAP 35 • RACE LEADERS: ROSBERG 1-32, 37-71; HAMILTON 33-35; VETTEL 36
* 10-PLACE GRID PENALTY
** 20-PLACE GRID PENALTY FOR USING FIFTH POWER UNIT
! INCLUDES 5s PENALTY FOR CROSSING WHITE LINE AT PIT EXIT

It looked, at first, as though Williams could take the race to Mercedes at Silverstone, but Felipe Massa and Valtteri Bottas were both to be disappointed and the silver arrows moved ahead to enable Lewis Hamilton score his third win on home soil.

Hamilton claimed his eighth pole in nine attempts. Yet, had Nico Rosberg not struggled for grip from his front left tyre in the final third of the lap, pole would have been his. The best of the rest, Williams' Felipe Massa, was 0.724s further back.

So, surely, all Mercedes clearly had to do to secure victory was to be in front into the first corner? Indeed, but they weren't, as Massa accelerated between the two Mercedes to enter Abbey in front. To make matters worse, Massa was followed through by team-mate Valtteri Bottas. Mercedes had to react fast and Hamilton dived past Bottas for second in The Loop.

There was trouble behind, as Daniel Ricciardo hit Romain Grosjean's Lotus at Village, punting it into Pastor Maldonado's sister car. Fernando Alonso spun trying to avoid the accident and took out team-mate Jenson Button. With Felipe Nasr's Sauber not having started because of gearbox failure, there were just 16 cars left before the safety car was deployed.

When the safety car pulled off, Massa came under immediate attack from Hamilton, but he went too hard into Club and ran wide, letting Bottas regain second.

Bottas was faster than Massa, but couldn't find a way by and Hamilton sat not far behind, waiting. After the first pitstops, the order was Hamilton, Massa and Bottas. The Finn was left rueing the fact the team hadn't let him attack Massa early on, as he was sure his pace advantage with heavy tanks would have helped him get by.

With Hamilton in front, it seemed that Williams' tactics had cost them, as the Englishman edged away. Rosberg was still fourth after their first stops, but rain fell with 15 laps to go and he passed first Massa, then Bottas, before they pitted again to secure Mercedes' 17th one-two in 28 races.

Williams then missed out on a podium, as Vettel changed to intermediates before they did and was able to claim third place.

Hamilton lets rip with the bubbly after a great afternoon's work that produced his third home win.

SILVERSTONE ROUND 9

DATE: **5 JULY 2015**

Laps: **52** • Distance: **190.262 miles/306.198km** • Weather: **Warm & bright, rain later**

Pos	Driver	Team	Result	Stops	Qualifying Time	Grid
1	**Lewis Hamilton**	Mercedes	1h31m27.729s	2	1m32.248s	1
2	**Nico Rosberg**	Mercedes	1h31m38.685s	2	1m32.361s	2
3	**Sebastian Vettel**	Ferrari	1h31m53.172s	2	1m33.547s	6
4	**Felipe Massa**	Williams	1h32m04.568s	2	1m33.085s	3
5	**Valtteri Bottas**	Williams	1h32m30.923s	2	1m33.149s	4
6	**Daniil Kvyat**	Red Bull	1h32m31.684s	2	1m33.636s	7
7	**Nico Hulkenberg**	Force India	1h32m46.473s	2	1m33.673s	9
8	**Kimi Raikkonen**	Ferrari	51 laps	3	1m33.379s	5
9	**Sergio Perez**	Force India	51 laps	2	1m34.268s	11
10	**Fernando Alonso**	McLaren	51 laps	3	1m34.959s	17
11	**Marcus Ericsson**	Sauber	51 laps	3	1m34.868s	15
12	**Roberto Mehri**	Marussia	49 laps	2	1m39.377s	20
13	**Will Stevens**	Marussia	49 laps	2	1m37.364s	19
R	**Carlos Sainz Jr**	Toro Rosso	31 laps/electrical	1	1m33.649s	8
R	**Daniel Ricciardo**	Red Bull	21 laps/electrical	2	1m33.943s	10
R	**Max Verstappen**	Toro Rosso	3 laps/spun off	0	1m34.502s	13
R	**Romain Grosjean**	Lotus	0 laps/collision	0	1m34.430s	12
R	**Pastor Maldonado**	Lotus	0 laps/collision	0	1m34.511s	14
R	**Jenson Button**	McLaren	0 laps/collision	0	1m35.207s	18
NS	**Felipe Nasr**	Sauber	0 laps/gearbox	0	1m34.888s	16

FASTEST LAP: **HAMILTON, 1M37.093S, 135.723MPH/218.425KPH ON LAP 29** • RACE LEADERS: **MASSA 1-18, 20; HAMILTON 19, 22-43, 45-52; BOTTAS 21; ROSBERG 44**

HUNGARIAN GP

This was the race that F1 needed to take it into its summer break, with place-changing galore and a few surprises as Sebastian Vettel dominated the grand prix for Ferrari and was joined on the podium by the Red Bull duo, with Mercedes struggling.

Once Mercedes had claimed the front row, with ease ahead of Sebastian Vettel, it was assumed that they would be able to add to their tally of seven wins in a row. However, the script changed on lap 1 when Vettel blasted past and team-mate Kimi Raikkonen leapt from fifth to second when he passed Nico Rosberg into Turn 2. Then Lewis Hamilton ran into the gravel at Turn 5 and fell to tenth.

Hamilton worked his way back to fifth before the first round of pitstops, and to fourth when he passed Daniel Ricciardo, but he was too far behind the leading trio.

The field was bunched up when a virtual safety car period was triggered after seventh-placed Nico Hulkenberg's front wing collapsed and went under his Force India's front wheels, causing it to charge headlong into the Turn 1 tyrewall, narrowly missing Valtteri Bottas' Williams. The real safety car was then sent out as the debris was cleared. This failure followed one for team-mate Sergio Perez in practice.

When the safety car withdrew, Hamilton was too eager to make up ground and clipped Ricciardo's tail. He was forced to pit for a new nose and also earned a drive-through penalty, from which he could recover only to sixth.

At this point, Raikkonen was struggling with a failing MGU-K that would lead to his retirement. Rosberg moved into second, but wasn't to keep it as Ricciardo had more pace and passed him with five laps to go. Sadly, there was contact, with Rosberg suffering a puncture and Ricciardo front-wing damage. Both had to pit and this elevated Daniil Kvyat to a career-best second.

Ricciardo was able to get back to the pits and rejoin to finish third. Max Verstappen claimed his best result by racing to fourth, but Rosberg had to limp around and was delayed so much that he fell to eighth.

McLaren got both cars into the points, with Alonso finishing fifth and Button ninth.

HUNGARORING ROUND 10 — DATE: 26 JULY 2015

Laps: 69 • Distance: 187.818 miles/302.264km • Weather: Warm & sunny

Pos	Driver	Team	Result	Stops	Qualifying Time	Grid
1	Sebastian Vettel	Ferrari	1h46m09.985s	2	1m22.739s	3
2	Daniil Kvyat	Red Bull	1h46m25.733s*	3	1m23.332s	7
3	Daniel Ricciardo	Red Bull	1h46m35.069s	3	1m22.774s	4
4	Max Verstappen	Toro Rosso	1h46m54.236s	4	1m23.679s	9
5	Fernando Alonso	McLaren	1h46m59.064s	3	1m24.563s	15
6	Lewis Hamilton	Mercedes	1h47m02.010s	4	1m22.020s	1
7	Romain Grosjean	Lotus	1h47m08.563s	3	1m24.181s	10
8	Nico Rosberg	Mercedes	1h47m08.861s	3	1m22.595s	2
9	Jenson Button	McLaren	1h47m17.013s	2	1m24.739s	16
10	Marcus Ericsson	Sauber	1h47m19.115s	3	1m24.843s	17
11	Felipe Nasr	Sauber	1h47m23.443s	3	1m24.997s	18
12	Felipe Massa	Williams	1h47m24.263s	3	1m23.537s	8
13	Valtteri Bottas	Williams	1h47m30.213s	3	1m23.222s	6
14	Pastor Maldonado	Lotus	1h47m35.127s**	4	1m24.609s	14
15	Roberto Mehri	Marussia	67 laps	3	1m27.416s	19
16	Will Stevens	Marussia	65 laps/vibration	3	1m27.949s	20
R	Carlos Sainz Jr	Toro Rosso	60 laps/engine	2	1m23.869s	12
R	Kimi Raikkonen	Ferrari	55 laps/engine	3	1m23.020s	5
R	Sergio Perez	Force India	53 laps/brakes	4	1m24.461s	13
R	Nico Hulkenberg	Force India	41 laps/front wing	2	1m23.826s	11

FASTEST LAP: RICCIARDO, 1M24.821S, 115.537MPH/185.939KPH ON LAP 68 • RACE LEADERS: VETTEL 1-21 & 23-69; RAIKKONEN 22
* 10 SECOND PENALTY FOR EXCEEDING TRACK LIMITS
** 10 SECOND PENALTY FOR OVERTAKING BEFORE THE SC1 LINE AFTER THE SAFETY CAR PERIOD

Vettel leads into Turn 1 and team-mate Raikkonen starts to line up a move on Rosberg into Turn 2.

BELGIAN GP

Lewis Hamilton didn't put a wheel wrong as he dominated this race, leaving Nico Rosberg a distant second and Sebastian Vettel extremely frustrated after his one-stop gamble ended in retirement with a late-race blow-out that handed third to Romain Grosjean.

There were two major blow-outs at the Belgian GP. The first came in second practice, when Nico Rosberg had his right rear fail on the approach to Blanchimont.

The second came on the penultimate lap when Ferrari's gamble of running Sebastian Vettel on a one-stop strategy failed as his right rear blew on the approach to Les Combes as he was pressed by Lotus' Romain Grosjean. So, Ferrari didn't get to celebrate its 900th grand prix in style. Vettel was livid with Pirelli, although rivals pointed out that they hadn't thought a one-stop strategy feasible, so blamed Ferrari.

Hamilton had no such worries, as he qualified on pole by 0.458s from Rosberg, with Valtteri Bottas a further 0.882s back for Williams and Grosjean an impressive fourth. The talk after qualifying, though, was of grid penalties, with Grosjean being demoted five places for having a gearbox change. The major penalties were given for the use of power units beyond the season's allocation of five per car, with McLaren's Jenson Button and Fernando Alonso being hit with 50- and 55-place grid penalties.

Hamilton fended off a challenge from Force India's fast-starting Sergio Perez into Les Combes before controlling the race. He was helped by Rosberg dropping to fifth at the start before getting back to second when Perez pitted on lap 8. Thereafter, he ran second, but could do nothing to take first.

Grosjean was delighted to take third, as were his financially beleaguered team. However, third should have been possible for Bottas, but Williams fitted one medium tyre with three softs at his first pit stop. To compound the problem, he was hit with a drive-through penalty and ended up ninth.

While many were talking of blow-outs, almost as many were raving about the move by Max Verstappen when he passed Marcus Ericsson around the outside at Blanchimont, a move that left every onlooker with their heart in their mouth.

SPA-FRANCORCHAMPS ROUND 11 DATE: 23 AUGUST 2015

Laps: **43** • Distance: **187.062 miles/301.048km** • Weather: **Warm & sunny**

Pos	Driver	Team	Result	Stops	Qualifying Time	Grid
1	**Lewis Hamilton**	Mercedes	1h23m40.387s	2	1m47.197s	1
2	**Nico Rosberg**	Mercedes	1h23m42.445s	2	1m47.655s	2
3	**Romain Grosjean**	Lotus	1h24m18.375s	2	1m48.561s	9*
4	**Daniil Kvyat**	Red Bull	1h24m26.079s	2	1m48.599s	12
5	**Sergio Perez**	Force India	1h24m34.384s	2	1m48.599s	4
6	**Felipe Massa**	Williams	1h24m35.670s	2	1m48.685s	6
7	**Kimi Raikkonen**	Ferrari	1h24m36.090s	2	no time	16*
8	**Max Verstappen**	Toro Rosso	1h24m36.463s	3	no time	18**
9	**Valtteri Bottas**	Williams	1h24m41.427s	3	1m48.537s	3
10	**Marcus Ericsson**	Sauber	1h25m11.621s	2	1m49.586s	13
11	**Felipe Nasr**	Sauber	1h25m22.698s	2	1m49.952s	14
12	**Sebastian Vettel**	Ferrari	42 laps/puncture	1	1m48.825s	8
13	**Fernando Alonso**	McLaren	42 laps	3	1m51.420s	19^^
14	**Jenson Button**	McLaren	42 laps	3	1m50.978s	20^
15	**Roberto Mehri**	Marussia	42 laps	2	1m53.099s	17
16	**Will Stevens**	Marussia	42 laps	2	1m52.948s	15
R	**Carlos Sainz Jr**	Toro Rosso	32 laps/withdrawn	2	1m49.771s	10
R	**Daniel Ricciardo**	Red Bull	19 laps/power unit	1	1m48.639s	5
R	**Pastor Maldonado**	Lotus	2 laps/transmission	0	1m48.754s	7
R	**Nico Hulkenberg**	Force India	0 laps/power unit	0	1m49.121s	11

FASTEST LAP: ROSBERG, 1M52.416S, 139.370MPH/224.295KPH ON LAP 34 • RACE LEADERS: HAMILTON 1-30, 32-43; ROSBERG 31
* 5-PLACE GRID PENALTY FOR CHANGING THE GEARBOX • ** 10-PLACE GRID PENALTY FOR FITTING SIXTH POWER UNIT
^ 50-PLACE GRID PENALTY FOR FITTING EIGHTH POWER UNIT • ^^55-PLACE GRID PENALTY FOR FITTING NINTH POWER UNIT

Sebastian Vettel was heading for third when he suffered this blow-out on the penultimate lap.

ITALIAN GP

Lewis Hamilton took pole, fastest lap and victory, while Nico Rosberg failed to finish, so he had every reason to beam after opening out a 53-point lead. As he celebrated, there was an investigation over his car's tyre pressures, but he was cleared of any wrongdoing.

When Lewis Hamilton describes a grand prix as "fantastic, a perfect weekend for me", you need to sit up and listen. Of course, he was not only caught up in the emotion of winning at such an historic track, but also by the fact that he had taken a huge stride towards a third title as team-mate Nico Rosberg left Monza empty-handed. However, with the future of the race in the balance, and the drivers up in arms about this, there was an extra level of appreciation of the fans, the atmosphere and the history of the place.

Hamilton took his 11th pole in 12 rounds, weathered a first-corner move by Sebastian Vettel, and was never headed. Fifty-three laps later, he had 25 more points in the bag.

Rosberg, on the other hand, made a mess of qualifying and would start fourth. Then things got worse as he dropped two places on the opening lap, falling behind Williams duo Felipe Massa and Valtteri Bottas. Rosberg then worked his way back to third place, and got to within 1.4s of Vettel near the end, but had to park up with three laps to run when his engine failed, elevating the Williams drivers to third and fourth.

Rosberg wasn't the only driver to stumble at the start. Kimi Raikkonen's Ferrari went into anti-stall, dropping him from second on the grid to 14th. He made it back to fifth place.

Having been hit with a 50-place grid penalty, Daniel Ricciardo did well to advance to eighth place, albeit lapped by Hamilton's flying Mercedes.

With the Lotus team teetering on the brink financially, and F1 ringmaster Bernie Ecclestone apparently having paid its staff's wages, the one thing it needed was a strong showing. Instead both of its cars retired on the opening lap. Romain Grosjean was hit from behind by Felipe Nasr's Sauber, while Pastor Maldonado damaged his E23 against Nico Hulkenberg's Force India, with the German being slowed as a consequence through the race.

Hamilton resisted Vettel's challenge into the first chicane and then pulled away to victory.

MONZA ROUND 12

DATE: **6 SEPTEMBER 2015**

Laps: **53** • Distance: **190.587 miles/306.720km** • Weather: **Bright & warm**

Pos	Driver	Team	Result	Stops	Qualifying Time	Grid
1	**Lewis Hamilton**	Mercedes	1h18m00.688s	1	1m23.297s	1
2	**Sebastian Vettel**	Ferrari	1h18m25.730s	1	1m23.685s	2
3	**Felipe Massa**	Williams	1h18m48.323s	1	1m23.940s	5
4	**Valtteri Bottas**	Williams	1h18m48.684s	1	1m24.127s	6
5	**Kimi Raikkonen**	Ferrari	1h19m09.548s	1	1m23.631s	3
6	**Sergio Perez**	Force India	1h19m13.471s	1	1m24.626s	7
7	**Nico Hulkenberg**	Force India	52 laps	1	1m25.317s	9
8	**Daniel Ricciardo**	Red Bull	52 laps	1	no time	19^
9	**Marcus Ericsson**	Sauber	52 laps	1	1m26.214s	12*
10	**Daniil Kvyat**	Red Bull	52 laps	1	1m25.796s	18
11	**Carlos Sainz Jr**	Toro Rosso	52 laps	2	1m25.618s	17!!!
12	**Max Verstappen**	Toro Rosso	52 laps	3	no time	20!!
13	**Felipe Nasr**	Sauber	52 laps	2	1m24.898s	11
14	**Jenson Button**	McLaren	52 laps	1	1m26.058s	15**
15	**Will Stevens**	Marussia	51 laps	1	1m27.731s	13
16	**Roberto Mehri**	Marussia	51 laps	1	1m27.912s	14
17	**Nico Rosberg**	Mercedes	50 laps/engine	1	1m23.703s	4
18	**Fernando Alonso**	McLaren	47 laps/electrical	2	1m26.154s	16!
R	**Romain Grosjean**	Lotus	1 lap/collision	0	1m25.054s	8
R	**Pastor Maldonado**	Lotus	1 lap/collision	0	1m24.525s	10

FASTEST LAP: HAMILTON, 1M26.672S, 149.512MPH/240.617KPH ON LAP 48 • RACE LEADERS: HAMILTON 1–53
* 3-PLACE GRID PENALTY FOR IMPEDING ANOTHER DRIVER, • ** 5-PLACE GRID PENALTY FOR EXCESS POWER UNIT USE
! 10-PLACE GRID PENALTY FOR EXCESS POWER UNIT USE • !! 20-PLACE GRID PENALTY FOR EXCESS POWER UNIT USE
!!! 35-PLACE GRID PENALTY FOR EXCESS POWER UNIT USE • ^ 50-PLACE GRID PENALTY FOR EXCESS POWER UNIT USE

With Mercedes off form, Sebastian Vettel triumphed for Ferrari, but the night time street race was a strange one as the safety car had to be deployed when a spectator took a stroll on the circuit. It closed the field up, but did it spoil Daniel Ricciardo's charge?

The signs had been there in the heat of the Malaysian GP, when Ferrari made its cars work better than Mercedes could on its tyres, and there was an even more marked advantage to Ferrari in Singapore. In fact, Red Bull also had the upper hand over Mercedes, outqualifying Hamilton and Rosberg with ease. Mercedes was perplexed and many felt that it simply couldn't get Pirelli's supersoft tyres into their best performance window in the high temperatures. This left Hamilton and Rosberg fifth and sixth on the grid.

Starting from pole position, Vettel got his Ferrari to Turn 1 first, followed by Ricciardo, Raikkonen and Kvyat.

The first safety car intervention came on lap 13, after a clash between Hulkenberg's Force India and Massa's Williams at Turn 3.

The safety car was called out again on lap 37 when a spectator was spotted walking along the edge of the track. Ricciardo reckoned that each deployment came at a time when he had a performance advantage over Vettel, thus costing him, but we will never know and the result was that he was forced to accept second place. His performance showed that his RB11's Renault engine wasn't as bad as the team had been making it out to be.

Raikkonen finished a distant third, 7s clear of Rosberg, who continued to struggle in race trim. At least the German finished, as Hamilton failed to score after losing fourth place when his engine lost power.

Kvyat lost position to the Mercedes drivers when the safety car first came out and another place to Bottas when it returned, and so ended up sixth.

With the drive of the race, Verstappen went on the charge after stalling on the grid and getting away last. Amazingly, he was up to eighth with two laps to go, but was struggling to pass Perez. Toro Rosso asked him to let team-mate Carlos Sainz Jr through to have a try and he refused.

106

Ricciardo joins Ferrari's Vettel and Raikkonen on the podium after a rare stutter by Mercedes.

MARINA BAY ROUND 13   DATE: 20 SEPTEMBER 2015

Laps: **61** • Distance: **191.896 miles/308.828km** • Weather: **Hot & humid**

Pos	Driver	Team	Result	Stops	Qualifying Time	Grid
1	Sebastian Vettel	Ferrari	2h01m22.118s	2	1m43.885s	1
2	Daniel Ricciardo	Red Bull	2h01m23.596s	2	1m44.428s	2
3	Kimi Raikkonen	Ferrari	2h01m39.272s	2	1m44.667s	3
4	Nico Rosberg	Mercedes	2h01m46.838s	2	1m45.415s	6
5	Valtteri Bottas	Williams	2h01m56.322s	2	1m45.676s	7
6	Daniil Kvyat	Red Bull	2h01m57.626s	2	1m44.745s	4
7	Sergio Perez	Force India	2h02m12.954s	2	1m46.385s	13
8	Max Verstappen	Toro Rosso	2h02m13.568s	2	1m45.798s	8
9	Carlos Sainz Jr	Toro Rosso	2h02m14.978s	3	1m46.894s	14
10	Felipe Nasr	Sauber	2h02m52.163s	2	1m46.965s	16
11	Marcus Ericsson	Sauber	2h02m59.625s	3	1m47.088s	17
12	Pastor Maldonado	Lotus	2h02m59.836s	3	1m47.323s	18
13	Romain Grosjean	Lotus	59 laps/saving gearbox	2	1m46.413s	10
14	Alexander Rossi	Marussia	59 laps	2	1m51.523s	20*
15	Will Stevens	Marussia	59 laps	2	1m51.021s	19*
R	Jenson Button	McLaren	52 laps/gearbox	3	1m47.019s	15
R	Fernando Alonso	McLaren	33 laps/gearbox	1	1m46.328s	12
R	Lewis Hamilton	Mercedes	32 laps/power unit	1	1m45.300s	5
R	Felipa Massa	Williams	30 laps/power unit	3	1m46.077s	9
R	Nico Hulkenberg	Force India	12 laps/collision	1	1m46.305s	11

FASTEST LAP: **RICCIARDO, 1M50.041S, 102.962MPH/165.701KPH ON LAP 52** • RACE LEADERS: **VETTEL 1–61**
* 5-PLACE GRID PENALTY FOR REPLACING GEARBOX

JAPANESE GP

Victory at the Japanese GP moved Lewis Hamilton on to 41 wins, to equal the final tally of his childhood hero Ayrton Senna. He showed equal determination in forcing his way past his team-mate Nico Rosberg on the opening lap at Suzuka to achieve it.

Rosberg claimed his second pole of 2015, but was given a helping hand as Daniil Kvyat crashed approaching the hairpin and brought out the red flags to end the session before his rivals had started their final runs.

Hamilton was less than happy about that, but he assumed a lead he thought was rightfully his before the opening lap was three corners old. Hamilton grabbed the inside line into Turn 1 and then ran side-by-side with Rosberg both through there and the following right-hander. Rosberg went wide, and was demoted by Sebastian Vettel and Valtteri Bottas He did get back past them, but not for several laps, by which time Hamilton was too far clear to be caught.

There are often incidents on the opening lap at Suzuka, and 2015 was no different, as Felipe Massa's Williams was hit by Daniel Ricciardo when the Australian tried to guide his Red Bull between the Williams and Raikkonen's Ferrari in a quest to grab fourth on the run to the first corner, and their slow return to the pit ended any hopes of points.

So, even though both Mercedes drivers were delighted that their team was back on form after its dip in Singapore, only one of them was smiling broadly afterwards: Hamilton, who was 19s clear at flag-fall.

Vettel displayed strong race form again and remained close enough to worry Rosberg in the latter stages, ending up just 1.8s adrift. Kimi Raikkonen collected the 12 points for fourth place, after undercutting Bottas at their second pitstops, ending up 13s down on his team-mate.

After being pushed back three places on the grid for his contact with Massa at the Singapore GP, Nico Hulkenberg drove well to rise from 13th to sixth. Having felt that he was being delayed by the Lotus duo, Force India brought Nico in early for his first pitstop, and the undercut worked in his favour. For Romain Grosjean and Pastor Maldonado, their haul of ten points for beleaguered Lotus was most welcome.

SUZUKA ROUND 14

DATE: **27 SEPTEMBER 2015**

Laps: **53** • Distance: **191.053 miles/307.471km** • Weather: **Hot & overcast**

Pos	Driver	Team	Result	Stops	Qualifying Time	Grid
1	Lewis Hamilton	Mercedes	1h28m06.508s	2	1m32.660s	2
2	Nico Rosberg	Mercedes	1h28m25.472s	2	1m32.584s	1
3	Sebastian Vettel	Ferrari	1h28m27.358s	2	1m33.245s	4
4	Kimi Raikkonen	Ferrari	1h28m40.276s	2	1m33.347s	6
5	Valtteri Bottas	Williams	1h28m43.254s	2	1m33.204s	3
6	Nico Hulkenberg	Force India	1h29m02.067s	2	1m34.390s	13*
7	Romain Grosjean	Lotus	1h29m18.806s	2	1m33.967s	8
8	Pastor Maldonado	Lotus	1h29m20.083s	2	1m34.497s	11
9	Max Verstappen	Toro Rosso	1h29m41.823s	2	No time	17*
10	Carlos Sainz Jr	Toro Rosso	52 laps	2	1m34.453s	10
11	Fernando Alonso	McLaren	52 laps	2	1m34.785s	12
12	Sergio Perez	Force India	52 laps	3	No time	9
13	Daniil Kvyat	Red Bull	52 laps	3	No time	20**
14	Marcus Ericsson	Sauber	52 laps	2	1m35.673s	15
15	Daniel Ricciardo	Red Bull	52 laps	2	1m33.497s	7
16	Jenson Button	McLaren	52 laps	2	1m35.664s	14
17	Felipe Massa	Williams	51 laps	3	1m33.337s	5
18	Alexander Rossi	Marussia	51 laps	2	1m47.114s	19
19	Will Stevens	Marussia	50 laps	3	1m38.783s	18
R	Felipe Nasr	Sauber	49 laps/Handling	2	1m35.760s	16

FASTEST LAP: : HAMILTON, 1M36.145S, 135.107MPH/217.434KPH ON LAP 33 • RACE LEADERS: HAMILTON 1-53
* 3-PLACE GRID PENALTY FOR SINGAPORE GP COLLISION • ** STARTED FROM THE PIT LANE

Hamilton (on the left) and pole-starter Rosberg charge side-by-side to the opening corner.

A throttle pedal problem for Nico Rosberg early in the race left Lewis Hamilton clear to take a win that put him on the verge of his third title, but he had to endure a scare that required intense monitoring when the team detected a problem with his car's rear wing.

For the third round in a row, Lewis Hamilton failed to claim pole position. As at Suzuka, it went instead to his Mercedes team-mate Nico Rosberg. This was imperative for the German in his quest to keep any fading hopes he may have had of winning the championship alive and the margin of a third of a second was an impressive one.

Rosberg duly converted this into the lead of the race. At Turn 2, though, there was incident, as slow-starting Nico Hulkenberg attempted to make up the ground he lost to his Force India team-mate Sergio Perez and spun, only to be clipped by Max Verstappen and Marcus Ericsson, with the Swede joining him on the sidelines as the safety car was deployed.

Only a few laps later, though, the race had its third retirement, and it was a key one. It was Rosberg, who was forced out by a sliding throttle pedal. This promoted Hamilton into the lead, Valtteri Bottas to second and Kimi Raikkonen to third. Then the safety car was brought into action again, as there had been a huge accident after Romain Grosjean dropped his Lotus out of Turn 3. He admitted that he took his hands off the steering wheel and closed his eyes once he'd lost control and felt he was fortunate to walk away from it.

Once the safety car withdrew, Hamilton had proceedings under control and Sebastian Vettel rose to second once they'd all made their one planned pitstop. Behind him, Perez had advanced to third by dint of making his one pitstop nearly 20 laps earlier during the second safety car period.

This left Daniel Ricciardo fourth, but he wasn't to remain there, his Red Bull RB11 retiring with a suspension failure. So Bottas and Raikkonen came back into the picture, and both passed Perez on the penultimate lap, only for Raikkonen to take a lunge at Bottas into Turn 4 at the last time of asking and punted the Williams into the wall. So, Perez made the podium after all.

SOCHI ROUND 15

DATE: **11 OCTOBER 2015**

Laps: **53** • Distance: **192.602 miles/309.963km** • Weather: **Overcast but warm**

Pos	Driver	Team	Result	Stops	Qualifying Time	Grid
1	**Lewis Hamilton**	Mercedes	1h37m11.024s	1	1m37.433s	2
2	**Sebastian Vettel**	Ferrari	1h37m16.977s	1	1m37.965s	4
3	**Sergio Perez**	Force India	1h37m39.942s	1	1m38.691s	7
4	**Felipe Massa**	Williams	1h37m49.855s	1	1m39.895s	15
5	**Daniil Kvyat**	Red Bull	1h37m58.590s	1	1m39.214s	11
6	**Felipe Nasr**	Sauber	1h38m07.532s	1	1m39.323s	12
7	**Pastor Maldonado**	Lotus	1h38m12.112s	1	1m39.811s	14
8	**Kimi Raikkonen**	Ferrari	1h38m23.382s	1	1m38.348s	5
9	**Jenson Button**	McLaren	1h38m30.491s	1	1m39.763s	13
10	**Max Verstappen**	Toro Rosso	1h38m39.448s	2	1m38.964s	9
11	**Fernando Alonso**	McLaren	1h38m42.234s	1	1m40.144s	19**
12	**Valtteri Bottas**	Williams	52 laps/collision	1	1m37.912s	3
13	**Roberto Mehri**	Marussia	52 laps	1	1m43.804s	18*
14	**Will Stevens**	Marussia	51 laps	2	1m43.693s	17
15	**Daniel Ricciardo**	Red Bull	47 laps/suspension	1	1m39.728s	10
R	**Carlos Sainz Jr**	Toro Rosso	45 laps/brakes	1	no time	20*
R	**Romain Grosjean**	Lotus	11 laps/spun off	1	1m38.787s	8
R	**Nico Rosberg**	Mercedes	7 laps/throttle	0	1m37.113s	1
R	**Nico Hulkenberg**	Force India	0 laps/collision	0	1m38.659s	6
R	**Marcus Ericsson**	Sauber	0 laps/collision	0	1m40.660s	16

FASTEST LAP: VETTEL, 1M40.071S, 130.723MPH/210.378KPH ON LAP 51 • RACE LEADERS: ROSBERG 1–6, HAMILTON 7–53
* 20-PLACE GRID PENALTY FOR USING EXTRA POWER UNITS • ** 35-PLACE GRID PENALTY FOR USING EXTRA POWER UNITS

Hamilton, in typical Cossack hat, celebrates the win that put him on the brink of a third title.

UNITED STATES GP

Lewis Hamilton was smiling after the race as his victory gave him his third drivers' title. Nico Roberg was not smiling. He was furious, as Hamilton had pushed him out of the way at the first corner on the opening lap and he later ceded the lead by going wide at Turn 12.

The third worst hurricane on record hit Mexico and brought heavy rain to Texas. It was thought unlikely that the race would go ahead but, with qualifying delayed until Sunday, everything got back on track, and Nico Rosberg made it three poles in a row.

To be sure of landing his third F1 title, Lewis Hamilton needed to win, so he pounced after Rosberg had made a poor start. Not only did he force his way up the inside into Turn 1, but he pushed Rosberg wide at the exit and the Red Bulls came by too. After the race, Mercedes would agree with Rosberg that the move had been too robust, but Hamilton was determined not to back down.

Daniil Kvyat and Daniel Ricciardo weren't prepared to let Hamilton escape. There was then a virtual safety car period as debris from lap 1 contact at Turn 1 between Fernando Alonso and Valtteri Bottas was cleared. Fired up, Rosberg went straight back to second when the period ended, but Kvyat then attacked Rosberg at Turn 20, both slid wide and Ricciardo assumed the position.

The Australian set about catching Hamilton and passed him on lap 15. Four laps later, Rosberg went by as well, then Hamilton pitted for slicks. Ricciardo stayed out for a further four laps before doing so. After the stops, Rosberg assumed the lead, but was delayed when the safety car came out for Marcus Ericsson's Sauber to be cleared. Rosberg streaked clear when the green flag was flown, before another virtual safety car period after Nico Hulkenberg's front wing failed and he clattered into Ricciardo. A few laps later, Kvyat brought the safety car out for a second time by crashing and Rosberg looked to have got it right again when they were released but, under pressure from Hamilton, slid straight on at Turn 12 and lost the lead. Then came another challenge, a charge from Sebastian Vettel, who had started 13th. He got right under Rosberg's wing, but could never find a way past and so the 2015 title was settled.

Hamilton emerges from the first corner in front, while Rosberg scrabbles to rejoin the track.

CIRCUIT OF THE AMERICAS ROUND 16

DATE: **25 OCTOBER 2015**

Laps: **56** • Distance: **191.634 miles/308.405km** • Weather: **Overcast & wet then drying**

Pos	Driver	Team	Result	Stops	Qualifying Time	Grid
1	**Lewis Hamilton**	Mercedes	1h50m52.703s	2	1m56.929s	2
2	**Nico Rosberg**	Mercedes	1h50m55.553s	2	1m56.824s	1
3	**Sebastian Vettel**	Ferrari	1h50m56.084s	3	1m58.596s	13**
4	**Max Verstappen**	Toro Rosso	1h51m15.062s	2	2m00.199s	8
5	**Sergio Perez**	Force India	1h51m17.116s	2	1m59.210s	5
6	**Jenson Button**	McLaren	1h51m20.761s	3	2m01.193s	11
7	**Carlos Sainz Jr**	Toro Rosso	1h51m23.322s***	3	2m07.304s	20
8	**Pastor Maldonado**	Lotus	1h51m24.976s	3	2m01.604s	12
9	**Felipe Nasr**	Sauber	1h51m32.960s	5	2m03.194s	15
10	**Daniel Ricciardo**	Red Bull	1h51m46.074s	3	1m57.969s	3
11	**Fernando Alonso**	McLaren	1h51m47.519s	3	2m00.265s	9
12	**Alexander Rossi**	Marussia	1h52m07.980s	3	2m04.176s	17
R	**Daniil Kvyat**	Red Bull	41 laps/spun off	2	1m58.434s	4
R	**Nico Hulkenberg**	Force India	35 laps/collision	2	1m59.333s	6
R	**Marcus Ericsson**	Sauber	25 laps/electrical	2	2m02.212s	14
R	**Kimi Raikkonen**	Ferrari	25 laps/brakes	2	1m59.703s	18**
R	**Felipe Massa**	Williams	23 laps/damper	1	1m59.999s	7
R	**Romain Grosjean**	Lotus	10 laps/crash damage	2	2m00.595s	10
R	**Valtteri Bottas**	Williams	5 laps/damper	2	2m00.334s	16*
R	**Will Stevens**	Marussia	1 lap/collision	0	2m04.526s	19!

FASTEST LAP: **ROSBERG, 1M40.666S, 122.506MPH/197.154KPH ON LAP 49** • RACE LEADERS: HAMILTON 1-14, 39-43, 48-56; RICCIARDO 15-21; ROSBERG 22-38, 44-47 • * 5-PLACE GRID PENALTY FOR CHANGING THE GEARBOX • ** 10-PLACE GRID PENALTY FOR USING ADDITIONAL POWER UNIT • ! 20-PLACE GRID PENALTY FOR USING ADDITIONAL POWER UNIT • *** 5S PENALTY FOR SPEEDING IN THE PITLANE

MEXICAN GP

This return to Mexico was a shot in the arm for F1 as the fans came in their hundreds of thousands and clearly loved being part of the show. On track, Rosberg qualified on pole again and came out on top over an unhappy Hamilton, who wasn't allowed to change strategy.

Pole, fastest lap and victory for Nico Rosberg suggest that he'd rediscovered his winning ways after an eight-race drought. However, Lewis Hamilton said that Mercedes was being "warm" to Nico – in other words favouring him.

Rosberg had a lead of 2.9s when he came in for the second of their two planned pitstops on lap 46. Then Hamilton was told to come in next time around and queried why, reckoning that this was his best chance to move ahead. So he stayed out for an extra lap before coming in, as the team talked of tyres being at their limit. Rosberg duly raced on to win as a furious Hamilton was kept in second.

The Red Bulls gave chase early on, Daniil Kvyat ahead of Daniel Ricciardo, but they couldn't match the Mercedes for pace. Behind them there had been a clash at the first corner, as Sebastian Vettel came across on Ricciardo and his Ferrari ended up with a right rear puncture. Vettel's race was not to get much better, as he had a spin as he regained positions after his pitstop, then he crashed out late in the race when still outside the points.

He wasn't the only one in the wars, as Raikkonen and Bottas came together as they had in Sochi. This time, with Raikkonen running sixth, as he had yet to pit, he was caught and on the verge of being passed fairly, but pulled across when Bottas was fully alongside. Raikkonen was out on the spot, but Bottas kept going and would end the day third after jumping Ricciardo when the safety car that came out while Vettel's Ferrari was shifted from its resting place at Turn 7 withdrew from the circuit

Although he finished only eighth after pitting just once for new tyres, Sergio Perez still earned the loudest cheer of the day for his feat of keeping cars on fresher rubber behind him after the safety car period bunched the field. Mexico loves F1 and it wasn't only Perez who appreciated their support.

Rosberg celebrates his first win since June, while Hamilton contemplates being runner-up.

MEXICO CITY ROUND 17

DATE: **1 NOVEMBER 2015**

Laps: **71** • Distance: **190 miles/305.354km** • Weather: **Warm & bright**

Pos	Driver	Team	Result	Stops	Qualifying Time	Grid
1	**Nico Rosberg**	Mercedes	1h42m35.038s	2	1m19.480s	1
2	**Lewis Hamilton**	Mercedes	1h42m36.992s	2	1m19.668s	2
3	**Valtteri Bottas**	Williams	1h42m49.630s	2	1m20.448s	6
4	**Daniil Kvyat**	Red Bull	1h42m51.610s	2	1m20.398s	4
5	**Daniel Ricciardo**	Red Bull	1h42m54.720s	2	1m20.399s	5
6	**Felipe Massa**	Williams	1h42m56.531s	2	1m20.567s	7
7	**Nico Hulkenberg**	Force India	1h43m00.898s	2	1m20.788s	10
8	**Sergio Perez**	Force India	1h43m09.381s	1	1m20.716s	9
9	**Max Verstappen**	Toro Rosso	1h43m10.267s	2	1m20.710s	8
10	**Romain Grosjean**	Lotus	1h43m12.972s	2	1m21.038s	12
11	**Pastor Maldonado**	Lotus	1h43m13.576s	2	1m21.261s	13
12	**Marcus Ericsson**	Sauber	1h43m15.218s	3	1m21.544s	14
13	**Carlos Sainz Jr**	Toro Rosso	1h43m23.810s	3	1m20.942s	11
14	**Jenson Button**	McLaren	1h43m24.252s	2	no time	20!
15	**Alexander Rossi**	Marussia	69 laps	2	1m24.136s	16
16	**Will Stevens**	Marussia	69 laps	2	1m24.386s	17
R	**Felipe Nasr**	Sauber	57 laps/brakes	3	1m21.788s	15
R	**Sebastian Vettel**	Ferrari	50 laps/spun off	2	1m19.850s	3
R	**Kimi Raikkonen**	Ferrari	21 laps/collision	0	1m22.494s	19**
R	**Fernando Alonso**	McLaren	1 lap/power unit	0	1m21.779s	18*

FASTEST LAP: **ROSBERG, 1M20.521 2S, 119.568MPH/192.426KPH ON LAP 67** • RACE LEADERS: **ROSBERG 1-25, 29-45, 49-71; HAMILTON 26-28, 46-48** *** 15-PLACE GRID PENALTY FOR USING EXTRA POWER UNIT ELEMENT & CHANGING GEARBOX • ** 35-PLACE GRID PENALTY FOR USING EXTRA POWER UNIT ELEMENTS & CHANGING GEARBOX • ! 55-PLACE GRID PENALTY FOR USING EXTRA POWER UNIT ELEMENTS**

BRAZILIAN GP

Lewis Hamilton was desperate to win in Brazil – the home of his childhood hero, Ayrton Senna – but it wasn't to be. Nico Rosberg led from the start and the team kept them on the same pitstop pattern, depriving Hamilton the chance to attack. No one else was in the hunt.

With the 2015 title already his, Lewis Hamilton was keen to achieve another ambition: to win the home grand prix of his childhood hero, Ayrton Senna. This quest didn't start well, as he arrived a day later than planned after colliding with a few parked cars in Monaco, when coming home from a party. Yet, he was still able to lap fastest in the first two practice sessions.

On the Saturday, team-mate Nico Rosberg moved ahead and was able to claim his fifth pole in succession. With Hamilton just under 0.1s behind, it was close, but not for those trying to keep up, with Ferrari's Sebastian Vettel all but a further half second slower.

Unable to beat Rosberg on the run to the first corner, ending up being squeezed in the outside line, Hamilton had to tuck in behind Rosberg and that was how they ran to their first pitstops. During the second stint, convinced that he was faster than Rosberg, Hamilton looked to have his strategy changed, as he felt there was no way to take the lead without doing so. The team said no and their order remained the same all the way to the finish. Team boss Toto Wolff disagreed with Hamilton's requests to change the timing of his pitstops, saying that, "Lewis would lose every time if he decided his own strategy."

The Mercedes were so dominant that Vettel could only aim at finishing third, which he managed with ease. Opting for a two-stop strategy rather than three, Kimi Raikkonen claimed fourth, half a minute further adrift, with fellow Finn Valtteri Bottas taking fifth. Felipe Massa wasn't so lucky in the second Williams, as he lost eighth place as his car's tyre temperatures on the grid before the race were 27 degrees higher than allowed.

Having qualified his Force India fifth, Nico Hulkenberg went on to finish sixth after a good battle with Daniil Kvyat. The other Red Bull ended up out of the points, as Daniel Ricciardo could only advance from 19th on the grid as high as 11th.

INTERLAGOS ROUND 18

DATE: 15 NOVEMBER 2015

Laps: **71** • Distance: **190.083 miles/305.909km** • Weather: **Hot & humid**

Pos	Driver	Team	Result	Stops	Qualifying Time	Grid
1	Nico Rosberg	Mercedes	1h31m09.090s	3	1m11.282s	1
2	Lewis Hamilton	Mercedes	1h31m16.846s	3	1m11.360s	2
3	Sebastian Vettel	Ferrari	1h31m23.334s	3	1m11.804s	3
4	Kimi Raikkonen	Ferrari	1h31m56.633s	2	1m12.144s	4
5	Valtteri Bottas	Williams	70 laps	2	1m12.085s	7*
6	Nico Hulkenberg	Force India	70 laps	2	1m12.265s	5
7	Daniil Kvyat	Red Bull	70 laps	2	1m12.322s	6
8	Romain Grosjean	Lotus	70 laps	3	1m13.913s	14
9	Max Verstappen	Toro Rosso	70 laps	3	1m12.739s	9
10	Pastor Maldonado	Lotus	70 laps	2	1m13.385s	15
11	Daniel Ricciardo	Red Bull	70 laps	3	1m12.417s	19!
12	Sergio Perez	Force India	70 laps	3	1m13.147s	11
13	Felipe Nasr	Sauber	70 laps	2	1m12.989s	13**
14	Jenson Button	McLaren	70 laps	3	1m13.425s	16
15	Fernando Alonso	McLaren	70 laps	3	no time	20!!
16	Marcus Ericsson	Sauber	69 laps	3	1m13.233s	12
17	Will Stevens	Marussia	67 laps	2	1m16.283s	18
18	Alexander Rossi	Marussia	67 laps	2	1m16.151s	17
D	Felipe Massa	Williams	70 laps/ excess tyre temperature	3	1m12.415s	8
R	Carlos Sainz Jr	Toro Rosso	0 laps/electrical	0	1m13.045s	10^

FASTEST LAP: HAMILTON, 1M14.832S, 128.808MPH/207.296KPH ON LAP 51 • RACE LEADERS: ROSBERG 1-12, 15-32, 35-47, 50-71; HAMILTON 13-14, 33-34, 48-49 • * 3-PLACE GRID PENALTY FOR OVERTAKING NUNDER RED FLAGS, • ** 3-PLACE GRID PENALTY FOR IMPEDING MASSA IN QUALIFYING • ! 20-PLACE GRID PENALTY FOR USING ADDITIONAL POWER UNIT ELEMENTS • !! 25-PLACE GRID PENALTY FOR USING ADDITIONAL POWER UNIT ELEMENTS • ^ STARTED FROM PITLANE

The drivers line up on the grid for a confused minute's silence after the Paris massacres.

ABU DHABI GP

Nico Rosberg rounded out 2015 by completing a hat-trick of poles and wins, with Lewis Hamilton again trying to adapt his race strategy to get ahead and failing. With Sebastian Vettel starting 15th, Kimi Raikkonen claimed his third podium of the year.

When Nico Rosberg took pole on F1's return to Mexico in the 17th round, he regained a little pride he had lost after Mercedes team-mate Lewis Hamilton had clinched his third F1 title. Going on to win, with Hamilton frustrated to be running behind, was a further fillip. Repeating this feat in Brazil showed this was no fluke, and so he was delighted when he made it six poles in the final six rounds in Abu Dhabi.

Key to Rosberg's race was making a good start and so it proved at Yas Marina, as the German was easily first into the opening corner, while Hamilton had to defend rather than attack as he came under pressure from Kimi Raikkonen and Sergio Perez. Thereafter, it was a case of déjà vu, with Hamilton having to try to out-think his rival.

The opening lap wasn't without incident, as Pastor Maldonado was punted off by Fernando Alonso, with the Spaniard insisting that this was the result of a push from behind by Felipe Nasr. Maldonado's Lotus was out on the spot and Alonso was hit with a drive-through penalty.

Hamilton realized he was going to have play the long game and made a decision to run a second stint ten laps longer than Rosberg's in order to have a shorter run to the finish on his third set of tyres. He had even asked his race engineer if it would be possible to run to the finish without making a second stop, but was ordered not to try it. Giving chase, he closed in, but it looked as though Rosberg always had enough in hand. The chase was then scuppered by Max Verstappen delaying Hamilton for a lap, for which the Dutch teenager was hit with a 20s time penalty.

Ferrari took third and fourth, with Raikkonen claiming the final step on the podium and Sebastian Vettel doing well to advance from 15th on the grid after the team banked on a lap in the first qualifying session being good enough to go through to Q2 and it wasn't.

YAS MARINA ROUND 19

DATE: **29 NOVEMBER 2015**

Laps: **55** • Distance: **189.805 miles/305.462km** • Weather: **Hot & dry**

Pos	Driver	Team	Result	Stops	Qualifying Time	Grid
1	**Nico Rosberg**	Mercedes	1h38m30.175s	2	1m40.237s	1
2	**Lewis Hamilton**	Mercedes	1h38m38.446s	2	1m40.614s	2
3	**Kimi Raikkonen**	Ferrari	1h38m49.605s	2	1m41.051s	3
4	**Sebastian Vettel**	Ferrari	1h39m13.910s	2	1m42.941s	15
5	**Sergio Perez**	Force India	1h39m34.127s	2	1m41.184s	4
6	**Daniel Ricciardo**	Red Bull	1h39m35.185s	2	1m41.444s	5
7	**Nico Hulkenberg**	Force India	1h40m03.793s	2	1m41.686s	7
8	**Felipe Massa**	Williams	1h40m07.926s	2	1m41.759s	8
9	**Romain Grosjean**	Lotus	1h40m08.376s	2	no time	18*
10	**Daniel Kvyat**	Red Bull	1h40m12.546s	2	1m41.933s	9
11	**Carlos Sainz Jr**	Toro Rosso	1h40m13.700s	2	1m42.708s	10
12	**Jenson Button**	McLaren	54 laps	2	1m42.668s	12
13	**Valtteri Bottas**	Williams	54 laps	3	1m41.656s	6
14	**Marcus Ericsson**	Sauber	54 laps	2	1m43.838s	17
15	**Felipe Nasr**	Sauber	54 laps	3	1m43.614s	14
16	**Max Verstappen**	Toro Rosso	54 laps!!	3	1m42.521s	11
17	**Fernando Alonso**	McLaren	53 laps	4	1m43.187s	16
18	**Will Stevens**	Marussia	53 laps	2	1m46.297s	19**
19	**Roberto Mehri**	Marussia	52 laps	1	1m47.434s	20!
R	**Pastor Maldonado**	Lotus	0 laps/collision	0	1m42.807s	13

FASTEST LAP: HAMILTON, 1M44.517S, 118.869MPH/191.302KPH ON LAP 44 • RACE LEADERS: ROSBERG 1-10, 12-30, 42-55; HAMILTON 11, 31-41
* 5-PLACE GRID PENALTY FOR CHANGING GEARBOX • ** 5-PLACE GRID PENALTY FOR FITTING ADDITIONAL POWER UNIT ELEMENT
! STARTED FROM THE PITLANE AFTER CAR MODIFIED IN PARC FERME • !! PENALISED 5S FOR GAINING AN ADVANTAGE BY LEAVING TRACK & 20S
FOR IGNORING BLUE FLAGS

Three wins on the trot gave Rosberg plenty of reasons to smile as he ended the year in style.

113

The two Mercedes cars, Nico Rosberg's left, sit in front of the podium after the Abu Dhabi Grand Prix. World Champion Lewis Hamilton, white cap, and Kimi Raikkonen, red, are about to be joined by the race-winning German.

An elated Lewis Hamilton, flying the flag, waves to his supporters at the Circuit of the Americas in Texas after his win in the United States GP guaranteed he would be World Champion for the third time in 2015.

FINAL RESULTS 2015

POS	DRIVER	NAT		CAR ENGINE	R1	R2	R3	R4	R5
1	LEWIS HAMILTON	GBR		MERCEDES F1 W06	1PF	2P	1PF	1P	2F
2	NICO ROSBERG	GER		MERCEDES F1 W06	2	3F	2	3	1P
3	SEBASTIAN VETTEL	GER		FERRARI SF15-T	3	1	3	5	3
4	KIMI RAIKKONEN	FIN		FERRARI SF15-T	R	4	4	2F	5
5	VALTTERI BOTTAS	FIN		WILLIAMS-MERCEDES FW37	NS	5	6	4	4
6	FELIPE MASSA	BRA		WILLIAMS-MERCEDES FW37	4	6	5	10	6
7	DANIIL KYVAT	RUS		RED BULL-RENAULT RB11	NS	9	R	9	10
8	DANIEL RICCIARDO	AUS		RED BULL-RENAULT RB11	6	10	9	6	7
9	SERGIO PEREZ	MEX		FORCE INDIA-MERCEDES VJM08	10	13	11	8	13
10	NICO HULKENBERG	GER		FORCE INDIA-MERCEDES VJM08	7	14	R	13	15
11	ROMAIN GROSJEAN	FRA		LOTUS-MERCEDES E23	R	11	7	7	8
12	MAX VERSTAPPEN	NED		TORO ROSSO-RENAULT STR10	R	7	17	R	11
13	FELIPE NASR	BRA		SAUBER-FERRARI C34	5	12	8	12	12
14	PASTOR MALDONADO	VEN		LOTUS-MERCEDES E23	R	R	R	15	R
15	CARLOS SAINZ JR	SPA		TORO ROSSO-RENAULT STR10	9	8	13	R	9
16	JENSON BUTTON	GBR		McLAREN-HONDA MP4-30	11	R	14	NS	16
17	FERNANDO ALONSO	SPA		McLAREN-HONDA MP4-30	-	R	12	11	R
18	MARCUS ERICSSON	SWE		SAUBER-FERRARI C34	8	R	10	14	14
19	ROBERTO MERHI	SPA		MARUSSIA-FERRARI MR03B	NQ	15	16	17	18
20	ALEXANDER ROSSI	USA		MARUSSIA-FERRARI MR03B	-	-	-	-	-
21	WILL STEVENS	GBR		MARUSSIA-FERRARI MR03B	NQ	NS	15	16	17
22	KEVIN MAGNUSSEN	DEN		McLAREN-HONDA MP4-30	NS	-	-	-	-

SCORING

1st	25 points
2nd	18 points
3rd	15 points
4th	12 points
5th	10 points
6th	8 points
7th	6 points
8th	4 points
9th	2 points
10th	1 point

POS	TEAM-ENGINE	R1	R2	R3	R4	R5
1	MERCEDES	1/2	2/3	1/2	1/3	1/2
2	FERRARI	3/R	1/4	3/4	2/5	3/5
3	WILLIAMS-MERCEDES	4/NS	5/6	5/6	4/10	4/6
4	RED BULL-RENAULT	6/NS	9/10	9/R	6/9	7/10
5	FORCE INDIA-MERCEDES	7/10	13/14	11/R	8/13	13/15
6	LOTUS-MERCEDES	R/R	11/R	7/R	7/15	8/R
7	TORO ROSSO-RENAULT	9/R	7/8	13/17	R/R	9/11
8	SAUBER-FERRARI	5/8	12/R	8/10	12/14	12/14
9	McLAREN-HONDA	11/NS	R/R	12/14	11/NS	16/R
10	MARUSSIA-FERRARI	NQ/NQ	15/NS	15/16	16/17	17/18

SYMBOLS AND GRAND PRIX KEY

ROUND 1................ AUSTRALIAN GP
ROUND 2.................MALAYSIAN GP
ROUND 3.................... CHINESE GP
ROUND 4..................BAHRAIN GP
ROUND 5..................... SPANISH GP

ROUND 6...................... MONACO GP
ROUND 7..................... CANADIAN GP
ROUND 8..................... AUSTRIAN GP
ROUND 9...................... BRITISH GP
ROUND 10 .... HUNGARIAN GP

ROUND 11 .... BELGIAN GP
ROUND 12 .... ITALIAN GP
ROUND 13 ....SINGAPORE GP
ROUND 14 ....JAPANESE GP
ROUND 15..................... RUSSIAN GP

ROUND 16 .... UNITED STATES GP
ROUND 17.................... MEXICAN GP
ROUND 18 .... BRAZILIAN GP
ROUND 19 .... ABU DHABI GP

D DISQUALIFIED   **F** FASTEST LAP   **NC** NOT CLASSIFIED   **NS** NON-STARTER   **P** POLE POSITION   **R** RETIRED   **W** WITHDRAWN

R6	R7	R8	R9	R10	R11	R12	R13	R14	R15	R16	R17	R18	R19	TOTAL
3P	1P	2P	1PF	6P	1P	1PF	R	1F	1	1	2	2F	2F	381
1	2	1F	2	8	2F	17	4	2P	RP	2PF	1PF	1P	1P	322
2	5	4	3	1	12	2	1P	3	2F	3	R	3	4	278
6	4F	R	8	R	7	5	3	4	8	R	R	4	3	150
14	3	5	5	13	9	4	5	5	12	R	3	5	13	136
15	6	3	4	12	6	3	R	17	4	R	6	D	8	121
4	9	12	6	2	4	10	6	13	5	R	4	7	10	95
5F	13	10	R	3F	R	8	2F	15	R	10	5	11	6	92
7	11	9	9	R	5	6	7	12	3	5	8	12	5	78
11	8	6	7	R	R	7	R	6	R	R	7	6	7	58
12	10	R	R	7	3	R	13	7	R	R	10	8	9	51
R	15	8	R	4	8	12	8	9	10	4	9	9	16	49
9	16	11	NS	11	11	13	10	R	6	9	R	13	15	27
R	7	7	R	14	R	R	12	8	7	8	11	10	R	27
10	12	R	R	R	R	11	9	10	R	7	13	R	11	18
8	R	R	R	9	14	14	R	16	9	6	14	14	12	16
R	R	R	10	5	13	18	R	11	11	11	R	15	17	11
13	14	13	11	10	10	9	11	14	R	R	12	16	14	9
16	R	14	12	15	15	16	-	-	13	-	-	-	19	0
-	-	-	-	-	-	14	18	-	12	15	18	-	-	0
17	17	R	13	16	16	15	15	19	14	R	16	17	18	0
-	-	-	-	-	-	-	-	-	-	-	-	-	-	0

117

R6	R7	R8	R9	R10	R11	R12	R13	R14	R15	R16	R17	R18	R19	TOTAL
1/3	1/2	1/2	1/2	6/8	1/2	1/17	4/R	1/2	1/R	1/2	1/2	1/2	1/2	703
2/6	4/5	4/R	3/8	1/R	7/12	2/5	1/3	3/4	2/8	3/R	R/R	3/4	3/4	428
14/15	3/6	3/5	4/5	12/13	6/9	3/4	5/R	5/17	4/12	R/R	3/6	5/D	8/13	257
4/5	9/13	10/12	6/R	2/3	4/R	8/10	2/6	13/15	5/R	10/R	4/5	7/11	6/10	187
7/11	8/11	6/9	7/9	R/R	5/R	6/7	7/R	6/12	3/R	5/R	7/8	6/12	5/7	136
12/R	7/10	7/R	R/R	7/14	3/R	R/R	12/13	7/8	7/R	8/R	10/11	8/10	9/R	78
10/R	12/15	8/R	R/R	4/R	8/R	11/12	8/9	9/10	10/R	4/7	9/13	9/R	11/16	67
9/13	14/16	11/13	11/NS	10/11	10/11	9/13	10/11	14/R	6/R	9/R	12/R	13/16	14/15	36
8/R	R/R	R/R	10/R	5/9	13/14	14/18	R/R	11/16	9/11	6/11	14/R	14/15	12/17	27
16/17	17/R	14/R	12/13	15/16	15/16	15/16	14/15	18/19	13/14	12/R	15/16	17/18	18/19	0

FORMULA ONE RECORDS

Rubens Barrichello wore a patriotically-liveried helmet for his 325th and final grand prix, on home ground at Interlagos, for Williams in 2011.

MOST STARTS

DRIVERS

325	Rubens Barrichello	(BRA)		Johnny Herbert	(GBR)
308	Michael Schumacher	(GER)	161	Ayrton Senna	(BRA)
285	Jenson Button	(GBR)	159	Heinz-Harald Frentzen	(GER)
256	Riccardo Patrese	(ITA)	158	Martin Brundle	(GBR)
	Jarno Trulli	(ITA)		Olivier Panis	(FRA)
254	Fernando Alonso	(SPA)		Sebastian Vettel	(GER)
247	David Coulthard	(GBR)	152	John Watson	(GBR)
232	Kimi Raikkonen	(FIN)	149	Rene Arnoux	(FRA)
230	Giancarlo Fisichella	(ITA)	147	Eddie Irvine	(GBR)
	Felipe Massa	(BRA)		Derek Warwick	(GBR)
216	Mark Webber	(AUS)	146	Carlos Reutemann	(ARG)
210	Gerhard Berger	(AUT)	144	Emerson Fittipaldi	(BRA)
208	Andrea de Cesaris	(ITA)	135	Jean-Pierre Jarier	(FRA)
204	Nelson Piquet	(BRA)	132	Eddie Cheever	(USA)
201	Jean Alesi	(FRA)		Clay Regazzoni	(SWI)
199	Alain Prost	(FRA)	128	Mario Andretti	(USA)
194	Michele Alboreto	(ITA)	126	Jack Brabham	(AUS)
187	Nigel Mansell	(GBR)	123	Ronnie Peterson	(SWE)
185	Nick Heidfeld	(GER)	119	Pierluigi Martini	(ITA)
	Nico Rosberg	(GER)	116	Damon Hill	(GBR)
180	Ralf Schumacher	(GER)		Jacky Ickx	(BEL)
176	Graham Hill	(GBR)		Alan Jones	(AUS)
175	Jacques Laffite	(FRA)	114	Keke Rosberg	(FIN)
171	Niki Lauda	(AUT)		Patrick Tambay	(FRA)
167	Lewis Hamilton	(GBR)	112	Denny Hulme	(NZL)
165	Jacques Villeneuve	(CDN)		Jody Scheckter	(RSA)
163	Thierry Boutsen	(BEL)			
162	Mika Hakkinen	(FIN)			

CONSTRUCTORS

908	Ferrari
781	McLaren
700	Williams
572	Lotus* (*nee* Toleman then Benetton then Renault*)
526	Toro Rosso (*nee* Minardi)
492	Lotus
435	Force India (*nee* Jordan then Midland then Spyker)
418	Tyrrell
409	Prost (*nee* Ligier)
402	Sauber (including BMW Sauber)
394	Brabham
383	Arrows
338	Red Bull (*nee* Stewart then Jaguar Racing)
303	Mercedes GP (*nee* BAR then Honda Racing then Brawn GP)
230	March
197	BRM
132	Osella
129	Renault

MOST WINS

DRIVERS

91	Michael Schumacher	(GER)	**14**	Jack Brabham	(AUS)	**9**	Mark Webber	(AUS)
51	Alain Prost	(FRA)		Emerson Fittipaldi	(BRA)	**8**	Denny Hulme	(NZL)
43	Lewis Hamilton	(GBR)		Graham Hill	(GBR)		Jacky Ickx	(BEL)
42	Sebastian Vettel	(GER)		Nico Rosberg	(GER)	**7**	Rene Arnoux	(FRA)
41	Ayrton Senna	(BRA)	**13**	Alberto Ascari	(ITA)		Juan Pablo Montoya	(COL)
31	Nigel Mansell	(GBR)		David Coulthard	(GBR)	**6**	Tony Brooks	(GBR)
27	Jackie Stewart	(GBR)	**12**	Mario Andretti	(USA)		Jacques Laffite	(FRA)
25	Jim Clark	(GBR)		Alan Jones	(AUS)		Riccardo Patrese	(ITA)
	Niki Lauda	(AUT)		Carlos Reutemann	(ARG)		Jochen Rindt	(AUT)
24	Juan Manuel Fangio	(ARG)	**11**	Rubens Barrichello	(BRA)		Ralf Schumacher	(GER)
23	Nelson Piquet	(BRA)		Felipe Massa	(BRA)		John Surtees	(GBR)
22	Damon Hill	(GBR)		Jacques Villeneuve	(CDN)		Gilles Villeneuve	(CDN)
20	Mika Hakkinen	(FIN)	**10**	Gerhard Berger	(AUT)			
	Kimi Raikkonen	(FIN)		James Hunt	(GBR)			
16	Stirling Moss	(GBR)		Ronnie Peterson	(SWE)			
15	Jenson Button	(GBR)		Jody Scheckter	(RSA)			

CONSTRUCTORS

224	Ferrari	**16**	Cooper	**1**	BMW Sauber
181	McLaren	**15**	Renault		Eagle
114	Williams	**10**	Alfa Romeo		Hesketh
79	Lotus	**9**	Ligier		Penske
51	Red Bull (including Stewart)		Maserati		Porsche
49	Lotus* (including Benetton, Renault II)		Matra		Shadow
45	Mercedes GP (including Honda Racing, Brawn GP)		Mercedes		Toro Rosso
			Vanwall		
35	Brabham	**4**	Jordan		
23	Tyrrell	**3**	March		
17	BRM		Wolf		
		2	Honda		

Jackie Stewart celebrates after winning the German GP in 1973. It was to be his 27th and last F1 win. Third-placed Jacky Ickx (right) looks on.

Jim Clark guides his Lotus through the Mexico City circuit's esses in 1967 after starting from pole position for the 32nd time (of 33).

DRIVERS

13	Michael Schumacher	2004		Ayrton Senna	1988		Jim Clark	1965
11	Lewis Hamilton	2014	**7**	Fernando Alonso	2005		Juan Manuel Fangio	1954
	Michael Schumacher	2002		Fernando Alonso	2006		Damon Hill	1994
	Sebastian Vettel	2011		Jim Clark	1963		James Hunt	1976
10	Lewis Hamilton	2015		Alain Prost	1984		Nigel Mansell	1987
9	Nigel Mansell	1992		Alain Prost	1988		Kimi Raikkonen	2007
	Michael Schumacher	1995		Alain Prost	1993		Nico Rosberg	2015
	Michael Schumacher	2000		Kimi Raikkonen	2005		Michael Schumacher	1998
	Michael Schumacher	2001		Ayrton Senna	1991		Michael Schumacher	2003
8	Mika Hakkinen	1998		Jacques Villeneuve	1997		Michael Schumacher	2006
	Damon Hill	1996	**6**	Mario Andretti	1978		Ayrton Senna	1989
	Michael Schumacher	1994		Alberto Ascari	1952		Ayrton Senna	1990

CONSTRUCTORS

16	Mercedes GP	2014	**9**	Ferrari	2001		Renault	2006
	Mercedes GP	2015		Ferrari	2006		Williams	1997
15	Ferrari	2002		Ferrari	2007	**7**	Ferrari	1952
	Ferrari	2004		McLaren	1998		Ferrari	1953
	McLaren	1988		Red Bull	2010		Ferrari	2008
12	McLaren	1984		Williams	1986		Lotus	1963
	Red Bull	2011		Williams	1987		Lotus	1973
	Williams	1996	**8**	Benetton	1994		McLaren	1999
11	Benetton	1995		Brawn GP	2009		McLaren	2000
10	Ferrari	2000		Ferrari	2003		McLaren	2012
	McLaren	2005		Lotus	1978		Red Bull	2012
	McLaren	1989		McLaren	1991		Tyrrell	1971
	Williams	1992		McLaren	2007		Williams	1991
	Williams	1993		Renault	2005		Williams	1994

MOST POLE POSITIONS

DRIVERS

68	Michael Schumacher	(GER)
65	Ayrton Senna	(BRA)
49	Lewis Hamilton	(GBR)
46	Sebastian Vettel	(GER)
33	Jim Clark	(GBR)
	Alain Prost	(FRA)
32	Nigel Mansell	(GBR)
29	Juan Manuel Fangio	(ARG)
26	Mika Hakkinen	(FIN)
24	Niki Lauda	(AUT)
	Nelson Piquet	(BRA)
22	Fernando Alonso	(SPA)
	Nico Rosberg	(GER)
20	Damon Hill	(GBR)
18	Mario Andretti	(USA)
	Rene Arnoux	(FRA)
17	Jackie Stewart	(GBR)
16	Felipe Massa	(BRA)
	Stirling Moss	(GBR)

	Kimi Raikkonen	(FIN)
14	Alberto Ascari	(ITA)
	Rubens Barrichello	(BRA)
	James Hunt	(GBR)
	Ronnie Peterson	(SWE)
13	Jack Brabham	(AUS)
	Graham Hill	(GBR)
	Jacky Ickx	(BEL)
	Juan Pablo Montoya	(COL)
	Jacques Villeneuve	(CDN)
12	Gerhard Berger	(AUT)
	David Coulthard	(GBR)
11	Mark Webber	(AUS)
10	Jochen Rindt	(AUT)

CONSTRUCTORS

208	Ferrari
154	McLaren
128	Williams
107	Lotus
58	Red Bull
53	Mercedes GP (including Brawn GP, Honda Racing, BAR)
39	Brabham
34	Lotus* (including Toleman, Benetton, Renault II)
31	Renault
14	Tyrrell
12	Alfa Romeo
11	BRM
	Cooper
10	Maserati
9	Ligier
8	Mercedes
7	Vanwall
5	March
4	Matra
3	Force India (including Jordan)
	Shadow
	Toyota
2	Lancia
1	BMW Sauber
	Toro Rosso

McLaren's Ayrton Senna and Alain Prost, here at Imola, won all but one of the 16 races in the 1988 season.

FASTEST LAPS

DRIVERS

76	Michael Schumacher	(GER)
42	Kimi Raikkonen	(FIN)
41	Alain Prost	(FRA)
30	Nigel Mansell	(GBR)
28	Jim Clark	(GBR)
	Lewis Hamilton	(GBR)
25	Mika Hakkinen	(FIN)
	Sebastian Vettel	(GER)
24	Niki Lauda	(AUT)
23	Juan Manuel Fangio	(ARG)
	Nelson Piquet	(BRA)
21	Fernando Alonso	(SPA)
	Gerhard Berger	(AUT)
19	Damon Hill	(GBR)
	Stirling Moss	(GBR)
	Ayrton Senna	(BRA)
	Mark Webber	(AUS)

18	David Coulthard	(GBR)
17	Rubens Barrichello	(BRA)
16	Felipe Massa	(BRA)
15	Clay Regazzoni	(SWI)
	Jackie Stewart	(GBR)
14	Jacky Ickx	(BEL)
	Nico Rosberg	(GER)
13	Alberto Ascari	(ITA)
	Alan Jones	(AUS)
	Riccardo Patrese	(ITA)
12	Rene Arnoux	(FRA)
	Jack Brabham	(AUS)
	Juan Pablo Montoya	(COL)
11	John Surtees	(GBR)

CONSTRUCTORS

232	Ferrari
152	McLaren
133	Williams
71	Lotus
54	Lotus* (including Toleman, Benetton, Renault II)
47	Red Bull
40	Brabham
32	Mercedes GP (including Brawn GP, BAR + Honda Racing)
22	Tyrrell
18	Renault
15	BRM
	Maserati
14	Alfa Romeo
13	Cooper
12	Matra
11	Prost (including Ligier)
9	Mercedes
7	March
6	Vanwall

MOST POINTS (THIS FIGURE IS GROSS TALLY, I.E. INCLUDING SCORES THAT WERE LATER DROPPED)

DRIVERS

1896	Sebastian Vettel	(GER)
1867	Lewis Hamilton	(GBR)
1778	Fernando Alonso	(SPA)
1566	Michael Schumacher	(GER)
1214	Jenson Button	(GBR)
1209.5	Nico Rosberg	(GER)
1174	Kimi Raikkonen	(FIN)
1071	Felipe Massa	(BRA)
1047.5	Mark Webber	(AUS)
798.5	Alain Prost	(FRA)
658	Rubens Barrichello	(BRA)
614	Ayrton Senna	(BRA)
535	David Coulthard	(GBR)
485.5	Nelson Piquet	(BRA)
482	Nigel Mansell	(GBR)
420.5	Niki Lauda	(AUT)
420	Mika Hakkinen	(FIN)
385	Gerhard Berger	(AUT)
360	Damon Hill	(GBR)
	Daniel Ricciardo	(AUS)

	Jackie Stewart	(GBR)
329	Ralf Schumacher	(GER)
326	Valtteri Bottas	(FIN)
310	Carlos Reutemann	(ARG)
307	Juan Pablo Montoya	(COL)
290	Nico Hulkenberg	(GER)
289	Graham Hill	(GBR)
287	Romain Grosjean	(FRA)
281	Emerson Fittipaldi	(BRA)
	Riccardo Patrese	(ITA)
277.5	Juan Manuel Fangio	(ARG)
275	Giancarlo Fisichella	(ITA)
274	Jim Clark	(GBR)
273	Robert Kubica	(POL)
266	Sergio Perez	(MEX)
261	Jack Brabham	(AUS)
259	Nick Heidfeld	(GER)
255	Jody Scheckter	(RSA)
248	Denny Hulme	(NZL)
246.5	Jarno Trulli	(ITA)

CONSTRUCTORS

6244.5	Ferrari
5017.5	McLaren
3338	Williams
3140.5	Red Bull (including Stewart, Jaguar Racing)
2788	Mercedes GP (including BAR, Honda Racing, Brawn GP)
2545.5	Lotus* (including Toleman, Benetton, Renault II)
1514	Lotus
919	Force India (including Jordan, Midland, Spyker)
854	Brabham
803	Sauber (including BMW Sauber)
617	Tyrrell
439	BRM
424	Prost (including Ligier)
333	Cooper
312	Renault
304	Toro Rosso
278.5	Toyota
171.5	March
167	Arrows
155	Matra

Sebastian Vettel scored on his debut in the 2007 US GP when he subbed for injured Robert Kubica and would go on to take four F1 titles.

MOST DRIVERS' TITLES

7	Michael Schumacher	(GER)		Alberto Ascari	(ITA)		Denny Hulme	(NZL)
5	Juan Manuel Fangio	(ARG)		Jim Clark	(GBR)		James Hunt	(GBR)
4	Alain Prost	(FRA)		Emerson Fittipaldi	(BRA)		Alan Jones	(AUS)
	Sebastian Vettel	(GER)		Mika Hakkinen	(FIN)		Nigel Mansell	(GBR)
3	Jack Brabham	(AUS)		Graham Hill	(GBR)		Kimi Raikkonen	(FIN)
	Lewis Hamilton	(GBR)	1	Mario Andretti	(USA)		Jochen Rindt	(AUT)
	Niki Lauda	(AUT)		Jenson Button	(GBR)		Keke Rosberg	(FIN)
	Nelson Piquet	(BRA)		Giuseppe Farina	(ITA)		Jody Scheckter	(RSA)
	Ayrton Senna	(BRA)		Mike Hawthorn	(GBR)		John Surtees	(GBR)
	Jackie Stewart	(GBR)		Damon Hill	(GBR)		Jacques Villeneuve	(CDN)
2	Fernando Alonso	(SPA)		Phil Hill	(USA)			

MOST CONSTRUCTORS' TITLES

16	Ferrari	2	Brabham		Brawn
9	Williams		Cooper		BRM
8	McLaren		Mercedes GP		Matra
7	Lotus		Renault		Tyrrell
4	Red Bull	1	Benetton		Vanwall

NOTE: To avoid confusion, the Lotus stats listed are based on the team that ran from 1958 to 1994, whereas the those listed as Lotus* are for the team based at Enstone that started as Toleman in 1981, became Benetton in 1986, then Renault II in 2002 and Lotus in 2012. The Renault listings are for the team that ran from 1977 to 1985, the stats for Red Bull Racing include those of the Stewart Grand Prix and Jaguar Racing teams from which it evolved, and those for Mercedes GP for the team that started as BAR in 1999, then ran as Honda GP from 2006 and as Brawn GP in 2009. Force India's stats include those of Jordan, Midland and Spyker, while Scuderia Toro Rosso's include those of its forerunner Minardi.

No circuit has a backdrop as beautiful as the Red Bull Ring in Austria, not that Marussia's Will Stevens had time to admire it in 2015.

2016 FILL-IN CHART

DRIVER	TEAM	Round 1 – 20 March AUSTRALIAN GP	Round 2 – 3 April BAHRAIN GP	Round 3 – 17 April CHINESE GP	Round 4 – 1 May RUSSIAN GP	Round 5 – 15 May SPANISH GP	Round 6 – 29 May MONACO GP	Round 7 – 12 June CANADIAN GP	Round 8 – 19 June EUROPEAN GP	Round 9 – 3 July AUSTRIAN GP
LEWIS HAMILTON	Mercedes									
NICO ROSBERG	Mercedes									
SEBASTIAN VETTEL	Ferrari									
KIMI RAIKKONEN	Ferrari									
FELIPE MASSA	Williams									
VALTTERI BOTTAS	Williams									
DANIEL RICCIARDO	Red Bull									
DANIIL KVYAT	Red Bull									
SERGIO PEREZ	Force India									
NICO HULKENBERG	Force India									
JOLYON PALMER	Renault									
PASTOR MALDONADO	Renault									
MAX VERSTAPPEN	Toro Rosso									
CARLOS SAINZ JR	Toro Rosso									
MARCUS ERICSSON	Sauber									
FELIPE NASR	Sauber									
FERNANDO ALONSO	McLaren									
JENSON BUTTON	McLaren									
WILL STEVENS*	Manor									
ALEXANDER ROSSI*	Manor									
ROMAIN GROSJEAN	Haas F1									
ESTEBAN GUTIERREZ	Haas F1									

SCORING SYSTEM: 25, 18, 15, 12, 10, 8, 6, 4, 2, 1 POINTS
FOR THE FIRST 10 FINISHERS IN EACH GRAND PRIX

*UNCONFIRMED AT TIME OF GOING TO PRESS

Round 10 – 10 July BRITISH GP	Round 11 – 24 July HUNGARIAN GP	Round 12 – 31 July GERMAN GP	Round 13 – 28 Aug BELGIAN GP	Round 14 – 4 Sept ITALIAN GP	Round 15 – 18 Sept SINGAPORE GP	Round 16 – 2 Oct MALAYSIAN GP	Round 17 – 9 Oct JAPANESE GP	Round 18 – 23 Oct UNITED STATES GP	Round 19 – 30 Oct MEXICAN GP	Round 20 – 13 Nov BRAZILIAN GP	Round 21 – 27 Nov ABU DHABI GP	POINTS TOTAL

The *Tifosi* couldn't celebrate a home victory in the Italian GP at Monza in 2015, but a Ferrari driver, Sebastian Vettel was second behind Mercedes' World Champion to be Lewis Hamilton, and a Ferrari "old boy" Felipe Massa took third for Williams.

The publishers would like to thank the following sources for their
kind permission to reproduce the pictures in this book.

Alamy: /W G Murray: 59T

LAT Photographic: 17, 21, 29, 33, 41, 45, 53, 59BL, 119, 120, 121; /Sam Bloxham: 30, 104, 128;
/Charles Coates: 11, 18, 23, 27, 31, 36, 37, 39, 50, 51, 92-93, 95, 96, 110, 123; /Glenn Dunbar: 10,
20, 22, 25, 48, 55, 61TR, 98, 100, 109, 111, 114-115, 124-125; /Steve Etherington: 12, 13, 14-15, 64-
65, 89, 102, 103, 105, 107, 113, 118; /John Harrelson: 59BR; /Andrew Hone: 3, 94, 97, 112; /Jed
Leicester: 113; /Zak Mauger: 76-77; /Alastair Staley: 16, 19, 24, 26, 32, 34, 35, 38, 40, 42, 43,
46, 47, 49, 52, 54, 101, 106, 108; /Steven Tee: 5, 6-7, 8-9, 28, 44, 56-57, 61TL, 62-63, 90-91, 99

Shutterstock: /Jaroslav Francisko: 61B

Every effort has been made to acknowledge correctly and contact the source and/
or copyright holder of each picture and Carlton Books Limited apologizes for any
unintentional errors or omissions that will be corrected in future editions of this book.